FROM OPEN DOOR
TO DUTCH DOOR

FROM OPEN DOOR TO DUTCH DOOR

An Analysis of U.S. Immigration Policy Since 1820

Michael C. LeMay

PRAEGER

New York
Westport, Connecticut
London

Library of Congress Cataloging-in-Publication Data

LeMay, Michael C., 1941–
   From open door to Dutch door.

   Bibliography: p.
   1. United States—Emigration and immigration—
Government policy—History. I. Title.
JV6493.L46   1987   353.0081'7   87-2368
ISBN 0-275-92492-0 (alk. paper)
ISBN 0-275-92628-1 (pbk. : alk. paper)

Library of Congress Catalog Card Number: 87-2368
ISBN: 0-275-92492-0 (hb); 0-275-92628-1 (pbk)

First published in 1987

Praeger Publishers, 521 Fifth Avenue, New York, NY 10175
A division of Greenwood Press, Inc.

Printed in the United States of America

∞

The paper used in this book complies with the Permanent Paper Standard
issued by the National Information Standards Organization (Z39.48-1984).

10   9   8   7   6   5   4   3   2   1

THIS BOOK, A LABOR OF LOVE,
IS DEDICATED TO MY MOTHER, MARIE,
THE DAUGHTER OF A GERMAN IMMIGRANT.
HER LIFE OF LOVE, DEDICATION, AND HARD WORK
IS A CONSTANT SOURCE OF INSPIRATION.

Contents

List of Tables and Illustrations   ix
Preface   xi
Acknowledgments   xvii

1 AN OVERVIEW OF U.S. IMMIGRATION POLICY   1
   The Importance of Immigration
   The Waves of Immigration
   The Four Phases of Policy
   Current and Future Trends
   Notes

2 THE OPEN-DOOR ERA, 1820–1880   20
   Introduction
   The Old Immigration Wave
   Nativist Political Reaction
   The Civil and Post-Civil War Years
   The Recessions of the 1870s:
     New Calls for Restrictionism
   Notes

3 THE DOOR-AJAR ERA, 1880–1920   38
   The Change in Immigrant Waves
   The New Immigrants' Patterns
   The First Restrictionist Laws
   The Depression of the 1890s and Subsequent Laws
   Further Attempts at Restrictionism
   The Pre-War Years
   The Post-War Years
   Notes

4 THE PET-DOOR ERA, 1920–1950   73
    The Immigration Act of 1917
    The Quota Act of 1921
    The Immigration Act of 1924
    The National Origins Act of 1929
    The Great Depression Decade
    The World War II Years
    Notes

5 THE DUTCH-DOOR ERA, 1950–1980   103
    Introduction
    The Immigration and Naturalization Act of 1952
    The Immigration and Nationality Act of 1965
    The 1976 Amendment to the Immigration and Nationality
        Act and the 1980 Refugee Act
    Notes

6 CURRENT LAW AND FUTURE TRENDS   118
    Introduction
    Recent Trends in Immigration
    Some Major Problems
    Recent Proposals to Revise Immigration Laws
    The Passage of the 1986 Act
    Conclusion
    Notes

    Appendix: Major Provisions of the Immigration Bill   154
    Bibliography   160
    Index   175
    About the Author   183

Mepi

BTG7, ae -90, 100
92
104, 115, 121-2, 125
127-8 131 133-4
137

and Illustrations

1.1 Rank Order of Immigration to the United States, By Nation of Origin, 1820–1980   2
1.2 Summary of U.S. Immigration Policy, 1783–1986   17
4.1 Comparison of Immigration Quotas Under 1890 Census and the National Origins Plan for Representative European Nations   90
4.2 Comparison of Quotas Allotted to Selected Countries Under Three Different Versions of the Quota System   91
4.3 Quota and Nonquota Immigration, 1930–1940   93
4.4 Sources of Immigration to the U.S., 1820–1947   96
4.5 Annual Immigrant Arrivals and Departures, United States, 1924–1948   101
5.1 Private Immigration and Nationality Bills   110
6.1 Resettlement of Refugees, 1975–1980   122

FIGURES

1.1 Immigrants Admitted to the U.S., by Region of Birth, 1820–1979   5
1.2 Trends in Immigration, By Phases, 1820–1980   8
2.1 The Origins of U.S. Immigration, By Region, 1821–1880   22
3.1 The Origins of U.S. Immigration, By Region, 1880–1920   40
4.1 Levels and Rates of U.S. Immigration, 1870–1979   75
4.2 The Origins of U.S. Immigration, By Region, 1920–1950   76
5.1 The Origins of U.S. Immigration, By Region, 1950–1980   105

BOXES

1.	An Immigration Officer Speaks	60
2.	Major Provisions of the Johnson-Reed Act	87
3.	Major Provisions of the Immigration Act of 1965	112
4.	Remarks of President Johnson on the 1965 Act	113
5.	Reagan's Proposed Immigration Reform Bill	138

Preface

This book is about United States immigration policy—what forces have shaped it, how and why various changes were made in it, and where it is headed in the future. It is designed as a supplemental book for courses dealing with the analysis of public policy. Hopefully, it will also be of interest to students of U.S. history who may wish to focus on this particular topic and study how and why that policy has changed over the course of our nation's history. Hopefully, too, it will be of interest to the general reader concerned with this important and timely topic.

The reader might well ask, why study immigration policy? This is a good question. I believe there are several appropriate responses to it.

First of all, U.S. immigration policy is a topic of substantive and timely interest. The United States is unique among the nations of the world in the degree to which it has absorbed immigrants! Since 1820, when we first began keeping count, more than 49.5 million persons have immigrated here. According to the 1980 census, the United States is now home to residents born in 155 other nations. A recent *Time* magazine special issue devoted to the new immigrants (July 8, 1985) noted that an amazing two-thirds of all the immigration in the world consists of people entering the United States. The influx of these millions of immigrants has in the past and continues today to have a profound impact on our nation's economy, culture, and politics. We are truly a nation of nations. We can best understand their impact upon us by studying the process of immigration. The magnitude of the problems associated with the immigration process, particularly with the estimated millions of undocumented aliens, has compelled renewed scholarly and media interest in the subject. It has led, also, to a recent review of our immigration policy. Congress has reacted to that concern with the passage of the Immigration Reform and Control Act of 1986. As citizens of this nation, we can best assess this new law in the light of an historical review and analysis of our past immigration policy.

A second reason to study immigration is that it is an *inherently interesting subject*. We are a nation of immigrants. The story of how we came to be such is one rich in human interest. The vast variety of groups who have mixed and intermingled here—if not "melted" into one—compels our interest. How immigration policy has influenced the composition of that mixture, and how that composition has in turn shaped immigration laws is a story which ought to be of significance to any student of public policy. This, in turn, suggests a third reason for this study.

Immigration policy is the type of subject that affords an excellent opportunity to gain a great deal of insight into the complexity of the policy process. As James Anderson defines it in his book, *Public Policy-Making* (New York: Holt, Rinehart and Winston, 1979), public policy is "a purposive course of action followed by an actor or set of actors in dealing with a problem or matter of concern" (Anderson: 3). He distinguishes the types of policy as distributive, regulatory, self-regulatory, or re-distributive. Immigration policy is an insightful example of regulatory policy—that is, one which involves the imposition of restrictions or limits on the behavior of individuals and groups (Anderson: 126-28). Not all regulatory policies are as clear-cut as immigration policy in the dramatic impact it has upon the social and political environment. Seldom can the student of the policy process see a more extensive result of a change in policy than is the case with the "gatekeeping" policy examined herein. We cite but two examples here to illustrate the point. In 1881, 11,900 Chinese immigrants entered the country, and over 39,500 came in 1882. But that number dropped to a paltry 8,031 in 1883 and a mere 23 by 1885—after passage of the Chinese Exclusion Act of 1882. In the decade before passage of the national origins quota system, over 8 million immigrants, nearly 71 percent of whom came from southeastern European countries, entered the U.S. This was the greatest number in the history of our nation. In the decade after passage of the quota system, our nation saw the smallest influx of immigrants for any decade since we began counting in 1820, and those from southeastern European nations had decreased to but 37 percent of that far smaller total.

Anderson analytically distinguishes a number of functional categories of activity which characterize the policy process—stages in that process, if you will. He identifies them as: problem formation, formulation, adoption, implementation, and evaluation (Anderson: 23-24). This analysis of immigration policy exemplifies every stage in that policy process. The story of how that policy has evolved and changed over time is a story that usefully exemplifies each category of activity in the public policy process for the student of public policy. These activities emerge clearly in the analysis and it makes their interplay apparent, elucidating the dynamic nature of that process for the student.

A fourth reason we might present to answer why one might study immigration policy is that it affords us insight into a particularly timely policy problem. This study is a *policy analysis,* not a *policy advocacy.* That is, it is concerned with the examination of the causes and consequences of public policy rather than advocating what government *should* do, promoting some particular policy proposal or response to a problem (Anderson: 8). Nonetheless, we can learn much from the *long-term* historical perspective to better assess the various pros and cons of the recent law revising immigration policy. While this book does not advocate any particular policy, it hopefully enables the reader to be better informed in making his/her own judgments as to the various merits of each side in the current debate over our immigration policy.

The approach of this study is to present an historical overview of United States immigration policy. Such an analysis identifies a number of *commonalities* in the story of our immigration policy and how it changed over time. Every period that preceded a significant change in immigration policy, for example, was one in which the country experienced a major recession or depression, be it the depressions of 1873, 1893, or 1920, the Great Depression of the 1930s, or the recent recession of 1981–82. Every such period was also one of social unrest and anxiety. The labor unrest and strife of the 1870s led to the immigration restrictions of the early 1880s, the first ever imposed. The "Red Scare" of 1919 immediately preceded the imposition of the quota system of the 1920s. The social turmoil of the civil rights era and the Vietnam War were associated with the changes in the Immigration Act of 1965, just as the cold-war era was reflected in the Immigration Act of 1952. Indeed, each post-war period—be it after the Civil War, World War I, World War II, the Korean War, or the Vietnam War—saw agitation leading to substantial changes in our nation's immigration policy.

Associated, too, with each major shift in that policy is a dramatic shift in the composition of the immigrant population. A change from Protestants from northwestern Europe to Catholics and Jews from southeastern Europe led to the imposition of the quota system to limit that influx. The need to deal with the "refugees" after World War II compelled yet another substantial change. More recently, the massive influx of Chicanos, Haitians, Vietnamese and other Asian people has led to new demands to modify our current immigration law.

Each major shift in immigration policy came only after one or more of the major political parties then dominant in American politics decided to advocate such change as an important plank in their party platform. Likewise, each major shift followed the formation of specific ad-hoc interest groups advocating or opposing such change: the Know-Nothing party in the 1840s; the Asian Exclusion League in the 1880s and 1890s; and in the 1920s, the Ku Klux Klan, the American Coalition, the Immigration Restriction League, and the American Protective League of True Americans did battle with the Hebrew Sheltering and Immigration Aid Society and the Anti-National Origins Clause League. In the 1980s, we see the emergence of FAIR [Federation for American Immigration Reform] and Zero Population Growth strongly advocating the need for change.

We see, too, in this long-term view of immigration policy, the recurrent arguments, like variations on a theme in a symphony, of proponents for a change in policy. Time and again, we hear concern expressed over the impact of immigration on wages and working conditions. Over and over again, one hears of the adverse impact of immigration from those advocating increased restrictions. They fear that the influx of newcomers will damage U.S. culture, social mores, and politics. The recurrent theme of whether or not each new wave of immigrants can, or should, assimilate into our culture is a motif heard throughout the history of our immigration policy. So, too, is the recurring concern expressed over the *method* by which we should screen immigrants. Advocates of change may suggest new methods: from "excluded categories" containing groups with certain undesirable physical or mental characteristics, to a "literacy test," to the imposition of a "quota system," to the development of an elaborate "system of preferences," on to the use of devices to reduce the economic incentives for immigration. What is consistent throughout, however, is that each shift is associated with the advocacy of some new "method".

The long-term review of immigration history shows that, throughout that history, four main elements of the immigration process figure prominently in the formulation of immigration policy: economics, race, nationalism, and foreign policy. Sometimes these elements work in harmony with one another, reinforcing each other. At other times they work in conflict with each other, and the contending forces seeking to influence immigration policy will each stress differing elements. But in all cases these four elements are the key to an understanding of U.S. immigration policy.

We see throughout the history of U.S. immigration policy coalitions of stable organized interest groups generally promoting an open-door approach to immigration policy or advocating the need for a restrictionist stance. Time and again, there is the coalition of business and "ethnic" associations in favor of unrestricted immigration doing battle with a coalition of organized labor, the American Legion, and various "patriotic" associations pressing for some new method to restrict the influx.

The period before each major shift also sees a spate of scholarly books and mass media programs concerned with the current immigration "problem". Such attempts to mold public opinion are followed by a significant shift in public sentiment in the direction of the new change in immigration policy.

Thus, we come to the basic approach used in this book. Through historical analysis, the book focuses upon the commonalities and themes evident in the story of U.S. immigration policy from 1820 to the present, highlighting the *interest groups* advocating or opposing change at any given time and the coalition of congressional forces they marshall in seeking to implement or oppose such a policy shift.

Interest groups are treated herein as organized bodies of individuals who share some goals and who try to influence public policy in order to better pursue those goals. The group theory of politics suggests that public policy is the product of a struggle among groups. It sees public policy as "the equilibrium reached in this [group] struggle at any given moment, and it represents a balance which the contending factions or groups constantly strive to weight in their favor" (Earl Latham, *The Group Basis of Politics,* New York: Octagon Books, 1965: 36). While certainly not the case in every public policy area, analyses of immigration policy underscoring its essential gatekeeping function clearly illustrate that it is one which reflects the interest of dominant groups. As groups gain and lose power and influence, policy is altered in favor of those gaining influence at the expense of those whose influence is waning (Anderson: 18). In the words of one proponent of group theory:

> The legislature referees the group struggle, ratifies the victories of the successful coalitions, and records the terms of the surrenders, compromises, and conquests in the form of statutes. Every statute tends to represent compromise because the process of accommodating conflicts of group interests in one of deliberation and consent (Latham: 35–36).

This study demonstrates that a review of the history of immigration policy shows a constant struggle for control of the immigration process. It is the story of periodic attempts to achieve a politically acceptable consensus about *procedural justice* in the matter of regulating the influx into our borders. We feel such analysis shows that ultimately the *disparities in power among competing groups* seeking to influence that balance or consensus is the *key to our understanding our immigration policy* (Kritz: 363). Clearly, the interplay among those groups is central to understanding the shifts in policy, the periodic reviews and revisions in policy and procedure designed to arrive at a new consensus as to how open or closed will be our doors at any given time.

The format of the book is as follows. Chapter 1 starts with a brief overview of U.S. immigration policy. It identifies various "waves" in the composition of immigration to this country. It distinguishes four distinct *phases* in immigration policy. Chapters 2 through 5 are each devoted to a discussion of a phase in policy: the "Open-Door Era," when there were virtually no restrictions on immigration; the "Door-Ajar Era," which saw the beginnings of restrictionism in policy; the "Pet-Door Era," when the national origins quota system dominated policy; and the "Dutch-Door Era." This last established a more open-door policy than the previous phase and allowed for an increase in total immigration but with a decided bias in favor of those who entered "at the top," in that they came in as special refugees from communism or possessed certain characteristics enabling them to come in under an elaborate system of "preferences."

The book closes with a discussion of current policy. It highlights recent changes in the flow of immigration that have led to a new political awareness of the "problem" of immigration. It critiques the recently passed Immigration Reform and Control Act of 1986 in the light of the historical overview presented in the preceding chapters. The long-term analysis of immigration policy affords insights into the advantages and disadvantages, as well as some of the likely impacts, of this latest revision in immigration policy. It suggests we are beginning a new era or phase of immigration policy, one which might well be called "The Revolving-Door Era."

Acknowledgments

An extensive book such as this leaves its author with a debt of gratitude to a great many persons who have preceded him. This is all the more the case when the work is of an historical nature. The contributions of the many scholars from whose work I drew when writing this book are acknowledged in the bibliography. In addition, there are several persons who deserve a special recognition.

The American Political Science Association and the American Historical Association provided me with a travel grant to attend the Project '87 seminar on Immigration and the Constitution at the University of Minnesota in the summer of 1986. That seminar—and its roughly two dozen participants—were very helpful. Professor Rudolph Vecoli, the seminar coordinator, and the Immigration History Research Center staff proved to be most gracious hosts and very helpful colleagues. I am indebted to Professor Vecoli for allowing me to use certain material cited herein.

Several colleagues read various drafts of the manuscript and offered useful suggestions to improve it: Ronald Hedlund, William McLeod, and John Wiseman.

Students in my American Public Policy Analysis class served as a captive audience upon whom I could test the materials as I developed them.

Any errors of fact or interpretation contained herein are, of course, solely the responsibility of the author.

FROM OPEN DOOR
TO DUTCH DOOR

1
An Overview of U.S. Immigration Policy

THE IMPORTANCE OF IMMIGRATION

The restoration of the Statue of Liberty, its centennial celebration, and the 1986 passage of a revised immigration law have refocused attention on immigration policy and its problems. Since 1820, when this nation formally began keeping track of immigration, more than 49.5 million persons have immigrated here.[1] According to 1980 census data, the United States is now home to residents born in 155 other nations. From 1820 to 1920 alone some 35 million came, mostly from Europe. A renewed influx in immigration and some especially vexing problems in policy designed to control that influx have led to increased scholarly interest in the topic. Such policy is controversial because the immigration process raises questions about its cultural, demographic, economic, and social impact.

Table 1.1 presents the number of immigrants since 1820 by rank order of the nation of origin. The massive level of immigration to the United States was the result of the correspondence between the needs of the overcrowded nations of Europe and Asia and the needs of a vastly underpopulated America.

The old world was experiencing massive and radical social and economic change engendered by overpopulation, requiring societal reorganization to deal with these problems. The old agricultural order changed from the feudal system's communal and subsistence farming to individually owned farms oriented to supplying an urban market economy. This led to the creation of a large mass of landless peasants from the British Isles to Russia. The Industrial Revolution, starting first in England and moving gradually across the European continent, added new strains to the social order as the old employment patterns disintegrated. Displaced artisans and farm workers alike joined the waves of immigrants to the United States.

1

TABLE 1.1
Rank Order of Immigration to the United States,
by Nation of Origin, 1820–1980

Rank/Nation of Origin:	No. of Immigrants:	Time Span:	Peak Decade:
1. Germany(1)	6,991,504	1830–1930	1881–1890
2. Italy	5,305,854	1880–1930	1901–1910
3. United Kingdom(2)	4,963,527	1820–1970	1881–1890
4. Ireland	4,691,954	1820–1920	1841–1850
5. Austria-Hungary(1,4)	4,317,897	1890–1920	1901–1910
6. Canada,Newfoundland	4,138,647	1840–1960	1921–1930
7. U.S.S.R.(4,5)	3,385,776	1880–1920	1901–1910
8. Mexico(8)	2,232,886	1900–1970	1961–1970
9. West Indies	1,831,126	1840–1970	1961–1970
10. Other Asia(13)	1,696,015	1880–1970	1951–1960, 1970–1980
11. Sweden(3)	1,273,457	1840–1930	1881–1890
12. Norway(3)	857,315	1840–1930	1881–1890
13. France	755,234	1820–1960	1921–1930
14. South America	738,456	1901–1970	1961–1970
15. Greece	665,527	1890–1920	1901–1910
16. China(14)	567,629	1850–1900	1881–1890
17. Poland(4)	523,084	1890–1930	1921–1930
18. Portugal	460,830	1870–1970	1921–1930
19. Japan(6)	415,159	1890–1910	1901–1910
20. Turkey	389,094	1890–1930	1901–1910
21. Denmark	365,042	1840–1930	1881–1890
22. Netherlands	361,994	1840–1930	1881–1890
23. Central America	351,540	1901–1970	1961–1970
24. Switzerland	350,590	1840–1930	1881–1890
25. Spain	264,715	1850–1960	1911–1920
26. India	204,930	1901–1980	1970–1980
27. Belgium	203,490	1880–1930	1921–1930
28. Romania(11)	173,984	1890–1930	1921–1930
29. Africa	157,252	1901–1960	1951–1960
30. Czechoslovakia(10)	138,574	1920–1940	1930–1940
31. Australia/ New Zealand	123,193	1870–1960	1941–1950
32. Yugoslavia(9)	117,509	1920–1960	1921–1930
33. Other America	109,462	1940–1960	1951–1960
34. Bulgaria(9)	68,142	1901–1930	1901–1910
35. Other Europe	55,919	1911–1960	1921–1930
36. Finland(10)	34,081	1840–1960	1881–1890
37. Pacific Islands	24,855	1880–1960	1881–1890
38. Lithuania(10)	3,936	1930–1970	1931–1940
39. Luxemburg(12)	2,932	1930–1970	1951–1960
40. Latvia(10)	2,622	1930–1970	1931–1940
41. Albania(10)	2,611	1930–1970	1931–1940
42. Estonia(10)	1,157	1930–1970	1931–1940

All Countries	= 49,655,952	Total Europe = 36,339,257
Total Americas	= 9,452,117	Total Asia = 3,272,827

Notes:
1. Data for Austria-Hungary was not reported until 1861. Austria and Hungary have been reported separately since 1905. From 1838-1945, Austria included in Germany.
2. United Kingdom: England, Scotland, Wales, and N. Ireland.
3. From 1820-1868 figures for Norway and Sweden were combined.
4. Poland reported separately from 1820-1898, and since 1920; otherwise Poland included in Austria, Hungary, Germany, and Russia.
5. From 1931-1963 U.S.S.R. divided into European and Asian, since 1964 total U.S.S.R. has been reported in Europe.
6. No record of immigration from Japan until 1861.
7. Prior to 1920, Canada and Newfoundland recorded as British N. America. From 1820-1898 figures include all British N. American possessions.
8. No record of immigration from Mexico from 1886-1893.
9. Bulgaria first recorded in 1899, reported separately since 1920. Since 1922 Serbs, Croats, and Slovenes recorded as Yugoslavia.
10. Countries added to list since W. W. I.
11. No record until 1880.
12. Figures from Luxemburg are available since 1925.
13. Beginning in 1952, Asia includes the Philippines. From 1934-1951, the Philippines are included in the Pacific Islands.
14. Beginning with the year 1957, China includes Taiwan.

Source: Data from INS, *1980 Statistical Yearbook*. Rank order table developed in LeMay, Michael, *The Struggle for Influence*, Lanham, Maryland: University Press of America, 1985, pp. 33-34.

Such population pressures contributed to economic disruptions and to religious and political persecution. Soon the various governments of Europe and Asia began to encourage emigration. When famine was added to such "push" factors, those leaving numbered in the millions. Push factors may account for why the tens of millions left Europe, but it was various pull factors that drew them to the United States.

The U.S. offered religious freedom to immigrants fleeing religious persecution. Its politically open society drew those escaping political persecution. The country's repute as a land of nearly boundless opportunity drew those compelled to flee the economic deprivation and often near-starvation conditions in their homelands. Open lands attracted the Europeans suffering from acute overpopulation. The U.S. needed to augment its population to defend itself from hostile Indians and from the potential threat of European colonial power.

The nation's burgeoning cities needed unskilled laborers. Many immigrants were drawn here expecting to find the streets paved with gold. Ironically, they found the streets unpaved and discovered *they* were to do the paving! Rapid industrialization was made possible by the cheap labor afforded by immigration, which kept wages down and enabled the accumulation of the large sums of capital. It provided a large pool of unskilled labor at the most opportune time.

THE WAVES OF IMMIGRATION

Traditionally, scholars dealing with this massive influx of immigration have categorized various periods of the immigration process into "waves." These distinctions are based on the size and character of the incoming groups that comprised each successive wave.

The first wave, from 1820 to 1880, witnessed over 10 million immigrants entering the United States. European nations comprised from 80 to 90 percent of that influx, with northwestern European nations predominating throughout the period, on the average comprising about 80 percent of the total influx. The predominance of northwestern European nations is clearly seen in Figure 1.1, which presents graphically the percentages of immigrants admitted to the United States by various regions of birth for selected periods from 1820 to present. Immigrants who came during this first wave have been commonly referred to as the "old" immigrants.

This first wave marked a sudden and dramatic increase in total immigration to the United States. From the end of the Revolutionary War to 1819 an estimated one hundred twenty-five thousand persons entered, most of whom were Protestants from the British Isles and northern Europe (Vialet:9). That began to change after the 1830s. Irish and German peasants came by the millions after the potato famines and the economic depressions of the 1840s. This sudden influx of Catholics led to an anti-Catholic reaction, which will be detailed more fully below.

The next major wave, which, since the time of the Dillingham Commission, has been commonly referred to as the "new" immigrants, occurred from 1880 to 1920. During this wave, a staggering 23.5 million immigrants flooded into the United States! They were predominately from southern central and eastern Europe. These new immigrants, being even more visibly different from the "native stock" than those of the first wave, set off a renewed xenophobic reaction that culminated in restrictive immigration laws marking the end of the second wave.

A third wave, lasting from 1920 to 1950, saw the total number of immigrants drop dramatically from about 23.5 million in forty year's time to just over 5.5 million in thirty year's time. This wave was also marked by several changes in the composition of the immigrant influx. European nations made up roughly 60 percent of the wave, with immigrants from northwestern European nations gradually rising from over 30 percent at the beginning of the period to nearly 50 percent by the end. Immigration from the Western Hemisphere rose to around 30 to 35 percent of the total.

FIGURE 1.1

Immigrants Admitted to the U.S., by Region of Birth, 1820–1979

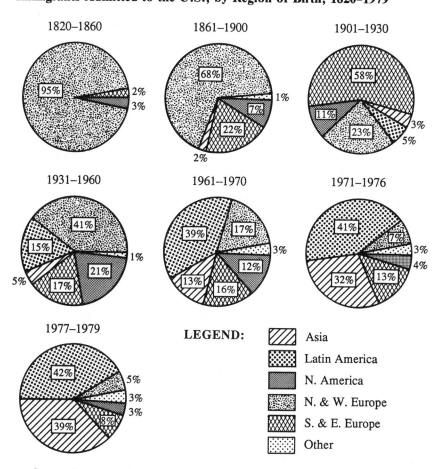

Source: PRB Population Bulletin Vol. 32, No. 4: 1977–79 data supplied by the Statistical Branch, U.S. Immigration and Naturalization Service, as cited in Bouvier, Leon F., 1981, "Immigration and Its Impact on U.S. Society," *Population Trends and Public Policy,* (No.2). Washington, D.C.: Population Reference Bureau, Inc. p. 2.

The latest wave, from 1950 to 1980, shows a renewed increase in total immigration, nearly doubling to almost 10 million in the thirty-year period. Western Hemisphere nations continue to predominate, rising to roughly half of the total wave. A dramatic increase in Asian immigration also distinguishes this wave.

U.S. immigration policy reflects the perceived needs of this nation as those needs shifted over time in response to changing economic conditions.

It reflects reactions to the changing nature and composition of the immigrant waves. Various economic, ethnic, foreign policy, and cold-war issues all played key roles in the debates over immigration policy.

The shifts in policy reflect conflicting value perspectives which tug and pull at one another, causing policy to oscillate in varying degrees between them. On the one hand is the perspective which values the immigrant as a source of industry and renewed vigor, a desirable infusion of "new blood" into the American stock, enriching the heritage and spurring new economic growth. This perspective forms the traditional base for a more open immigration policy. Almost every president, from Washington to Reagan, has affirmed that we are a nation of asylum for which immigration expresses and reconfirms the American spirit of liberty for all. As Professor Fuchs, one of the leading scholars of immigration puts it:

> In addition to the historical inheritance of asylum as one of the founding myths, the United States, as a leader of the Western Alliance of democracies against the Soviet Union, has become the champion of the human right to emigrate. Such advocacy, of course, implies the right to immigrate, too, even though it must be limited by practical necessity. In addition, there is the simple political fact of well-organized ethnic constituencies pushing for family reunification and refugee admissions (in Kritz: 289).

The other perspective calls for varying degrees of restrictions. Its proponents fear an influx of strangers who cannot, or in their view should not, be assimilated. These forces fear the dilution of U.S. culture. They fear that so vast an influx will destroy the economy or at least severely depress wages and working conditions. They advocate changes in policy to restrict immigration to avoid such dire effects. It is to an overview of those policy shifts we next turn our attention.

THE FOUR PHASES OF POLICY

Immigration policy performs a gatekeeping function and changes in that policy result in dramatic changes in both the size and composition of the flow. This gatekeeping function suggests the use of "door" imagery to characterize immigration policy. Just as the immigration influx was categorized into four waves, so immigration policy can be viewed as comprised of four distinct phases. Phase one, from 1820 to 1880, may thus be termed the "Open-Door Era." During this phase, policy entailed virtually no restrictions on immigration. Practically all who sought entrance were allowed in, and governmental policy was to reach out and seek immigrants. The second phase, the "Door-Ajar Era," lasted from 1880 to 1920. This phase saw the beginnings of restrictions, even while the door was still open to most. The third phase, the "Pet-Door Era," lasted from 1920 to 1950, a period when the national origins quota system formed the basis of our immigration policy. A restrictive policy approach to immigration, it allowed in only a favored few. The fourth and present phase is called the "Dutch-Door Era." It has established a more open policy than the previous phase, allowing for an increase in total immigration but with a decided bias favoring those who enter "at the top." Many are allowed in under special provisions and receive favored treatment. Figure 1.2 shows graphically these four phases and the major events and legislation that demark each phase. Each phase will be examined in greater detail in subsequent chapters, but will here be briefly summarized.

The Open-Door Era

The asylum view determined the policy-making of the first phase. With the successful establishment of an independent nation and then its newly revised Constitution in the 1790s, the official policy was to keep its gates open to all. Little opposition to this policy was even voiced at first. When the nation took its first census, in 1790, it recorded a population of 3,227,000, mostly the descendants of seventeenth- and eighteenth-century arrivals, or recent immigrants themselves. More than 75 percent were of British origin. About 8 percent were of German origin. The remainder were of Dutch, French, or Spanish origin, although approximately .5 million were black slaves and about the same number were Native Americans. This population occupied a land that was vast, sparsely settled, and obviously rich in soil and natural resources. The population density in 1790 was only 4.5 persons per square mile (Select Commission, *Staff Report*: 165). There was an obvious need for labor to build the cities, clear the farms on the frontier, and push back the Indians. Additional population was desired to strengthen the country's defenses against Indians and to avoid coming under control of European colonial powers. The U.S. Constitution enshrined the prevailing sentiment among most U.S. citizens at the time—that their nation was a brave and noble experiment in freedom. They felt this freedom should be broadly shared by any and all who desired to be free regardless of their former nationality.

President George Washington summed up the prevailing view and policy when he stated that

> The bosom of America is open to receive not only the opulent and respectable stranger, but the oppressed and persecuted of all Nations and Religions; whom we shall welcome to a participation of all our

FIGURE 1.2
Trends in Immigration, by Phases, 1820–1980

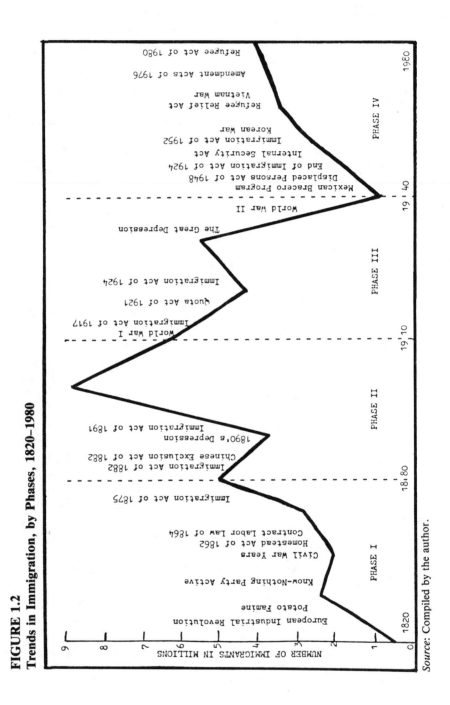

Source: Compiled by the author.

8

rights and privileges, if by decency and propriety of conduct they appear
to merit the enjoyment (Sic., in Rischin, p. 43).

The Constitution, however, said little about immigration. Article 1
prohibited Congress from limiting the states from importing slaves until
1808, but allowed a tax on importation of slaves for up to ten dollars per
person. It further granted to Congress the power to set a uniform rule
regarding naturalization and to make such laws as were necessary and proper to execute that power. It contained the "commerce clause," giving Congress the power to regulate commerce with foreign nations and among the
states. Subsequent Supreme Court cases interpreted that language in a manner which significantly impacted upon immigration policy.

In the 1790s, Congress began passing laws regulating naturalization.
The first act was very liberal, requiring only a two-year residency and the
renunciation of former allegiances. In 1795, however, turmoil in Europe
raised anew fears about foreign influence, and Congress passed a more
stringent naturalization act. It required a five-year residency period and a
renunciation of titles of nobility as well as allegiances. In 1798, Congress,
then under the control of the Federalist party, raised the period of residency
to fourteen years. They pushed through the Alien Acts, which allowed the
president to deport any alien considered to be a threat to the nation. The
Federalist party acquired an anti-immigrant image that contributed to the
party's decline. The substantial influx of newcomers who quickly became
citizens and joined the ranks of voters rejected the party in large numbers.
In 1810, the party made an effort (which proved to be too little, too late) to
attract immigrants with the tune

Come Dutch and Yankee, Irish Scot,
With intermixed relation,
From whence we came, it matters not;
We all make now, one nation.
(Roucek and Eisenberg: 5)

These acts were permitted to expire, however, when the Jeffersonian
Democratic Republicans replaced the Federalists in power. In 1802, a new
act re-established the five-year provision of the 1795 Act. In 1819, Congress
passed a law requiring a listing of all entering ship passengers which indicated their sex, occupation, age, and the "country to which they
belonged" (Select Commission, *Staff Report*: 169).

The wave of Catholic immigrants coming during the 1830s and 1840s
set off a dramatic anti-foreign reaction. They were easy scapegoats upon
which to lay the blame for the problems facing a rapidly changing U.S.
society as it began to urbanize and to industrialize. They were alleged to be

importing crime, poverty and drunkenness. Social reformers, who desired "to preserve the nation's institutions," and Protestant evangelicals, who sought to "save the nation's purity," joined forces to form such anti-immigration associations as the Secret Order of the Star Spangled Banner and the Know-Nothing political party (Jones: 147–276).

These groups advocated restrictive immigration policies and more stringent naturalization laws. The xenophobic fever even led to violent anti-Catholicism. Inflamed by a spate of virulent anti-Catholic literature, violent attacks on churches and convents took place during riots in such places as Baltimore, Boston, Cincinnati, Hartford, Louisville, Philadelphia, Providence, New Orleans, New York, San Francisco, and St. Louis (see Beals, and Billington).

Such nativist sentiment, however, did not prevail over public policy. The more economically and politically powerful of the native stock continued their potent support for open and unlimited immigration. The need for cheap labor to supply the explosively expanding cities and factories with manpower was the determining factor in public policy. Economic needs, coupled with the philosophic idealism regarding America as the land of opportunity and freedom, prevailed over the narrow views of the anti-Catholic movement.

The discovery of gold in California, in 1848, drew a vast population to the nation's west coast. The post-Civil War period created a virtually insatiable need for immigrants. The transcontinental railroad building boom opened up vast lands to settlement. Massive numbers of unskilled laborers were needed to mine the coal and ore, and to work in the mills spurred to new levels by Civil War generated production.

These forces, however, drew an influx of Chinese to the west coast and the composition of European immigrants started to change, with those from south, central and eastern Europe beginning to outnumber northwestern Europeans. These changes in the flow of immigration, coupled with economic recessions and a depression during the 1870s, created new political pressures for restriction. The banning of the immigration of convicts and prostitutes was passed in 1875, and the 1880s ushered in a new phase in immigration policy.

The Door-Ajar Era

Ironically, at the very time that the Statue of Liberty was first being erected, symbolizing our nation as being open to all the "poor and oppressed" of the world, the "new" immigrants were engendering fear and dislike among many of the native stock. Their more "alien" characteristics—strange coloring, physiques, customs, and languages—

aroused anew fears that these strangers would be unable to assimilate. A spate of pseudo-scientific studies by historians, sociologists and biologists attacked the newcomers as biologically and racially inferior. Such racist fervor led to the first blatantly restrictionist immigration law, the Chinese Exclusion Act of 1882.

Nativist arguments that the new immigrants were racially inferior and more inherently likely to become criminals or diseased were given popular credence. Such arguments undercut the earlier and prevailing tradition of welcome to "all the poor and the oppressed." Restrictive immigration policies reflected four historical trends which culminated in the 1880s and 1890s: 1) the burgeoning cities and rapid industrialization, which led to visibly corrupt urban political machines catering to the immigrant ethnic voters; 2) the official closing of the U.S. frontier; 3) the persistence among the "new" immigrants to maintain their culture and traditions far longer and more visibly than did the "old" immigrants; and 4) the greater religious divergence from Protestantism among the new immigrants who, unlike the "old" ones, were more overwhelmingly Catholic, Jewish, or Greek Orthodox.

The Immigration Act of 1882 also barred the immigration of "lunatics, idiots, convicts, and those liable to become public charges." The act added new categories of exclusion that reflected the hysteria of the nativist movement: those suffering from "loathsome or contagious diseases" and persons convicted of crimes involving "moral turpitude" were denied entry. The law also provided for the medical inspection of all new arrivals.

Passage of the 1882 act, however, did not satisfy the restrictionists. The continued and increasing influx during the 1880 decade led to further efforts to change immigration policy. They began to focus on a new area of regulation—that of literacy.

The first literacy bill was introduced into Congress in 1895, where it quickly passed both houses but was vetoed by President Cleveland. In 1906, another comprehensive immigration act was proposed that included both a literacy test for admission and an English-language test for naturalization. The restrictionists forces were joined by labor unions in advocating this new policy. The unions were increasingly wary of the economic threat to their wage scales and working conditions implicit in unrestricted immigration. Business leaders, however, opposed the new law. They wanted to avoid any limitation of new and cheaper labor sources.

The restrictionist forces succeeded in all but the passage of the literacy requirements for entry or naturalization. English-language proficiency was accepted for citizenship. In 1907, Congress also passed a law creating a joint Congressional/Presidential Commission to study the impact of immigration. Begun in 1909, the Dillingham Commission operated under the pseudo-scientific, racist theories prevalent at the time. The commission's recommendations, published in 1911, called for a literacy test and other restrictive legislation.

The war in Europe, however, was generating economic growth and labor demands in the U.S., both of which ran counter to restrictive policy. The growing political power of the new immigrant groups, coupled with business demand for new labor, preserved a more "free-entry" policy. In 1912, Congress once again passed a literacy test bill, but President Taft successfully vetoed it. In 1915, another such bill was passed, once again being vetoed, this time by President Wilson.

After the U.S. entered World War I in 1917, Congress finally passed a bill and successfully overrode yet another veto. The 1917 law finally made literacy an entrance requirement. It codified a list of aliens to be excluded, virtually banning all immigration from Asia. The xenophobic reactions during the war years contributed significantly to the success of the restrictionists. A frenzy of anti-German activity culminated in an "Americanization" movement to "educate" the foreign born into U.S. language and customs. Between 1819 and 1921, twenty states passed laws creating Americanization programs. Even industry, for the first time, joined the movement. This resulted in a new phase of immigration policy, the national origins quota system.

The Pet-Door Era

When industry, exemplified by such groups as the National Association of Manufacturers, and industrial giants like the International Harvester Company, and such prominent business leaders as Henry Ford, joined labor unions and the nativist political groups all calling for restrictionist immigration policy, a change in policy became inevitable.

Two restrictionist groups—organized labor and a group known as the "100 Percenters"—called for the suspension of all immigration. While labor supported the suspension of immigration because it feared the competition for jobs that occurred with the entry of aliens enhanced by the realignments occurring in the post-War economy, the "100 Percenters" were nativists who simply feared that European ideas, most notably the "red menace" of Bolshevism, would contaminate U.S. institutions, customs and society.

The Senate led the way with a law designed to reduce total immigration and change the composition of those entering. A bill, the Quota Act of 1921, was similar to one originally sponsored by Senator Dillingham of the earlier immigration commission. It was designed to ensure access for immigrants from northwestern Europe while restricting those from south/central/eastern Europe. In 1921, Congress passed, and President Harding signed into law, a measure introducing the concept of national origin quotas. In 1924, this approach was expanded upon with the enactment of the Johnson-Reed Act, more commonly known as the National Origins Act. This law provided for an annual limit of 150,000 Europeans, a total ban on Japanese, the issuance of visas against set quotas rather than on arrival, and the creation of quotas based on the contribution of each nationality to the overall U.S. population, rather than on the foreign-born population. The bill provided for the admission of immigrants, until 1927, by annual quotas of 2 percent of the nationality's proportion of the U.S. population in 1890. It was amended in 1929, when the national origins quotas themselves were set.

The Immigration Act of 1924, which remained in force until 1952, rejected the open-door tradition of U.S. immigration policy. That new policy, plus the decline in emigration during the Great Depression, dramatically reduced overall immigration for nearly three decades. In 1925, Congress created the border patrol as an effort to halt illegal aliens, an estimated half-million of whom entered during the 1920s (Chiswick: 13).

It was not until the 1940s that any pressure for change in the restrictionist immigration policy began to be felt and voiced. A slight relaxation in such policy was induced by World War II. The need for the labor of aliens after the U.S. entered the war led to the establishment of the "bracero" program. This temporary work program imported workers, mostly from Mexico, to fill war-time needs (Craig: 1971). In response to the war-time alliance with China, Congress repealed the sixty-year ban on Chinese immigration. Finally, as news of Nazi atrocities became widespread at end of the War, President Truman issued a directive admitting 40,000 war refugees. Congress responded to the problems of soldiers who had married overseas by passing the War Brides Act in 1946. This law allowed 120,000 alien wives, husbands and children of members of the armed forces to immigrate to the United States separate from the quota system.

The post-war years witnessed the emergence of the executive branch in taking a more active role in all policy-making, including a greater role in shaping immigration policy. President Truman initiated the nation's first refugee law, the Displaced Persons Act. It was pushed for by such groups as the American Jewish Committee, for Citizens Committee on Displaced Persons and even supported by the American Federation of Labor. Its most outspoken opponent was the American Legion. It passed Congress in 1948. This law ultimately allowed for the admission of over 400,000 displaced persons through the end of 1951 by "mortgaging" their entry against future immigration quotas.

It served as the precursor to the final phase of U.S. immigration policy, the "Dutch-Door Era," when special provisions allowed for the easier entry of various favored groups.

The Dutch-Door Era

The cold-war era saw additional "refugee" measures enacted by the Congress. In 1956 and 1957, legislation was passed allowing Hungarian "refugee-escapees" displaced by that failed revolution to enter. It established that category for refugees from Communist-dominated countries or countries in the Middle East. Congress passed the Refugee Fair Share Act in 1960, which provided for a temporary program for World War II refugees and displaced persons in the U.N. refugee camps.

Such special refugee-related acts did not alter the national origins quota approach but rather were exceptions to that approach allowing for groups to be given favored treatment under special circumstances because of the cold-war inspired anti-Communist atmosphere.

In 1952, the Immigration and Nationality Act, also known as the McCarran-Walter Bill, was passed. This act consolidated previous immigration laws into a single statute, but retained the basic national origins quota system. It further set up a system of "preferences" for certain skilled labor and for relatives of U.S. citizens and permanent resident aliens. It set a numerical limit of 150,000 on immigration from the Eastern Hemisphere and retained the unlimited number for the Western Hemisphere. The act set up a small quota for overall Asian immigration. President Truman vetoed it, but Congress overrode him. In 1953, the president appointed a commission to study immigration and naturalization policy. It recommended a liberalized approach harkening back to a more open-door policy. In 1962, Congress enacted the Migration and Refugee Assistance Act to aid the president in these matters. Some of the commission's recommendations were finally passed in the Immigration and Nationality Act of 1965, which was the most significant revision of immigration policy since the 1924 law.

The new law reflected the "civil-rights era" just as the McCarran-Walter Act had earlier reflected the cold-war period. The healthy and expanding economy of the 1960s eased fears of job competition and organized labor favored the more liberal policy (Kritz: 304). The new law abolished the national origins quota system, replacing it with an overall total of 160,000 to be distributed on the basis of a 20,000 persons limit per country for all nations outside the Western Hemisphere. It placed an overall limit of 120,000 on Western Hemisphere countries without individual national limits. Finally, it established a seven-category system of preferences for the Eastern Hemisphere, giving first preference to reuniting families, and a high preference to certain desired occupational skills.

The ending of the "open-door" policy for Western Hemisphere nations was a compromise necessary to get the bill passed. The ending of the "bracero" program and the closing of the open-door for the Western Hemisphere soon led to an increasing backlog of applicants from Latin

America, and to renewed problems of illegal aliens coming in from those countries. Congress reacted to such pressures by passing, in 1976, an amendment to the 1965 law that set immigration levels for both hemispheres, and applied the 20,000 per-country limit to both. In 1978, Congress amended the law to set a worldwide limit of 290,000, but it kept the seven-category preference system and the per-country limits of the 1965 law.

Special "parole" programs to handle the Cuban, Vietnamese and Soviet refugees were enacted instead of any blanket revision in immigration policy, which clearly could not keep up with the pressures by would-be immigrants to enter. Such authority became increasingly inadequate to handle what was becoming a recurring "special" situation, however, and concern over the "refugee" question led to further Congressional action, the Refugee Act of 1980. It was intended to correct deficiencies in existing policy by providing an ongoing mechanism for the admission and aid of refugees. It removed previous geographic ideological restrictions and set the total allocation for such refugee admissions at 50,000 annually through 1982. It set up a system for reimbursement to states and voluntary associations for financial and medical assistance they provided to refugees. It signaled renewed concern for re-examining immigration policy.

CURRENT AND FUTURE TRENDS

The 1970s was a decade of "stagflation," an economy troubled by both high inflation and high unemployment. These economic conditions and the continued illegal immigration issues have led to calls for a major revision in immigration policy. In 1984 alone, the U.S. Immigration and Naturalization Service (INS) apprehended over 1.2 million undocumented aliens, an astonishing 34 percent increase over two years. Rather broad support for a new policy and for a bipartisan effort underlies this development. It has become increasingly clear the the United States cannot adequately control its more than 5,000 miles of border. The combined illegal and legal immigration is at a rate that exceeds the peak years of the early 1900s, representing as much as 40 to 50 percent of our annual population increase.

Several key issues are raised by these numbers and were stressed in the recent debate over immigration policy. At what should be set the overall ceiling on legal immigrants, including immediate relatives and refugees? How broad should be the amnesty for undocumented aliens? How tough should we attempt to make the enforcement program? Should we reestablish a temporary worker program to relieve pressures for undocumented immigration? How should our nation deal with the asylum episodes such as the 1980 Cuban boatlift? Should we continue to distinguish political refugees from economic migrants?

These questions, of course, are all interrelated in practical as well as political terms. To be generous on entry requirements it was necessary to emphasize border control. A tough immigration policy also had to be viewed as compassionate. To avoid cutbacks on *legal* immigrants and refugees, policymakers had to enact stronger enforcement measures against *illegals*. Politically, stronger enforcement measured an amnesty program, but to make amnesty meaningful required the prospect of more effective enforcement.

The new direction in policy exemplified by the Immigration Reform and Control Act of 1986 may signal a new phase. It entails a new balance in the opposing values pursued over the years. On the one hand, it attempts to control the influx of workers by strengthening the border patrol and cutting down on incentives for new entrants by placing stiff penalties on potential employers—fines and even prison terms for employers who *knowingly* hire, refer, or recruit undocumented aliens for employment. The stiffer sanctions are balanced by the amnesty provision. The number of such undocumented aliens here has been variously estimated at from 2 to 10 million.[2]

Several Hispanic and religious organizations, by contrast, have openly defied current law over this issue. A sanctuary movement involving hundreds of congregations across the nation has developed largely since 1982. The U.S. Committee for Refugees, a private group, protests the unwillingness of the INS to grant asylum to thousands of Salvadorians as part of our foreign policy with respect to El Salvador (Murphy: 8–9).

Whether the new law will actually discourage aliens from coming here is certainly arguable. It may simply spur renewed and expanded business in "forged papers" so that the undocumented aliens can still get the jobs and the employer would be off the legal hook by being able to claim that all their workers had "papers." Nonetheless, this approach of attempting to decrease immigration by attempting to decrease economic incentives for immigration portends a new direction in immigration policy. This approach, plus the new law's provision to extensively expand a temporary-worker program, suggest a new phase in U.S. immigration policy. Perhaps it will be one that could be characterized as the "Revolving-Door Era."

Illegal immigration and the complex refugee issues have made the immigration policy problem a more complex and unpredictable one by intensifying the moral links to the "American Creed." It illustrates again, as this brief review of the history of that policy shows, society's constant struggle with the immigration process and its periodic attempts at achieving politically acceptable procedural justice. Ultimately, the key to understanding immigration policy is the disparities in power among the competing groups seeking to influence that balance. The interplay among such groups determines how open or closed will be the doors at any given time (Kritz: 363).

TABLE 1.2
Summary of U.S. Immigration Policy, 1783–1986

1783	George Washington proclaims America's open-door policy.
1798	Alien and Sedition Acts passed giving President arbitrary powers to seize and expel resident aliens suspected of subversive activities.
1819	For the first time, the U.S. government begins to count immigrants.
1855	Opening of Castle Garden immigration depot in N.Y. to process mass immigration.
1864	Congress passes law legalizing the importing of contract laborers.
1875	The first federal restrictions on immigration prohibits prostitutes and convicts.
1882	Congress curbs Chinese immigration.
.	Congress excludes convicts, lunatics, idiots and persons likely to become public charges, and places a head tax on each immigrant.
1885	Legislation prohibits the admission of contract laborers.
1886	Statue of Liberty dedicated.
1891	Ellis Island opened as immigration processing center.
1897	Literacy test law vetoed by President Cleveland.
1903	List of excluded immigrants expands to include polygamists and political radicals such as anarchists.
1906	Naturalization Act makes knowledge of English required.
1907	Congress establishes Dillingham Immigration Commission. Head tax on immigration increased; added to the excluded list are those with physical or mental defects that may affect their ability to earn a living, those with tuberculosis, and children unaccompanied by their parents. Gentlemen's Agreement between U.S. and Japan restricts Japanese immigration.
1917	Congress requires literacy in some language for those immigrants over 16 years old, except in cases of religious persecution. Bans virtually all immigration from Asia.
1921	Quotas are established limiting the number of immigrants from each nationality to three percent of the number of foreign-born persons of that nationality living in the U.S. in 1910. Limit on European immigration set at about 350,000.
1924	Nationality Origins Law (Johnson-Reed Act) sets temporary annual quotas at two percent of nationality's U.S. population as determined in 1890 census and sets an upward limit of 150,000 upon immigration in any one year from non-Western Hemisphere countries.
1929	Quotas of 1924 permanently set to be apportioned according to each nationality's proportion of the total U.S. population as determined by the 1920 census.
1939	Congress defeats refugee bill to rescue 20,000 children from Nazi Germany despite willingness of American families to sponsor them, on the grounds that the children would exceed the German quota.

TABLE 1.2 (continued)

1942	Bilateral agreements with Mexico, British Honduras, Barbados and Jamaica for entry of temporary foreign laborers to work in the U.S.--Bracero Program.
1943	Chinese Exclusion Act repealed.
1946	Congress passes War Brides Act, facilitating immigration foreign-born wives, husbands and children of U.S. armed forces personnel.
1948	Congress passes Displaced Persons Act (amended in 1950), enabling 400,000 refugees to enter the U.S.
1950	Internal Security Act increases grounds for exclusion and deportation of subversives; aliens required to report their addresses annually.
1952	Immigration and Nationality Act of 1952 (McCarran-Walter Act).
1953	Refugee Relief Act admits over 200,000 refugees outside of existing quotas.
1954	Ellis Island closed.
1957	Refugee-Escapee Act defines refugee-escapee as any alien who fled from any Communist country or from the Middle East because of persecution or the fear of persecution on account of race, religion or political opinion.
1960	Cuban Refugee Program established.
1964	U.S. ends Bracero Program.
1965	Immigration and Nationality Act of 1965.
1975	Indochinese Refugee Resettlement Program begins.
1976	Immigration and Nationality Act amendments of 1976: -extends the 20,000 per-country limit and the seven-category preference system to the Western Hemisphere. -maintains separate annual ceiling of 170,000 for the Western Hemisphere.
1978	Immigration and Nationality Act Amendments of 1978 combine the ceilings of both hemispheres to a worldwide total of 290,000, with the same seven-category preference system and the 20,000 per-country limit uniformly applied. Congress also establishes the Select Commission on Immigration and Refugee Policy. Congress passes law excluding and deporting Nazi persecutors.
1980	Refugee Act establishes clear criteria and procedures for the admission of refugees.
1981	Select Commission issues report, U.S. Immigration Policy and the National Interest.
1983-	
1984	Simpson-Mazzoli bill debated in media and Congress, passing both Houses in different versions.
1986	Immigration Reform and Control Act passed and signed into law.

Source: Adaped from: Select Commission on Immigration and Refugee Policy. *Final Report*. (Washington, D.C.: U.S. Government Printing Office, March 1, 1981), pp. 88–89.

The interplay among such competing groups is the central theme of this study. Each subsequent chapter will examine, in greater detail than this brief overview allows, a phase of U.S. immigration policy. Chapter 6 will examine recent trends in immigration and the new law and will speculate upon some of its likely effects. We will close this chapter with Table 1.2, which provides an overall summary of U.S. immigration policy from 1783 to date.

NOTES

1. This chapter draws heavily from two sources: Vialet and The Select Commission on Immigration and Refugee Policy, *Staff Report*: 161–220.
2. A Bureau of Census study for the Select Commission puts their number at 3 to 6 million. A New York *Times* article in January of 1980 set it at 11 million. A 1985 National Academy of Sciences Report estimates it at 2 to 4 million. For a summary of the 1986 law, see Appendix I.

2

The Open-Door Era, 1820–1880

INTRODUCTION

The United States is unique as a nation in the degree to which it has absorbed immigrants from other nation-states. No other nation in the world has experienced as many and as varied an influx of various ethnic groups. Our initial policy was to keep an open door, welcoming all. Indeed, as a nation comprised of a group of states, we positively reached out and sought to draw to our shores immigrants from Europe.

As stated earlier, the Constitution said little about immigration policy. It granted to Congress the power to establish a policy for naturalization. The key phrase in that article was that Congress could "make such laws as were necessary and proper to execute that power." Section 8 granted to Congress the power to regulate commerce, which was later interpreted to include immigration. Thus, the Supreme Court generally has been expansive in interpreting the powers of Congress to regulate immigration, and has been restrictive when it comes to state governmental laws or actions with respect to immigration and the rights of aliens.

The Constitution's nonexistent or vague language on citizenship, naturalization and immigration followed the tradition of the Articles of Confederation, which left ot the states the right to determine citizenship. It took the development of further laws and Supreme Court cases to elaborate upon the meaning of the vague language.

Congress acted quickly on its Constitutional authorization. In 1790, it passed its first law regulating naturalization by requiring simply a two-year period of residency and renunciation of former allegiances. In 1795, Congress slightly revised the law, increasing to five years the period for naturalization, but still maintaining a very liberal approach to immigration and naturalization.

In June of 1798, the fear that French "radicals" who had immigrated here might instigate turmoil along the lines of what the Federalists feared would be like the excesses of the French Revolution, led Congress to pass the first congressional act concerning "aliens." The law gave President John Quincy Adams the authority to deport any alien found guilty of seditious activities. Although the president never invoked those powers, this first example of xenophobia portended subsequent legislation that was more effectively restrictive. The act stated

> That it shall be lawful for the President of the United States at any time during the continuance of this act, to order all such aliens as he shall judge dangerous to the peace and safety of the United States, or shall have reasonable grounds to suspect are concerned in any treasonable or secret machinations against the government thereof, to depart out of the territory of the United States. (1 Stat. 570, 1798)

That law was permitted to expire in 1800, however, and had little impact on the actual immigration flow during this first phase of policy. The Jeffersonian Democrats, in 1802, passed a law reinstating the five-year provision. In 1819, Congress enacted a bill that required the enumeration of all immigrant passengers according to the country from which they came. The nation, for the first time, began keeping track of the immigration flow. State governments, however, were still primarily responsible for the actual processing of immigrants.

Figure 2.1 shows the origins of immigrants by region for the decades from 1820 to 1880. The next section will briefly sketch the immigration patterns of the primary groups who comprised the so-called "old" immigration wave.

THE OLD IMMIGRATION WAVE

The old immigrants came mainly from the northern and western countries of Europe and include Germans, Irish, and Scandinavians. Arriving most heavily during the period from 1820 to 1880, they came in two great surges. The first, between 1845 and 1854, was dominated by the Irish and the Germans. During the second, from 1865 to 1875, the British and Scandinavians also figured heavily along with the Irish and German groups.

German immigration reached nearly 7 million, making it the largest single source of immigrants to the United States after that from the British Isles. Roughly 40 million persons in the U.S. today claim some German ancestry. Although Germans immigrated steadily and in heavy numbers throughout our history, three major currents within that flow are

FIGURE 2.1

The Origins of U.S. Immigration, by Region, 1821–1880

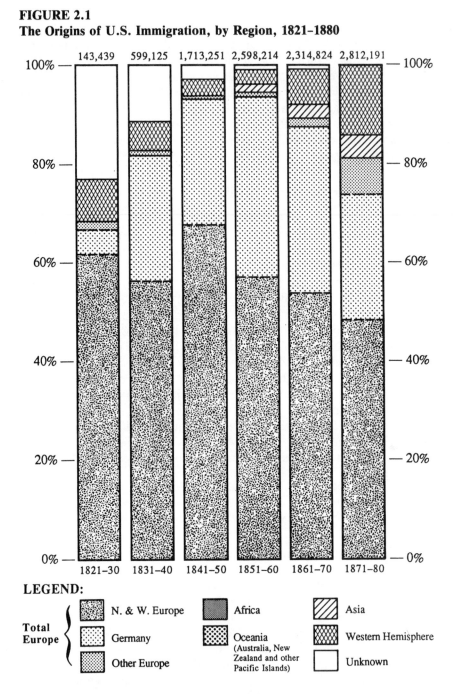

LEGEND:

Total Europe:
- N. & W. Europe
- Germany
- Other Europe

- Africa
- Oceania (Australia, New Zealand and other Pacific Islands)

- Asia
- Western Hemisphere
- Unknown

Source: U.S. Bureau of Census, *Historical Statistics of the United States, Colonial Times to 1970*. 2 Vols., Washington, D.C.: U.S. Government Printing Office, 1975.

commonly distinguished: the colonial period, when they immigrated mostly for religious and economic reasons; from 1848 to the Civil War, when they came for *political* and economic reasons; and the post-Civil War period, when they came mostly solely for economic opportunity, often having been actively recruited by one of several major industries, various state governments, the railroads, or friends and relatives already living here. Although the native stock treated them as one people, they were a diverse group splintered by regional strife and along religious lines.

During the colonial era, German immigration was distinguished by the movement of entire communities bound together by religious creeds not accepted in their homelands. They came in groups as Mennonites, Dunkers, Lutherans, Calvinists, and a few Jews. Geographically, they were Palatines, Salzburgers, Württenburgers, and Hanoverians. They sought out and cultivated some of the richest farmlands in colonial America; their granaries served as the "breadbasket" of the Revolution. Initially scattered thinly among the native population, they were united only by their language and exercised little political clout and showed not much interest beyond their local and private affairs.

The Revolutionary War changed all that. Although widely scattered, they still comprised the largest single nationality group after the British. They felt no special loyalty to the crown and were often unfriendly toward the Tories who favored continued union with England. While at first reluctant to become involved, they were easy converts to the cause of independence. Several German regiments were raised and fought prominently and well in the war. Their war-time service was widely recognized and helped accelerate their acceptance. It became their first major step towards assimilation. As their general social and economic conditions improved, they began to take a more active part in public affairs. Politically, they tended to affiliate with the Democrats, reflecting their small-farmer backgrounds. They were less at home with the "eastern seaboard establishment."

During the 1830s and 1840s, Germans emigrated for different reasons. By then the agricultural revolution hit central Europe, and particularly the southeastern area of Germany. Changes in inheritance laws forced the division of agricultural lands among all the children. A population explosion and these economic changes led to many farmers occupying farms too small for even subsistence farming. While some turned to manufacturing of clocks, tools, and the like, even this left them overly vulnerable to economic change. When the potato famine that plagued Europe in the late 1840s struck, their choice was often reduced to emigration or starvation.

Fortunately for them *and* the United States, these events coincided with the opening of the U.S. midwest. State governments, railroads, shipping lines, and manufacturers here began to entice immigration. The development of steamship lines made the journey cheaper and less arduous. Texas, the Great Lakes, and the Ohio River Valley all became home to some of these new settlers. Midwestern cities virtually exploded in population. Places such as Chicago, Detroit, Milwaukee, Cincinnati, and St. Louis led the way to a region of land stretching from New York to Maryland to the Mississippi River that became known as the "German belt."

The political turmoil and the 1848 revolutions led many German intellectuals to flee to America. These "Forty-Eighters," as they came to be known, made major contributions to the liberal movement in the states where they settled. Their influence far exceeded their relatively small numerical strength of some 10,000 because they became leaders of the German-American communities. They started German-language newspapers, reading societies, theatres, and related cultural activities. The full extent of their influence is a debated point (see Fuchs: 32–49), but they undoubtedly gave important leadership to the labor movement here. They were also instrumental in the nation's conservation movement. Forty-eighter Carl Schurz, for example, led the drive to save virgin forest land and became the first Secretary of the Interior in 1877.

They were also prominent in the anti-slavery movement and were instrumental in the founding of the Republican Party. They took credit—an inflated claim—for the election of Lincoln, who shrewdly had invested in a German-language newspaper.[1]

During and after the Civil War, German immigrant labor filled the desperately needed slots in the northern industrial labor force opened by the war. The booming economy drew labor to the areas of high demand. This became a major factor in the Germans' rapid absorption into the mainstream of U.S. life. The largest influx of German immigration came after the Civil War. The Homestead Act of 1862 provided the inducement of free land to the overcrowded population of the homeland. Western states advertised for German farmers who had a reputation for being hard-working and very productive. State governments were joined by the railroads, who sent agents to Germany to induce immigrants to settle and develop the abundant railroad lands. An additional draw was that the U.S. became a haven from the military conscription during the years of the German wars of unification.

German immigrants did face some opposition, of course, most notably the Know-Nothing party of the 1850s. They also came into conflict with the Irish. German Catholics immigrated at the same time as the large wave of Irish Catholics. The latter dominated the clergy and hierarchy of the Catholic Church in the U.S. until the early 1900s, when clergy of German background finally began to fill some leadership roles.

Irish immigration can also be traced back to the colonial period, when they settled mostly in Pennsylvania and Maryland. By 1790, the Irish comprised about 2 percent of the nation's population of just over 3 million. Their numbers and their Catholicism generated the first strong and overt discrimination. After 1830, when the Irish began fleeing the political and religious persecutions under British rule, Irish immigration swelled to a flood. Today, approximately 13 million U.S. citizens claim Irish descent, representing about 6.5 percent of the total population. Roughly two-thirds of them reside in the east, concentrated in New York, Massachusetts, Pennsylvania and New Jersey.

The potato famine of the late 1840s precipitated a massive migration, when the choice was literally to emigrate or to starve. Between 1847 and 1854, about 1.2 million Irish came to the United States. This wave peaked in 1851, when nearly .25 million arrived. This famine-induced emigration was critical in that it created a sudden and quite literal deluge of immigrants all settling into the urban areas of the east and activating existing prejudice. Their sheer numbers, their Catholicism, their obvious poverty, and their open anti-British feelings all contributed to the native stock's antagonism towards the Irish. Perhaps equally important, because of their poverty, the millions arriving from rural backgrounds were trapped in the nation's seaboard cities.

Coming with high rates of illiteracy and few job skills, they were forced into unskilled labor. They acquired lower-class status precisely at the time when the United States was developing class consciousness.[2] They were viewed, then, as a special threat, a great concentration of "indigent foreigners," and a lower class of people who formed the first huge pool of manual labor (O'Grady: 65). The Irish became the first group to face overt job discrimination. Advertisements in Boston, New York and other eastern cities for some time included the line, "No Irish Need Apply." They accepted whatever work was open to them—unskilled jobs such as stevedores, teamsters, ditch diggers, dokers, and terriers. They formed the construction gangs that razed or erected the buildings of an explosively expanding city. They built the roads, canals and railroads connecting the east with the midwest and beyond. Such jobs were, of course, seasonal, low-paying and subject to the constant threat of job competition. Labor competition was, at least partially, a factor that led to the beginnings of problems in race relations—the Irish regarding the blacks and Chinese as special menaces to their own vary precarious position.

To break out of their minority status and move up from the lowest rung of the socioeconomic ladder, involvement in the U.S. labor movement and the use of politics became the chosen path of the Irish. While few of them had experience in labor union affairs, their unstable working position led them into many labor associations. They were the early leaders in the formation of unions from New York to San Francisco, which included the entire gamut of skilled craftsmen from tailors to bricklayers, shoemakers, carpenters and longshoremen, as well as "unskilled laborers." In the 1850s these unions operated solely at the local level, but by the 1860s they began to appear at the national level. In 1861, Martin Burke helped form the American Miners Association. By the late 1870s, a second-generation Irish-American, Terrance Powderly, gained control of the first truly effective national level labor union, the Knights of Labor. Peter J. McGuire, the "Father of Labor Day," helped form the American Federation of Labor in 1886 (O'Grady: 163).

The tens of thousands who annually poured into the U.S. during the 1840s and 1850s contributed to the burgeoning of U.S. cities. This massive urbanization required rapidly increasing local governmental work-forces, especially police departments. The incoming Irish were quick to join, and some rose to levels of responsibility quite rapidly. By 1863, a John A. Kennedy led a New York City's police force. In the 1870s, a New York City detective of Irish descent, one Michael Kerwin, became Police Commissioner. The success of the Irish, however, was even less spectacular than that of the Scandinavians.

Scandinavians were among the first European people to explore America, with Viking explorations and minute settlements dating back to the period of 800 to 1050. In the mid-1600s several settlements of persons from the Scandinavian region were established in what is now Delaware. A few immigrants continued to come from Norway, Sweden and Denmark during colonial times, but their numbers were not substantial until after the Civil War. From then on, motivated by such factors as religious dissension, disenfranchisement, crop failures, and related economic factors, Scandinavians emigrated in large numbers, and most of them came to the United States. Total Scandinavian immigration to the United States was approximately 2.5 million. The Swedes hit their peak in 1910, the Norwegians in the 1920s. Although the Norwegians, Swedes and Danes came from countries with diverse governments, traditions and spoken languages, their physical similarities and a tendency to settle together here led to the use of the term "Scandinavian" to refer to all three groups.

On the whole, they were a very successful group of immigrants. As was true of virtually all immigrants, they were willing to work hard. Moreover, they arrived in better financial shape than most groups, which enabled them to escape the poverty and slums—as well as the accompanying stigma—of the eastern seabord cities. By 1880, the average Scandinavian immigrant was bringing about $60 to $70 dollars with him. These sums often enabled Scandinavians to reach the midwest, where they could take advantage of the cheap land and put their farming skills to use. Farming, however, was not their only trade. They went into business, commerce, manufacturing, finance and the professions. In their frontier settlements, they quickly and successfully established their own stores, shops, factories and banks.

During the "Open-Door Era," they mostly settled in the midwestern states whose soil and climate were akin to that of their homelands. Successful settlements drew others. Minnesota, Wisconsin, Iowa, Illinois and the Dakotas all saw dramatic increases in their populations, reflecting the Scandinavian influx.

Perhaps their entrance into this country in smaller numbers and their settlement into the interior account for their slower involvement in politics. At first they struggled, as did the other settlers on the frontier, with simply establishing viable settlements. Political involvement only came after they had built their homes, learned the language and customs, and achieved a modicum of economic and social success. By 1870, Scandinavian immigrants had a fairly clear understanding of American-style politics. They tended to be very patriotic. They often learned the rules of U.S. politics by organizing new townships, working the town machinery, carrying on local elections, levying and collecting taxes, and laying out new roads. In the early stages of political development, more than one-fifth of the men participated in town affairs.

Several other groups arrived in significant numbers during the period between 1820 and 1880. The Dutch, French, Scots, Scotch-Irish and Welsh are commonly grouped among the "old" immigrant groups. They generally exemplify patterns similar to those discussed above. Another group, the Chinese, showed a considerably different pattern.

Total immigration from the Netherlands was just over 350,000. Although more than half that total occurred after 1880, they are generally grouped among the "old" immigrants because they came in significant numbers during the earlier period and their greatest impact on U.S. society was during the colonial and early independence period. Dutch influence was most strongly felt in New Jersey and New York. Brooklyn, the Bowery, and the Bronx, for example, all take their names as derivatives of Dutch words.

Religious dissenters from the Netherlands founded colonies in Michigan and Iowa in 1846. Their departure coincided with the potato blight and economic depression that hit their homeland, as it did much of Europe, in the late 1840s. These religious separatists established a settlement that became Holland, Michigan. It served as the prototype for a new wave of immigrants who were settling in Wisconsin and Illinois, as well as Michigan and Iowa, because the soil and climate were so favorable.

The unifying force among Dutch settlements was religion rather than national identity. Subsequent schisms resulted in the formation of the Dutch Reformed Church, the Christian Reformed Church, and the Netherlands Reformed Church. The Holland, Michigan settlement was particularly successful. Dutch settlers there achieved a high social status, in part reflected by their founding of Hope College. The Christian Reformed

Church, a more conservative group, emulated their example by founding Calvin College in Grand Rapids.

Dutch settlers, whether urban or rural, were quick to acquire middle-class status in income and occupations. As Professor Parrillo summarizes their experience:

> Although most of the Dutch immigrants have come to the United States during the same period as the southern, central, and eastern Europeans, they have not encountered ethnic antagonism and they have assimilated more easily. Their physical features, their religion, their comparatively small numbers, and their more urbanized backgrounds have enabled them to both adapt and to gain approval from the dominant society more easily than other groups. (Parrillo: 127)

France has been the source of a large and rather continuous flow of immigrants. French-Americans fall into three distinct subgroups, each with a somewhat different pattern of immigration/assimilation: 1) immigrants from France proper; 2) French Louisianans, or "Cajuns," who were expelled from Acadia French Canada by the British in 1755; and 3) French Canadians who settled primarily in New England. The total number of immigrants from France was over 738,000.

The colonial era immigrants from France were dominated by the Huguenots, Protestants who were fleeing religious persecution. most of them readily converted to the Anglican Church here, and that fact, coupled with their rapid adoption of English, eased their assimilation. They did experience some antagonism due to the comparatively frequent hostilities between England and France that spilled over into animosities in the colonies. Such friction, however, was generally short-lived. Their marginal status did encourage them to anglicize as quickly as possible by changing their names and customs, and by learning English. Full assimilation into their new life was clearly a desired goal of this group. When the Revolutionary War made France an ally against Great Britain, their assimilation was greatly facilitated. It was the French diplomat, De Crevecoeur, who first used the concept of the United States as the asylum for the poor of Europe and who first popularized the concept of America as being "the melting pot" (Rischlin: 24; and Parrillo: 128).

By contrast, the French Revolution led to thousands of French aristocrats immigrating to the United States. Unlike their earlier compatriots, this group kept to themselves and avoided the native stock, whom they felt were socially inferior. They rejected assimilation and citizenship. Most returned to France after the fall of Napoleon. The French Revolution also briefly aroused anti-French feelings here as Americans began to fear and detest the excesses of that revolution. This sentiment was especially strong among Federalist Party members and contributed to their pushing through the Alien and Sedition Acts.

The Louisiana French, who became part of the United States by absorption in the Louisiana Purchase in 1803, afford yet another pattern. They have exhibited an exceedingly strong and persistent subculture that has absorbed other ethnic groups in the area, largely through intermarriage and their matriarchical socialization process.

The French Canadians also exhibit a persistent subculture. Overpopulation at home and the diminishing size of agricultural land, which had been subdivided for generations, finally led many to start immigrating here in the 1830s. Their peak periods were between 1860 and 1900, when an estimated 300,000 emigrated, settling for the most part in the mill and factory towns of New England. Other substantial settlements are in New York, Michigan, Illinois, and Wisconsin. Like the Louisiana French, their family and church structures seem to account for their persistent subculture and very slow rates of assimilation (Parrillo: 131).

The Scots, Scotch-Irish and Welsh all evidence similar patterns of immigration and assimilation. They all started their immigration during the colonial period and all have assimilated rather easily. Their religious preference for Presbyterianism, Episcopalianism, and Anglicanism helped to promote their reputations for following a strict moral code, the development of the "Protestant work ethic," and a wide-spread reputation for frugality and honesty, all of which made them easily accepted by the Calvinist New Englanders. They settled in heavy numbers in Pennsylvania, the Carolinas, and New England. They worked frequently as farmers or miners. In the latter occupation, they were often desired as skilled workers who served as superintendents and foremen.

They did experience some anti-immigrant feeling. Since they often settled in larger numbers in what were then the frontier regions, the native stock sometimes feared they might become the dominant group. The native labor force perceived them as an economic threat because of their job skills, which made them highly desired as workers by some of the native elite.

Such was not the case, however, with the Chinese. They are a unique case among the older immigrant groups in that they suffered a racial stigma. They alone among the "old" immigrants, for instance, were the target of specific restrictive laws.

The discovery of gold in California in 1849 served as a powerful "pull" force and proved to be a major factor influencing Chinese immigration here. Perhaps equally important were several "push" factors as well: floods and typhoons that devastated their home communities, particularly in the Toishan Province of China, and drove many young Chinese men to Hong

Kong and Canton, from which a large number of the most adverturesome made the trip here.

In addition to being attracted here by the gold rush, many of the Chinese young men were recruited to work on the railroads, particularly the Union Pacific, which was building the railroads from west to east. Some 400,000 Chinese eventually immigrated here, with over half of those arriving during the peak years between 1850 and 1880. Specifically, the immigration figures for those three decades are 41,397 for the period from 1851 to 1860, 64,301 for the period from 1861 to 1870; and 123,201 for the period from 1871 to 1880 (Dinnerstein and Reimers: 163). Unlike the groups from northwestern Europe, which usually included large numbers of females, the Chinese immigrants were on average 90 percent young males. They settled in the west, especially California, but not exclusively so. Some settled as far south and east as Mississippi.

In the west, Chinese immigrants were forced into those jobs that were the least desired—jobs shunned by whites. They tried but were often driven out of jobs in the mines and farms. Large numbers took on jobs considered to be "women's work." In the female-scarce west, such jobs were plentiful. When the railroad jobs for which the Chinese immigrant came over under contract ran out and they found themselves quite literally "trapped" in the United States, they were forced into domestic service. They eventually opened restaurants and laundries. By 1884, however, the Chinese still comprised nearly half of California's unskilled agricultural workers.

The Chinese immigrants' willingness to serve as scabs and strikebreakers quickly caused severe difficulties with organized labor groups. The Chinese refused to join the Knights of Labor. That fact, plus their service as strikebreakers for the Union Pacific railroad in Wyoming, led to severe conflicts in 1875, and again in 1885. In September of 1885, for example, a riot in Rock Springs, Wyoming, by union-led white rioters left 28 Chinese laborers killed, 15 others seriously wounded, and several hundred expelled from town.

A fear of the "Yellow Peril" developed along the entire west coast and led to various legal restrictions culminating in the exclusion of Chinese immigration. The successful implementation of restrictive legislation against the Chinese exemplifies the reaction of nativist groups to a perceived "threat" of the foreign influx. It is to a discussion of that nativist movement we next turn our attention.

NATIVIST POLITICAL REACTION

The successive "waves" of the old immigrants did not go unnoticed by the native majority. Many WASPS (white Anglo-Saxon Protestants) accepted and welcomed the immigrants. Numerous state governments and business, particularly the railroads and various manufacturing concerns, which were just beginning to develop, and the transatlantic shipping lines, welcomed or actively recruited the immigrants. But not all the native stock reacted so favorably. The American party, founded on July 4th, 1845, was a specific anti-immigrant party whose main platform was a total rejection of the foreigner. In its declaration of principles, the party stated

> The danger of foreign influence which threatens the gradual destruction of our national institutions has not failed to arrest the attention of the Father of His Country. Not only in rendering the American system liable to the poisonous influence of European policy—a policy at war with the fundamental principles of the American Constitution, but also its still more fatal operation in aggravating the virulence of partisan warfare—has awakened deep concern in the minds of every intelligent man from the days of Washington to now. (O'Connor: 122)

The most prominent nativist movement became known as the Know-Nothing party. Originally called the Order of the Star Spangled Banner, the party had its beginnings as a secret patriotic society founded in New York in 1849. It achieved its earliest successes in Massachusetts and Pennsylvania. In the 1854 elections, it added striking successes in Rhode Island, New Hampshire, Connecticut, Delaware, Maryland, Kentucky and Texas. The party also wielded a strong influence in Virginia, Georgia, Alabama, Mississippi and Louisiana (Smith 1956,: 141 and Nevins: 329).

As John Higham notes so well, the nativists themselves described their philosophy as "Americanism." He notes

> "The grand work of the American Party," proclaimed one of the Know-Nothing journals in 1855," is the principle of nationality . . . we must do something to protect and vindicate it. If we do not it will be destroyed."
> Here is the ideological core of nativism in every form. Whether the nativist is a workingman or a Protestant evangelist, a southern conservative or a northern reformer, he stood for a certain kind of nationalism. He believed—whether he was trembling at a Catholic menace to American liberty, fearing an invasion of pauper labor, or simply rioting against the great English actor William Macready—that some influence originating abroad threatened the very life of the nation from within. Nativism, therefore, should be defined as intense opposition to an internal minority on the ground of its foreign (i.e., "un-American") connections (Higham, 1955: 4.)

In the 1856 elections, the Know-Nothing party ran a presidential candidate, former President Millard Fillmore. Its platform was too narrowly based on an anti-immigrant, anti-Catholic stance to succeed nationally. It was silent on the slavery issue altogether. Thus the party merely played the role of spoiler in the election. Fillmore received 874,534 votes and carried only the state of Maryland.

Deep-rooted feelings caused many of the native stock to oppose immigrants by joining the new militantly nativist party. The massive immigration following the potato famines aroused fear and hostility among the nativists, which fed the movement and contributed greatly to the party's rapid rise and temporary success. The slavery question, which ultimately led to the demise of the party, loosened ties so that many voters who were unwilling as yet to cast their lot with either the pro-slavery Democrats or the anti-slavery forces forming the Republic party, found a temporary home in the Know-Nothing party.

In order to join one had to be a native-born American and a Protestant. The individual had to swear an oath to vote for whomever or whatever the party told him to vote. If asked their goals or stands on a position, they were instructed to reply, "I know nothing," which gave rise to the party's popular name. On occasion, some party members would close one eye and place a thumb and forefinger over the nose. This signified "eye nose nothing" (Bailey: 135).

The movement attracted the working class, who feared their jobs would be taken and institutions and order of society would be undermined by the vast influx of foreigners. They feared the increasing political threat as the electoral clout of the immigrant bloc vote was becoming increasingly evident in the beginnings of what would eventually emerge as the urban machine. These fears, of course, were not entirely unfounded. The new immigrants were flocking to the cities, causing unbelievable overcrowding and providing a massive and cheap labor pool. Employers were quick to determine that the new immigrants would do almost any job for very low pay (and thus continued to advocate a totally open-door policy with respect to immigration.) It was widely felt that large-scale immigration led to overall low-pay rates and deplorable working conditions.

Others were attracted to the movement out of a deep-seated fear of the Catholicism so evident among large portions of the immigrants flooding in since the late 1840s. They joined the movement and rose up ". . . to burn Catholic convents, churches and homes, assault nuns, and murder Irishmen, Germans and Negroes" (Beals: 9). A violent hate campaign was unleashed in many cities where immigrants were concentrated. In New York, mobs of Irish and Know-Nothings clashed, leaving two dead. In Newark, an estimated 2,000 Protestants and Catholics squared off, leaving one dead, many wounded, and a Catholic Church burned down. in 1855, Know-Nothings and Germans in Louisville clashed in an intense riot which left twenty dead and hundreds wounded. In Baltimore, where the party was particularly strong, numerous clashes took place and a riot in 1854 resulted in eight dead (Hofstadter and Wallace: 93, 313). A spin-off group of the Know-Nothings, called the "Plug Uglies," was often responsible for the physical violence of the period.

Obviously, not all U.S. citizens reacted so negatively. Ralph Waldo Emerson attacked the xenophobic hysteria and the nativist movement by stressing what he considered to be the advantages of what he called the "smelting pot theory."

> I hate the narrowness of the Native American Party. It is the dog in the manger. It is precisely opposite to true wisdom. . . . Well, as in the old burning of the Temple of Corinth, by the melting and intermixture of silver and gold and other metals, a new compound more precious than any, called Corinthian brass, was formed; so in this continent—asylum of all the nations—the energy of Irish, Swedes, Poles, and Cossacks, and all the European tribes—of the Africans, and of the Polynesians, will construct a new race, a new religion, a new state, a new literature, which will be vigorous as the new Europe which came out of the smelting pot of the Dark Ages, or that which earlier emerged from the Palasogic and Etruscan barbarianism. (cited in Orth and Ferguson: 299–300)

Obviously, however, many native U.S. citizens were afraid of just that development. Those to whom the nativist movement appealed did not want a new race, nor a new religion, nor a new language, state or literature. They, along with the party and movement, advocated—unsuccessfully—a change in immigration policy in order to restrict the influx and force for change.

Rapid in its rise, the party experienced an equally rapid decline. Its 1855 convention split wide-open over the slavery issue. Its northern members were anti-slavery; its southern wing would not budge from its pro-slavery stand. Attempted reconciliation failed, signaling serious trouble for the party. After the 1856 election, it essentially disintegrated, with its southern wing going Democratic (and later secessionist), and the northern members joining the Republicans.

THE CIVIL AND POST-CIVIL WAR YEARS

The prevailing forces in U.S. society that determined what the immigration policy would actually be were not the nativists. A coalition of past immigrant groups, organized into various ethnic associations and increasingly voting as a bloc, plus the politicians of the major political parties that sought and catered to that vote, and the leading forces in business, particularly the growing segment of northern manufacturing concerns, all advocated continuation of an open-door stance.

When nativist forces succeeded, in New York and Massachusetts, in enacting state laws that imposed restrictions and taxed passenger shipping lines for each immigrant brought in, the Supreme Court struck down the state laws. In the *Passenger Cases* (1849) and the *Henderson v New York* case (1876), the Supreme Court ruled against these state attempts to restrict immigration. The Court's majority declared that Congress alone had the right to regulate immigration.

Southern, western and midwestern states, of course, did not want to restrict the influx of immigrant labor. On the contrary, they sought immigrants in order to open up and develop their lands. Nearly every state outside of the northeast region hired agents or appointed boards of immigration to lure new settlers from Europe. Michigan began the practice in 1845. By the end of the Civil War, southern and western states joined in the practice, each hoping to divert some of the renewed influx. By the 1870s, twenty-five of the then thirty-eight states took some sort of official action designed to promote immigration. South Carolina went so far as to grant a five-year tax exemption on all real estate bought by immigrants (Higham 1955: 16).

Railroads, which were pushing development into the empty west, needed immigrants to buy the railroad lands and ensure future revenues by growing the crops or raising the cattle that would be shipped by rail. The Illinois Central, the Burlington, the Northern Pacific and other lines sent agents to northern Europe to attract immigrants. Other real estate interests promoted comparable campaigns.

Indeed, virtually every business enterprise hoped to make money from the immigration flow. Merchants looked to the tens of thousands of immigrants entering the nation annually after the Civil War as an ever-growing supply of new customers, and organized various associations to attract them. The San Francisco Board of Trade, for example, formed the Immigration Association of California, which established hundreds of contracts with agents in Europe. The mining industry in Pennsylvania and out west in the Rockies was especially dependent upon immigrant labor. By 1870, a third of the work force in manufacturing was from immigrant labor sources. That proportion remained constant until the 1920s. New England manufacturers recruited labor in Canada, and others did so in Europe (Higham 1955: 16–17).

The national government favored open immigration, and during the post-Civil War years considered various ways to assist it. The Republican party's platform in 1868 and 1872 advocated continued encouragement of immigration, although in the end official promotion was left to the states. The national government did pass one program that greatly induced immigration, although that was not its stated purpose. In order to encourage the opening and settlement of the west, the Congress enacted, in 1862, the Homestead Act. In the words of President Lincoln, when he signed the law, "so that every poor man may have a home," the act gave a settler 160 acres of land if he worked it for five years (*We Americans*: 156). A claim had to have a house with a window. The rule requiring a 12 by 12 house did not specify feet, and a 12 by 12 inch house sheltered many an owner only from the law. Ingenious devices such as that or building a cabin on wheels to roll from claim to claim were used to stake claims under the law.

Congress, of course, realized that more than free land was needed to settle the west, and it chartered two companies to build railroads, one from the east, the other from the west, to meet at a junction point. It granted each company 10 to 20 square miles of land for each mile of track built. The Union Pacific hired armies of Irish laborers to work westward from Omaha. Starting in California, 7,000 Chinese laborers built their way across the Sierra Nevada, east through Nevada, and into Utah. In 1869 the two met in Promontory, Utah, completing the first transcontinental rail line. Within a decade and a half, four twin bands of steel girded the continent and opened up the vast lands of the Great Plains to settlement. It was these lands, free or cheap, which drew millions, many of whom were immigrants.

By the early 1870s, with the development of agricultural devices such as the gang plow and reapers, mechanical threshers, and well-drilling equipment and windmills to supply water, an invasion of the western lands was under way. Fueled by a population from the east, and with many immigrants coming from Germany and Scandinavia, the frontier was pushed westward. The population of Kansas grew by nearly .5 million in the decade from 1880 to 1890, while Nebraska's did so by more than 600,000. The Dakotas grew by more than 400 percent a decade, reaching nearly 600,000 by 1890. Even Wyoming and Montana attracted tens of thousands. The cornucopia of free land was a beacon drawing millions to our shores.

In 1864, Congress passed the Contract Labor Law, an attempt to revive an eighteenth-century technique for stimulating the influx of laborers from Europe. The law authorized employers to pay the passage and bind the services of prospective migrants. While the law did not long outlive the war which spawned it, it underscored the hunger for population that grew ever more ravenous in the following years. Congress repealed the law in 1868 in favor of a laissez-faire policy. The repeal was pushed by organized labor which feared the lowering of wages encouraged by the importation of contract labor (Higham, 1955: 46).

THE RECESSION OF THE 1870s:
NEW CALLS FOR RESTRICTIONISM

A movement in the direction of restrictions on immigration began to build in the later post-Civil War years. Labor unrest gripped the coal fields of Pennsylvania between 1865 and 1875. Strikes, lockouts and suspensions signaled a period of unrest punctuated by violence. Mine owners reacted by importing more docile laborers from Hungary and Italy in the 1870s. That decade saw the beginning of a dramatic shift in immigration populations away from northwestern Europeans to those coming from south/central/eastern European nations. The "new" immigrants seemed to be both a symbol of and the agents for a widening gulf between capital and labor.

A long and severe economic depression during the 1870s fueled a renewal of anti-immigrant fervor and a revitalization of the nativist movement. When Italian strikebreakers were hired by the Armstrong Coal Works, in 1874, they touched off riots resulting in the deaths of four Italian immigrants (LeMay: 60).

A rekindling of anti-Catholicism was also sparked during the later post-Civil War years. A substantial nativist fear of "Rum, Romanism, and Rebellion" was exacerbated by the new influx. Catholics comprised only 1 percent of the total population in 1790. They were only 7 percent in 1850. By 1900, however, the 12 million Catholics here were 16 percent of the total population! Their ratio had more than doubled. The nativists perceived of them growing at an alarming rate (LeMay: 53).

A growing dismay over the corrupt urban machines also fueled anti-immigrant sentiment. "Boss Tweed," a great hulking Scotch-Irishman, organized the Tweed Ring that captured the Tammany Hall organization. Controlling New York's Democratic Party through Tammany Hall, the Tweed Ring plundered the city of millions of dollars from 1865 to 1871. Antimachine reformers began calling for restrictions on immigration.

Several states began to restrict immigration. The Supreme Court reiterated its ban on state and local regulations of immigration in the *Henderson* v. *Mayor of New York* case (92 U.S. 259, 1975). But the heightened public concern over the influx of immigrants, and the changing nature of that influx, coupled with the Supreme Court's decision emphasizing that Congress had the sole power to regulate commerce (including immigration), culminated in the first restrictions on immigration passed by the national government. In 1875, Congress enacted a statute which banned the entry of prostitutes and convicts (Vecoli and Lintelman: 103). Although the law was a weak one in terms of any real restrictions on the flow of immigration and did nothing to alter the nature of the composition of the influx in terms of nation of origin of the newcomers, it did signal that the forces advocating restrictions were gaining strength and legislative effectiveness. It clearly presaged the door-ajar era, when the beginnings of restrictionism in immigration policy were enacted. It is to a discussion of that era that the next chapter turns.

NOTES

1. These claims are cited in Parrillo: 133; and Louis Adamic: 181. They are disputed by the research of Schafer: 32–49. Not all German immigrants were enthusiastic supporters of the war. Rippley discusses several rural counties in Wisconsin where the Germans remained loyal to the Democratic Party. He cites the antidraft riots among Germans of Milwaukee, and in Ozaukee and Washington counties nearby.

2. Parrillo: 137. Dinnerstein and Reimers cite the fact that by 1860 some two-thirds of the domestics in Boston were Irish. See also Oscar Handlin's, *Boston's Immigrants* (Cambridge: Harvard University Press, 1979).

3

The Door-Ajar Era, 1880–1920

THE CHANGE IN IMMIGRANT WAVES

Although immigrants from south/central/eastern European nations had arrived in the United States during colonial times and throughout the 1820–1880 era, their numbers and influence were comparatively small until after 1880. Indeed, 1896 represents the turning point; that is, the year at which the numbers of immigrants from south central Europe exceeded those from northwestern Europe for the first time.

The fact that these newcomers were far different in their physical and cultural features than previous groups and, of course, than the majority society, plus the fact that they arrived in sufficient numbers to preserve their cultural and social identities within the various ethnic enclaves of the burgeoning cities of the U.S., all worked to increase the prejudice and discrimination they experienced. Professor Lieberson puts it in this way.

> What accounted for the exceptionally unfavorable response to the newcomers from these more distant parts of Europe? Several new forces were operating: religious issues; concentration in urban centers; implicit and often explicit racial notions; anxiety about assimilation; and the threats to existing institutions posed by the enormous numbers arriving. These concerns, later aggravated by domestic issues during World War I as well as the social and political tumult that followed, eventually led to the end of an unrestricted migration policy in the 1920s. (Lieberson: 21.)

In addition to the millions of Catholics arriving, many of the newcomers were Greek or Russian Orthodox, or Jews. More than 2 million Jews fled Europe during this period, about 90 percent of whom came to the United States. Jewish population here rose from around 250,000 in 1877 to over 4 million in 1927. (Dinnerstein and Reimers: 37–38)

As with the earlier era, several push and pull factors were at work in this vast migration, which saw some 27 million immigrants leave Europe and come to the United States. One push factor was the urbanization/industrialization revolutions spreading across Europe. These changes brought with them severe political, social, and economic disruptions. The newcomers were fleeing the horrendous conditions prevalent in their homelands: high birth rates, overpopulation, and cholera and malaria epidemics. These conditions in turn led to political unrest and often repression. European governments, in turn, coping with revolutionary pressures brought on by the forces of overpopulation, chronic poverty, the decline of feudalism and its resulting social and economic dislocations, as well as the economic shift from agrarian to industrial concerns, found that emigration was an expedient policy, and openly encouraged the waves of immigrants bound for the U.S.

Unrest in Czarist Russia contributed yet another push factor. Jews became the scapegoats for all that country's ills. Government-sponsored pogroms, begun in 1881 with the assassination of Czar Alexander II and continuing for some thirty years thereafter, forced many Jews to flee. Those brutal campaigns of beatings, killings and lootings were exemplified by the 1903 pogrom in Kishineff, Russia. Some 2,750 families were affected; 47 persons were killed, another 424 were wounded. Scores of Jewish homes were burned down, and their shops pillaged (Dinnerstein and Reimers: 38).

A number of pull factors were also involved. Transatlantic travel via the steamship lines facilitated the journey. Letters from friends and relatives in the United States induced many to come. Finally, the promise of the "golden opportunity" afforded by the U.S. was the beacon that drew millions.

On arrival, however, they often found themselves trapped in the teeming urban centers. Slum-bred cholera epidemics forced the general mortality rate of the city of New York to rise dramatically. The tenement slum dwellers of the city's East Side comprised the world's most densely populated district. It had some 290,000 persons to the square mile which far exceeded the 175,800 persons per square mile of Old London. The great influx also contributed to the virtual explosion of cities. Chicago, for instance, grew from less than 10,000 in population in 1848 to more than 1,690,000 in 1900. That was equivalent to building a new city capable of housing a population in excess of 80,000 persons a year, every year for that fifty-year period! The immigrant newcomers accounted for a significant portion of that explosive growth rate. By 1920, for example, the new immigrant groups comprised 44 percent of New York's population, 41 percent of Cleveland's, 39 percent of Newark's, and 24 percent of Boston's, Buffalo's, Detroit's, Philadelphia's and Pittsburgh's.

Figure 3.1 shows the origins of U.S. immigration by region of the world for the decades 1880 through 1920, the Door-Ajar era. The following

FIGURE 3.1
The Origins of U.S. Immigration, by Region, 1880–1920

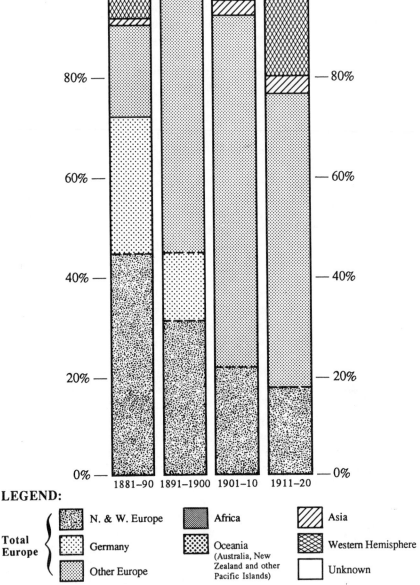

LEGEND:

Total Europe {
N. & W. Europe
Germany
Other Europe
}

Africa
Oceania (Australia, New Zealand and other Pacific Islands)

Asia
Western Hemisphere
Unknown

Source: U.S. Bureau of Census, *Historical Statistics of the United States, Colonial Times to 1970*. Washington, D.C.: U.S. Government Printing Office, 1975.

section of this chapter will highlight the immigration patterns of t'
ethnic groups comprising the "new" immigrant wave.

THE NEW IMMIGRANTS' PATTERNS

Italian immigration is a phenomenon almost exclusively of the period
after 1870. Some 5.3 million immigrants came from Italy, making it second
only to Germany as the nation of origin of immigrants from other than the
British Isles.

There was, however, some colonial and pre-Civil War immigration
from Italy. The pre-Revolutionary War immigration by Italians was lightly
scattered throughout Virginia, Georgia, the Carolinas, New York and
Florida. Some political repression in the 1780s led to a number of Italian intellectuals and revolutionaries immigrating. Pre-1880 Italian immigrants
were almost exclusively from northern Italy and they had considerable impact on the areas within which they settled. By 1848, two Italian immigrants
had been elected to the Texas state legislature. A year later, Secchi de Casali
started *L'Eco d'Italia*, a prominent Italian-language newspaper in New
York that supported the Whig Party and later the Republicans (see Iorizzo
and Mandello: 26). By the early 1850s, there was an Italian settlement in
Chicago where they served as saloon keepers, restauranteurs, fruit venders,
and confectioners, as well as common ditchdiggers and commissioned artists. At the same time, they were also lured to California by the gold rush.
Instead of mining, however, most of these immigrants became wine
growers, vegetable farmers and merchants, giving rise to "the Italio-
American folklore that, 'the miners mined the mines, and the Italians mined
the miners . . .' " (Ibid: 13). These early Italian immigrants were often
skilled craftsmen who came seeking better economic opportunity. This
changed radically after 1870.

The "Risorgimento," which resulted in the unification of Italy in 1870,
also sparked a mass exodus which saw nearly 9 million Italians cross the
Atlantic to both North and South America seeking the socioeconomic bet-
terment denied them by the movement they had supported at home. The
previous trickle of Italian immigrants, mostly from northern Italy, became
a flood from the country's south. From 1881 to 1910, more than 3 million
Italians came to the United States. Most of them settled in the cities of the
industrial northeast. By 1930, New York City's Italian residents numbered
over a million and comprised 15.5 percent of the city's total population
(*The Italians of New York*: viii). Today an estimated 7.2 million Italian-
Americans comprise about 3.5 percent of the total population of the United
States.

As with other groups arriving during this era, several push and pull factors influenced Italian immigrants to undertake the arduous and uprooting migration to the United States. Most were fleeing the shackles of poverty. The contrast in wages was considerable. Italian miners earnings ranged from 30 to 56 cents per day. General laborers received $3.50 for a six-day work week, compared to $9.50 for a 56-hour week in the states. Carpenters in Italy were payed 30 cents to $1.40 per day, or $1.80 to $8.40 for a six-day week. That same worker in America took home an average $18.00 for a 50-hour wek (*Italian-Americans*: 43–44; and *The Italians of New York*: 36–49).

Other push factors were the floods, volcanic eruptions and earthquakes that plagued Italy and contributed to its bleak agricultural outlook. Southern Italy was also especially hard hit by phylloxera, a disease which killed off agricultural plants on a scale similar to the Irish potato blight of the 1840s, and by severe and frequent outbreaks of malaria. Other Italians fled the country to avoid military service.

The pull factors were even more important. Again, the steamship lines made the journey faster, easier and cheaper. The glowing reports from relatives, friends and village acquaintances about the wealth of opportunity drew others. Returning "Americani," some of whom made the trip back and forth, had sufficient money not only to return temporarily back to Italy for brides, but also to attract many others to emulate their success in the U.S. State governments, such as those of California, Illinois, Louisiana, New York and Pennsylvania, hired agents to contract for laborers to come. And come they did. From 1890 to 1914, they arrived in excess of 100,000 annually, and for that period a total of more than 3 million Italians arrived here. So massive was the migration that

> One author told the humorous and probably apocryphal tale of a mayor who greeted the Prime Minister of Italy then touring the provinces: "I welcome you in the name of five thousand inhabitants of this town, three thousand of whom are in America and the other two thousand preparing to go (*The Italian-Americans*: 48).

The Southern Italian immigrant was often a sojourner—coming here with the intention of earning sufficient money to return to Italy and buy land back in his native village. As with the Chinese, Italian immigrants were predominantly young males. Of the millions who emigrated, roughly half did return, some having accomplished the goal, others having met defeat. But even those who remained in the U.S. often cherished the goal of returning to Italy some day. The persistence of that mentality slowed their acculturation. Why learn English, why become a citizen, why Americanize, if one were going back to the old country if not this year then next? In villages in Southern Italy even today one finds these "Americani" who, after fifty years, have returned to live on their social security benefits (Dinnerstein and Jaher: 202).

In the U.S., most settled in the nation's central cities. They found work in a wide variety of occupations: common laborers, digging the canals and waterways then under construction, digging the sewer systems and laying the pipes for the water supply, fruit and vegetable farming and vending, and working in manufacturing, such as the shoe and match industries. The latter recruited laborers but soon found that the "chain" migration was so effective that they no longer needed agents to recruit laborers, who were drawn by word of mouth or by letters from the friends and relatives who had preceeded them.

Some did settle in rural areas and occupations. In California, they so dominated the fruit and vegetable truckfarming business that Del Monte became a household word. In 1881, they sparked the development of the wine industry there as they did in upstate New York. In 1850, Louisiana had more Italians as laborers in the cotton fields than any other state, and New Orleans had a larger proportion of Italians than any other city. But by 1920, New York City led the nation with its more than .5 million Italian residents.

The massive wave of Italian immigrants arrived precisely when the U.S. was experiencing an economic downturn. The turbulent socioeconomic unrest following the Panic of 1873 and the subsequent depression led to rising anti-Semitism, emerging Jim Crowism, and a growing antipathy towards immigrants, who were often viewed by the native stock as radicals and criminals who filled our ever-growing slums, fueled class conflict, and fed the developing urban machine and its blatantly corrupt politics.

They did seem to be filling the cities. By the 1910 census, first- and second-generation Italian immigrants accounted for 77 percent of Chicago's foreign inhabitants, 78 percent of New York's, and 74 percent of Boston's, Cleveland's, and Detroit's (*Italians in Chicago*: xi).

The late 1880s and 1890s saw depression-induced violence sweeping the nation and directed at Italians. They suffered lynchings, murders and mob violence during the 1870–1920 period.

To assist them in adjusting to life here, a wide variety of self-help associations were founded, some soon after their arrival. In San Francisco, an Italian Mutual Aid Society was begun in 1857. The Society of Italian Union and Fraternity was started in New York in 1857. By 1912, New York City had 258 such societies, including the nation's most influential, the Society for Italian Immigrants, founded in 1901 (Iorizzo and Mandello: 95). By 1919, Chicago had 80 associations, including the influential Union Sicilian, the Columbian Federation, and the Order of the Sons of Italy in

America (Nelli: 172). Often begun as burial societies or mutual aid associations to help find work and housing, they soon developed into a wide variety of organizations providing a host of services and forming the basis of Italian-American social life.

Crime-related organizations emerged in a similar fashion. The mob violence directed against Italians often contributed to a rise of criminal activities in part as self-protective associations. Careers in crime became a "curious ladder of social mobility" (Vecoli, 1969: 205). When the urban machines and crime organizations linked during the period from 1910 to 1930, crime became associated with political party activity. It provided, too, a source of political leadership, as in Chicago, where Colosimo, Torrio, and Al Capone emerged (Nelli: 113–14). Crime also became a source of the derogatory stereotyping of all Italians as criminals. That image, plus the 1913 Depression, helped the revival of anti-Italian immigrant fervor by such groups as the Ku Klux Klan in the early 1900s, and led to a resurgence in the use of perjorative terms such as "wop" and "dago."

Wars had an impact on Italian-American assimilation as well. Although to a lesser extent than did the Irish, Italian-Americans won some initial, if short-lived, respectability among the native stock through their service in the Civil War. New York City sent a regiment—the Garibaldi Guard—to fight for the Union. Their war record was substantial and beneficial. In addition, some 100 Italians served in the Union Army, three of whom achieved the rank of General (*The Italian-Americans*: 30). The effects of World War I, when some 300,000 Italian-Americans served, were also pronounced.

Italian-Americans came to political activity more slowly than did the Irish, and often the two groups came into direct, occasionally even violent, conflict. Initially, Italian-American politicians emerged from various political clubs. They ran as Democrats, Republicans, Socialists, Independents, and Progressives. Prior to the 1920s, their activity was aimed at the local level. They often supported machine candidates. In New York, political activity included the creation, in 1925, of the Italian Federation of Democratic Clubs and of the Fascist League of America. Political leadership emerged out of the *padroni* system. In New York, these included several prominent Republican party leaders: Marnel, D'Angelo, Lapetino, Gualtieri and, later, LaGuardia. (*The Italian-Americans*: 138–58). In Chicago, the first state-level Italian-American politician was a Democrat, Charles Cois, who was elected to the state legislature in 1918. Several prominent Italian-American politicians served in local and judicial positions as Republicans at the same time. Nationally, Italian-Americans generally supported the Democratic candidates, but in Chicago they had a running battle against ward boss John Powers, called by them Johnny DePow and Gianni Pauli (Nelli: 99).

In 1912, anti-Wilson sentiment swung many of them away from the Democratic ticket. In New York, Republican Fiorello LaGuardia emerged as the leader of the Italian-American community. He was elected to the U.S. House of Representatives in 1915 and, after a distinguished war service, again in 1918. In 1920, he won the seat vacated by Al Smith.

Greeks have been coming to America since colonial times also—a scattering of explorers, sailors, cotton merchants, gold miners, and the like. There was even the ill-fated settlement of New Smyrna in Florida as early as 1768 (Moskos: 3–5). Greeks arrived in significant numbers, however, after the 1880s. Their peak immigration period was between 1900 and 1920, when some 350,000 arrived. The majority were young, unskilled males from the villages in the Penoponesus province of Greece. As with other SCE groups, various push and pull factors led to their migration. Political persecution played a role, although economic conditions were the primary push factor. A rapid increase in the Greek population produced an excess that the land could simply no longer support. By 1931, despite heavy migration, there was still 870 persons per square acre of cultivated land (Thernstrom: 431). Another push factor was the Balkan War of 1912–13 between Greece and Turkey. Many fled the compulsory military service in what they considered to be a Turkish tyranny.

Many Greeks, as with the Italians and Chinese, came as sojourners. They came hoping to earn enough money to provide substantial dowries for the prospective brides in their families. The fact that 95 percent were young males meant that many returned home for brides.

Better jobs in the U.S. were the single most important pull factor. The flood of Greek immigrants who arrived during this period followed one of three major routes: 1) West to work on railroad construction gangs or in the mines; 2) To New England to work in the textile and shoe factories; and 3) To New York, Chicago, and other large industrial cities to work in the factories, as busboys, dishwashers, bootblacks, and peddlers. Like the Italians, they were often exploited by a padrone system. The padrone found them jobs, helped with language problems, and settled disputes. Often the padrone's "clients" were young boys sent to them directly.

The system was highly profitable for the padrones, who made an average of $100 to $200 per year per boy, and in some cases as much as $500 per year per boy. The boys themselves would earn about $100 to $180 per year in wages.

A sizable number of Greek immigrants managed to start their own businesses, concentrating on confectionaries, candy stores, and restaurants. After World War I, for instance, there were an estimated 564 Greek restaurants in San Francisco alone. After World War II, there were 350 to 450 Greek-American confectionary shops and eight-to-ten candy manufacturing concerns in Chicago (Parrillo: 207; Moskos: 17–20).

As with Italians, Greeks did often travel back and forth to their homeland, many making the trip several times before finally settling in the United States. This back-and-forth migration undoubtedly slowed their acculturation rate. It led to a mutual lack of understanding and severe conflict with majority society. In 1904, in Chicago, for example, inexperienced Greeks, unaware of the conditions of a strike, served as strike-breakers. A wave of anti-Greek hysteria and a period of severe anti-Greek press followed. In the west, a virulent nativist movement directed a campaign against the Greek immigrants. In McGill, Nevada, three Greeks were killed in a riot in the summer of 1908. In Utah, the Mormons seemed particularly anti-Greek. The Utah press branded them as "a vicious element unfit for citizenship." In 1917, a Greek was accused of killing Jack Dempsey's brother and almost lynched in Salt Lake City. In 1923, in Price, Utah, local citizens rioted, attacking Greek stores and forcing the American-born girls who worked there to return home. The Ku Klux Klan was especially active in Utah in the early 1920s, and the Greeks were singled out as special targets (Moskos: 17). In Omaha, in 1909, a sizable Greek community of seasonal workers led to a strike-breaking situation. During the period of heightened tensions, a false arrest incident involving a Greek immigrant led to a scuffle in which the policeman died. An ugly riot the next day caused thousands of dollars of damage to the Greek section of the city (Burgess: 162–63).

Incidents such as these contributed to a growing anti-Greek sentiment. Even supposedly scholarly work, such as that of sociologist Henty Pratt Fairchild, reflected this negative image. His work stereotyped Greeks, as it did Italians, as being disproportionately of the "criminal type," and he despaired of their ever being able to assimilate.

Their acculturation was slow. They tended to live in small colonies where they could socialize and practice their religion. The Greek Church, the Greek-language press, such as the *Atlantis*, and the more than 100 Greek societies all encouraged cohesiveness. The largest and most notable of the Greek societies, the American Hellenic Educational Progressive Association (Ahepa), was founded in 1922. Its purpose was to preserve the Greek heritage and to help immigrants understand the American way of life.

Immigrating overwhelmingly in the late nineteenth and early twentieth centuries, the various eastern European groups traditionally discussed as "the Slavic peoples," were often treated alike and experienced many similarities in their immigration and acculturation patterns. They can be grouped into three regions of nations: the eastern Slavs, which include the Russians, White Ruthenians and Ukranians; the western Slavs, which include the Poles, Czechs, Slovaks and Lusatian Serbs; and the southern Slavs, those primarily of the Balkan Penninsula, which include the Slovanians, Croations, Montenegrins, Serbs, Macedonians and Bulgarians.

During colonial times, a few Slavic settlers reached the New Amsterdam and New Sweden colonies, and some Moravians joined the Quaker colony in Pennsylvania. The earliest Russian colonists date back to 1747, when a group settled in Alaska's Kodiak Island. Some colonial-period Ukranians were missionaries in California. Polish-Americans proudly stress the role of Generals Pulaski and Kosciusko as Revolutionary War heroes. Excepting these and the few who arrived after the Civil War, however, almost all Slavic immigrants came after the 1870s. Increasingly large numbers arrived from 1890 until 1921, when a new immigration act sharply curtailed their influx.

Slavic immigrants who came after 1880 tended to settle in the industrial centers of the northeast, some 80 percent of whom located in an area bounded roughly by Washington, D.C., in the southeast, St. Louis in the southwest and by the Mississippi River, Canada, and the Atlantic Ocean. Two-thirds of them can be found in New York, New Jersey, New England, and Pennsylvania. There are also sizable numbers in Illinois and Ohio. They settled largely in New York, Chicago, Detroit, Cleveland, Boston, Philadelphia, Milwaukee, Buffalo, Baltimore, Pittsburgh, Providence, San Francisco and Los Angeles.

Occupationally, the Slavic immigrants tended to replace German and Irish immigrants in the mines and factories of the midwest and Pennsylvania, and in the slaughterhouses in Chicago. Like the Italians and Greeks, the Slavic immigrants were often sojourners, comprising the majority of the more than 2 million aliens who returned to Europe between 1880 and 1914.

They all experienced severe segregation, frequently manifested in ghettoization and considerable economic hardship. The fact that their young boys worked from a young age and typically for sixty hours per week meant that they all evidenced a slower rise up the socioeconomic ladder. Their peasant backgrounds, and longer periods of economic deprivation that led to child labor and therefore less formal educational achievements among the second generation, are factors contributing to their slow rate of acculturation.

An estimated 2 million Hungarians came between 1871 and 1920, although about half returned before World War I. By 1920, for example, New York had 76,000 Hungarian immigrants residing there. Cleveland's Hungarian population was so large it was referred to as "an American Debucan," and it grew remarkably fast, in twenty years increasing from 8 to 18 percent of that city's foreign-born population (Weinberg: 174–75).

Wherever they settled they created strong ethnic enclaves with a persistent subculture. Their community, called Buckeye, encouraged the retention of their cultural identity. They clustered together, creating their own shops and small businesses: butcher shops, confectionaries, bakeries, hardware, clothing stores, taverns, pharmacies and the like.

They also concentrated in the factories and heavy industries as unskilled labor, particularly in the nation's iron, steel, and rubber works. Like the Greeks, they often used a padrone system, especially for getting work in work-gangs employed as stone cutters in the quarries, or as farm laborers in the south. Conditions were often bad. In the 1920s, they worked an average 60-hour week for $10.50 (Weinberg, 1971: 177). They were also sometimes mistreated by their bosses. In Georgia, for example, where they worked in the lumber camps, they were whipped. One particular situation led to the bosses being charged under anti-peonage laws, with ironic results.

> As the Hungarian peon recalled, a peculiar kind of justice was enacted. "Of all things that mixed my thinking in America," the Hungarian later wrote, "nothing was so strange as to find that the bosses who were indicted for holding us in peonage could go free on bail, while we, the laborers who had been flogged and beaten and robbed, should be kept in jail because we had neither money nor friends." (Dinnerstein and Reimers: 45)

In those areas where they settled in sufficiently large numbers to be visible and to be perceived as a threat, anti-Hungarian feelings developed among the native stock. The perjorative terms of "Hunky" and "Bohunk" resulted. They, too, and especially those working in the mines, were involved in the labor agitation of the 1890s. A violent incident in Hazelton, Pennsylvania, occurred in 1897. A posse, headed by a sheriff who was a former mine foreman, opened fire on a group of unarmed strikers, most of whom were Hungarian, killing twenty-one and wounding another forty. There was general agreement among other mine foremen that, had the strikers not been foreign born, there would have been no bloodshed (Parrillo: 131).

After World War I, when immigration restrictions were enacted with quotas, it became clear to Hungarians that their transient status was detrimental to them, and they ended their sojourner pattern. With the 1920s, those seeking naturalization rose dramatically, and they also began to become involved in politics, typically voting Democratic.

Estimates on the number of Polish immigrants vary widely since the official records did not always count them directly. Various estimates put them anywhere from about 875,000 to over 1.5 million. Estimates of Polish-Americans vary from 6 to 15 million.[1]

Most of those who immigrated were farm laborers, unskilled workers, and domestic servants. Less than 7 percent were classified as skilled. A fourth of them were illiterate, and virtually all came with less than $50.00 in their possession (Lopata: 3). They were typically young males, often sojourners. Their attachment to the homeland was perhaps enhanced by the fact that the ills of life in Poland could be blamed upon foreign occupation. Resentment of their own upper class seemed less than typically found among other Slavic groups.

Nearly a third managed to get into truck farming in the northeast and midwest, and into corn and wheat farming in the north central midwest and in the Panna Maria settlement in Texas, which was founded in 1854 entirely of Polish immigrant families. Most, however, settled in Buffalo, Chicago, Milwaukee, Pittsburgh, Detroit and New York. Chicago, with over 360,000 Poles, ranks after Warsaw and Lodz as the third largest Polish center in the world.

Men and boys shared common labor jobs, such as working the coal mines for a sixty-hour week to earn $15.00! It was common for children to complete but two years of high school before working full time. Polish-Americans thus showed a slow upwardly mobile pattern.

The most influential institutional mechanism in Polonia (as the Polish-American community is called) is the church. Numerous scholars have noted it as the unrivaled instrument for the organization and unification of the Polish-American community.[2] As with Italian-Americans, Polish-Americans often had difficulties adjusting to the Irish-dominated Catholic Church. Protests against that power structure took several forms: 1) parish mutual-aid societies joining the Polish Roman Catholic Union (PRCU), which was organized in 1873; 2) the Polish National Alliance, founded in 1880; and 3) the Polish National Catholic Church (PNCC), begun in 1897 and reformed in 1904. Today, there are 150 independent Polish parishes unified into the PNCC, plus an unknown number of isolated parishes split from Rome but which have not yet joined the PNCC.

An important institutional mechanism grew from the Polish mutual-aid societies and the Polish language press they developed. These served as strong links to the homeland, and the Polish government tried to manipulate and influence Polonia through them. Polonia, in turn, attempted to effect both immigration policy and Poland's emigration laws. It sent money and manpower to Poland, and exerted influence on U.S. foreign policy.

Over the years, more than 10,000 such mutual-aid societies were organized. They were especially active in the American Liberty Loan fund drives. The Polish National Department, for example, was created just before World War I. It became the mechanism through which Polish-Americans channeled more than twenty-million dollars into all aspects of the Polish cause. That amount was in addition to the 67 million dollars they used to purchase American Liberty Bonds during the War. Polonia sent 28,000 volunteers to fight in World War I. Between World War I and 1918, Polish-Americans invested over $18 million in Polish Government Bonds.

The earliest Russian immigration to the U.S. was in the mid-1700s, occurring mainly in Alaska and California. In 1792, the first Russian Orthodox Church was built in the U.S. As early as 1812, a sizable Russian settlement was begun in Sonoma, California, which lasted some thirty years before the entire group of several hundred returned to the homeland at the request of the czar.

It was after 1870, however, that the first really sizable wave of Russian immigration began. In the 1870s, some 40,000 Mennonites arrived. During the period from 1899 to 1913, 51,000 Russian immigrants arrived, some 45 percent of whom were Russian Jews fleeing pogroms. The peak years of Russian immigration were between 1881 and 1914. The 1917 Russian Revolution virtually stopped all Russian emigration. By 1910, nearly 60,000 Russian-born immigrants lived in the United States, more than half of whom lived in New York and Pennsylvania.

They worked in the mines and mills, and in the slaughterhouses of Chicago. In New York City, they worked in the clothing industry and in cigar and tobacco manufacturing. As with other Slavic groups, Russian immigrants held unskilled worker jobs in construction and with the railroads. Except for the United Mine Workers and the IWW, they tended to be nonunionized. Their pay was typically low-scale: In 1909, they worked for an average of twelve hours a day for $2.00. As late as 1919, Russian immigrants in Chicago earned only $12.00 to $30.00 per week (Davis: 17–37).

Russian immigrants also sought refuge in church and mutual-aid associations. By 1916, the Russian Orthodox Church in the U.S. had nearly 100,000 members in 169 parishes in 27 districts. They had nearly 7,000 students in 126 schools. Like the Poles, they split off as independent churches to escape the strong control of the archbishop, who in this case resided in Russia. By 1920, there were such independent churches established in Chicago; Detroit; New York; Boston; Philadelphia; Baltimore; Bayonne City, New Jersey; and in Lawrence, Massachusetts. The Russian Orthodox Society of Mutual Aid, founded in 1895, grew to 188 Brotherhoods with over 7,000 members. Likewise, the Russian Brotherhood Society, begun in 1900, grew to over 3,000 members by 1917. These groups provided health insurance, death benefits, and helped to secure jobs. After the 1917 Revolution, however, the avowedly political association, the Society to Help Free Russia, was formed. This group was anti-Bolshevik.

Russian immigrants dominated several unions: the clockmaker's, men and women's garment workers, the Society of Russian Bookmakers, and the Society of Russian Mechanics. More importantly, some 200 Russian socialistic, anarchistic, and radical clubs were started as of 1917, the largest of which was the Union of Russian Workers. These groups inflamed anti-Russian and anti-Bolshevik attitudes among their new countrymen, and contributed to a wave of prejudice, discrimination, and sometimes violence. In 1919, when the American Communist Party was formed, and a splinter group, the American Communist Labor Party, began in 1920, an hysterical reaction was set-off leading to the infamous "Palmer Raids," which eventually led to the arrest of thousands and the deportation of some 500 immigrants.

A related reaction was the suppression of the Russian language press. From 1900 to 1920, a total of 52 Russian-language papers were published. By 1921, only five such Russian dailies were still being published, the oldest having begun in 1902. The fifth daily, the radical *Novi Mir* (The New World), was suppressed by the U.S. government in 1921. The suppression led many immigrants to return to Russia and it cut-off future immigration here. It also slowed the acculturation of those who remained here. The anti-Bolshevik attitude spilled over, moreover, and affected other Slavic groups, such as the southern Slavs.

Data regarding immigration of eastern European Jews to the United States is even more sketchy than for the other SCE European groups. About 40 to 50 percent of all SCE Europeans entering the United States during the period from 1870 to 1930 were Jewish. One source estimates their immigration from 1899 to 1973 at nearly 2.5 million (Dinnerstein and Reimers: 172–74). Jews immigrated for many of the same push and pull factors that motivated other Slavic groups, plus the added push incentive of religious/political persecution, which was ultimately the most compelling cause. Jewish immigrants came in family groups intending to stay here. They settled mostly in ports of entry: New York, Philadelphia, and Baltimore. They lived in low-rent sections near those cities' business districts that quickly developed into ghetto-like areas.[3]

Jewish immigrants were better suited to the environment they found here than were the other eastern European immigrants groups. They generally had a more urban background and better job skills, which eased their acculturation into U.S. life. Sixty-seven percent of Jewish males immigrating here were classified as skilled workers, compared to an average of 20 percent for all other groups (Dinnerstein and Reimers: 44).

They were soon active in the union movement, especially in the garment industry. The Amalgamated Clothing Workers (ILGWU) were predominately Jewish and Italian. By World War II, about 60 percent of the ILGWU members were Jewish, and Dressmakers Local 22 of New York City was 75 percent Jewish. About half of the city's Jewish labor force worked in the trade. Other occupations they filled included cigar manufacturing, bookmaking, distilling, printing, and skilled carpentry. In the unskilled category, they tended towards peddling and sales. A 1900 census study found Jewish immigrants in the professions to be the highest of all non-English speaking immigrants (Leventman: 40; Bayor: 14–15; and LeMay: 92).

Anti-Semitism was experienced here, but it was nothing like the pogroms from which they fled in Russia. In colonial America, they were commonly disenfranchised, such voting restrictions lasting until 1877 when New Hampshire became the last state to end them. Anti-Semitic attitudes were prevalent, however, and were reflected in the popular culture, which commonly stereotyped Jews as avaricious scoundrels. Such anti-Semitism was generally easily dealt with by the German-Jews while their numbers remained small. Such Jews were generally middle-class. They initially feared the influx of eastern European Jews, seeing their vast migration as the cause of a new and more virulent outbreak of anti-Semitism. They were basically correct in their assessment. As the prejudice escalated, however, the German-Jews closed ranks with the newcomers and helped them to adjust.

In the 1870s, the largely latent anti-Semitism broke out into the open. In New York, in 1877, Jews were blackballed from the New York Bar Association. In 1878, New York college fraternities followed suit. The Saratoga Springs resort began to bar them and soon a host of private clubs, resorts, and private schools were doing likewise. The Ku Klux Klan revived during the early 1900s and became a leading anti-Semitic force.

Pogroms broke out in Russia in 1903 and 1906, inspiring the American Jewish community to organize to help their brethren. The American Jewish Committee began to raise money for those still suffering in Europe. In 1913, the B'nai B'rith's Anti-Defamation League (ADL) was formed. By 1909, more than 2,000 Jewish charities in the U.S. spent over $10 million that year alone. They organized orphanages, educational institutions, homes for unwed mothers and for delinquent children. They set up hospitals and recreational facilities, and supported the Jewish Theological Seminary. They began a host of Yiddish language newspapers. Between 1885 and 1915, 150 such papers were begun, including the highly influential *Daily Forward* (Howe: 518–51).

In both their religious and family lives, Jewish immigrants stessed formal education. Advanced learning was especially emphasized for males. Professional occupations were held up as the ideal, being highly valued for their secure incomes and high social prestige not only within the Jewish community but in the broader culture as well.

Education became the tool by which they secured a future, as Jewish immigrants used their occupations and an economic route to achieve security in middle-class status and as the means of acculturation into U.S. society. "By 1915, Jews comprised 85 percent of the student body of New York's free but renowned City College, one-fifth of those attending New York University, and one-sixth of the students at Columbia." (Dinnerstein and Reimers: 53).

THE FIRST RESTRICTIONIST LAWS

The effects of this new and massive wave of immigration, and its changing composition, were significantly and rather quickly felt. A strong movement to restrict immigration was under way by the mid-1870s, and achieved a degree of success in the early 1880s. Professor Bennett notes and summarizes the shift in policy during this period as follows:

> The developments of the era 1880–1920 . . . turned national policy from attempts to adjust immigration problems by treaty and executive agreement back to legislation, from attempts to restrict immigration by qualitative restrictions alone to restriction of numbers as well, and continued the established policy to discriminate among potential immigrants on the basis of other considerations if it appeared to Congress that a particular race or class of immigrants offered less change of readily assimilating into the dominant pattern of American life. (Bennett, Marion, 1963, 39).

The first targets of the restrictionist movement, and their first national legislative success, concerned the Chinese. Anti-Chinese sentiment began building in California as early as the 1850s. Violent crimes against Chinese immigrants working in the mine fields there were largely unpunished since, by 1849, a Know-Nothing judge serving on California's Supreme Court had ruled that the Chinese were forbidden to testify against white men (LeMay: 184).

The California legislature imposed various legal barriers upon them during the 1850s. In 1855, it passed the Foreign Miners Tax, which imposed a four-dollar per month tax, which increased each year the foreign miner did not become a citizen. Since the Chinese were barred from becoming naturalized citizens, the tax effectively expelled them from the mining work camps. They were also forbidden entry into public schools, denied the right to testify in court against whites, and forbidden to marry whites. By 1865, calls for immigration restrictions against them began. In 1867, the Democratic Party swept the offices of California elections by running on an anti-Chinese platform. The Panic of 1873 inspired fears of "the Yellow Peril." In 1867, the Workingmen's party won control of San Francisco. It called for an end to all Chinese immigration. By the 1870s, anti-Chinese sentiment was so strong on the West Coast that it was virtual political suicide to take their side.

Violence against them was also employed. In 1871, a riot in Los Angeles killed 21 Chinese immigrants. In 1876, the Trukee Raid took place. There whites burned down a Chinese home and shot the inhabitants as they fled the flames. The whites tried for the crime were acquitted. The Order of Caucasians was formed advocating the elimination of Chinese through the use of violence. In the early 1880s, they led mobs killing Chinese, driving many from their homes and otherwise terrorizing them in Denver, Tacoma, Seattle, and Oregon City (LeMay: 186).

Organized labor, particularly the Teamsters, became a major force behind the violently anti-Chinese movement. The Workingmen's Convention, the People's Protective Alliance, and Kearney's Workingmen's Party of California all joined labor in leading the campaign for legal restrictions of Chinese immigration. Sinophobia was so strong in California that in 1878 its constitution was amended to place legal restrictions upon them. West Coast politicians and organized labor pushed for federal legislation to restrict their immigration.

Some state and even some local governments had begun imposing a tax on immigrants as a means of restricting their influx. Those taxes were declared unconstitutional by the Supreme Court in the *Henderson* v. *Mayor of New York* case in 1875. That ruling set off a six-year campaign agitating for a federal tax law. Such a bill was opposed by the steamship lines, various business and manufacturing associations, and the representatives in Congress from the various western and midwestern states that still wanted and needed open immigration to attract the population increases they desired. In the early 1880s, New York threatened to close down Castle Garden, then *the major* reception depot for immigrants entering the country, if Congress did not act (Jones, Maldwyn, 1960, 250–51).

The movement to pass legislation in Congress, however, met with opposition from the executive branch. The imperial designs of our foreign policy dictated our relations with China. This brought the executive branch to a position opposing California's desires to restrict immigration. When Congress passed a Chinese Exclusion Act in 1879, it was vetoed by President Hayes on the grounds that it violated (as it so clearly did) the Burlingham Treaty of 1868 (Bennett, M., 1963: 16). Pressure to restrict their continued influx, however, kept building.

In the Senate, Charles Sumner of Massachusetts sponsored an amendment to the Fourteenth and Fifteenth Amendments that would have allowed for the naturalization of Chinese. It was defeated 14 to 30, with 28 abstentions (Ringer: 628). Senator Sargent of California introduced a resolution to renegotiate the Burlingham Treaty. Those negotiations took place in 1880. The new treaty was ratified by the Senate in May of 1881 and formally proclaimed by President Arthur in October of that same year.

Immediately after the ratification of the new treaty, Congress passed a new law suspending all Chinese immigration for twenty years. President Arthur vetoed that bill as well. Congress then passed a second bill, in May of 1882 (22 Stat. 58), which became known as the Chinese Exclusion Act. It stopped virtually all Chinese immigration for ten years (although it did allow for some brides to be brought in to "reunite families"). The impact of the law was immediate and dramatic. In 1881, nearly 12,000 Chinese immigrants entered the country, and nearly 40,000 came in 1882 (before the law took effect). That figure dropped to 8,031 in 1883 and a mere 23 by 1885! (LeMay: 185–86). It also prohibited their naturalization (Bennett M., 1963: 17).

The restrictionists were not satisfied with this limited ban on one aspect of immigration. They began pushing for more sweeping legislation. In August of 1882, Congress passed the first general immigration law with an avowedly (though still rather limited) restrictionist goal. The Immigration Act of 1882 (22 Stat. 214) excluded "any convict, lunatic, idiot, or any person unable to take care of himself or herself without *becoming a public charge*." That "public charge" clause, as we shall see, later became an administrative tool to significantly restrict immigration during periods of recessions and depressions. The Immigration Act of 1882 designated the Secretary of the Treasury responsible for the administration of the law and imposed a tax of 50 cents per-head on immigration. Its enforcement, however, was left to *state* boards or officers designated by the Secretary of the Treasury (Jones M., 1960: 251).

In 1885, Congress passed the Alien Contract Labor Law (23 Stat. 332), better known as the Foran Act. Organized labor, particularly the Knights of Labor, which had supported the Chinese Exclusion Act, had worked hard to enact a bill at the national level that would prohibit contract labor. The Order of American Mechanics, along with patriotic, veteran, and fraternal associations, began a strident anti-immigration campaign (Divine: 3). The American Protective Association, formed in Clinton, Iowa, in 1887, went on to become the largest and most powerful of the Protestant secret anti-Catholic societies. It adopted a strong restrictionist stance. The late 1880s saw social scientists, such as Richmond Mayo-Smith and geologist Nathaniel Shaler, questioning the economic value or need of immigration and advocating use of the ability of a group to assimilate into our society as a criterion for assessing the desirability of immigrant groups (Jones M 1960: 257–58). Their writings presaged the more blatantly racist restrictionist arguments of the early 1900s.

Ironically, the Statue of Liberty was dedicated in October of 1886, precisely when the anti-immigration mood was rising so sharply and when organized nativism was reviving. That mood contrasted sharply with the sentiment expressed in the famous poem, "The New Colossus," written by Emma Lazarus and dedicated to the Statue of Liberty, which was inscribed on her base:

Not like the brazen giant of Greek fame,
With conquering limbs astride from land to land; Here
at our sea-washed, sunset gates shall stand

A mighty woman with a torch, whose flame
Is the imprisoned lightning, and her name
Mother of Exiles. From her beacon-hand
Glows world-wide welcome; her mild eyes command
The air-bridged harbor that twin cities frame.
"Keep, ancient lands, your storied pomp!" cries she
With silent lips. "Give me your tired, your poor
Your huddled masses yearning to breathe free,
The wretched refuse of your teeming shore.
Send these, the homeless, tempest-tossed to me.
I lift my lamp beside the golden door!"
(As cited in Vecoli and Lintelman: 99)

The mid-1880s were a period of increased labor strife, radical agitation, and renewed nativism. The Molly McGuires used a violent campaign against the mine owners in Pennsylvania. The Haymarket Riot in Chicago, in May of 1886, preceded by only a few months the formation of a new nativist political party—the American party—in California. The passing of the frontier—it was officially declared at an end with the Census of 1890—and the growing class conflict of the 1880s contributed to a growing xenophobia. Congress, in 1884, amended the Chinese Exclusion Act by further tightening up its restrictions regarding the bringing in of brides of resident Chinese aliens and it required all such permanent residents to acquire a "reentry certificate"—that period's version of a green card—before traveling to China if they planned on re-entering the United States. That practice was fairly common among Chinese resident aliens, as they went back to China to get brides (miscegenation laws forbade their marrying white women here), bury family members with their ancestors, and the like. In 1887, Joseph Pulitzer, of the New York *World*, vigorously attacked the management of Castle Garden as one of his crusading ventures. In the summer of 1888, Congressman Ford of Michigan offered a resolution calling for a select committee to investigate the administration of immigration in New York and elsewhere. Castle Garden was officially closed on April 18, 1890 (Pitkin: 10–13). Clearly, sentiment was growing that we really did not want the "huddled masses of wretched refuse of their teeming shores, the homeless and tempest-tossed."

In 1888, Congress again amended the Chinese Exclusion Act. The Scott Act, as it was called, not only reaffirmed the ban of the original act, but extended it by banning the *return* to the U.S. of any Chinese laborer who had gone back to China (Ringer: 655). The Scott Act set up a Supreme Court case that challenged the Chinese Exclusion Act and dealt with the legal status of the Chinese immigrant as a permanent alien: *Chae Chan Ping* v. *United States* (130 U.S. 1889). Chae Chan Ping was a laborer who had resided in San Francisco for twelve years. He returned to China in 1887. He had in his possession a certificate for reentry as required by the law of 1884. A year later, when he was attempting to return, he was blocked, due to the passage of the Scott Act. He sued, taking his case to the Supreme Court. The Court upheld a lower court's ruling affirming the legality of the Scott Act. The Supreme Court's majority decision reflects the racism of the period and alludes to the "Yellow Peril" theme. In the words of Justice Field, author of the majority opinion, it was the

> highest duty of every nation to preserve its independence, and give security against foreign aggression and encroachments. [This was true] . . . no matter in what form such aggression and encroachment come, whether from the foreign nation acting in its national character or from the vast hordes of its people crowding in upon us. The government, possessing the powers which are to be exercised for protecting its security, is clothed with authority to determine the occasion on which the powers shall be called forth; and its determination, so far as the subjects affected are concerned, are necessarily conclusive upon all its departments and officers (130 U.S. 1889: 606).

Despite the ex post facto nature of the Scott Act, at least as it was being applied to Chae Chan Ping, and despite the obvious lack of due process afforded all Chinese laborers thus affected by the act (many of whom as long-standing resident aliens had significant property investments here that were in essence being taken from them without due process), the Court ruled in favor of Congress' right and power to make such immigration laws as it saw fit. Aliens did not have the rights of citizens and were, therefore, not governed or protected by the due process clause. In the words of Professor Ringer: "In the final analysis, then, the Chinese immigrant—no matter how long he was in the United States—had no vested right of return once he left this country, and could be barred from re-entry by an Act of Congress as could any first arrival." (Ringer: 673)

THE DEPRESSION OF THE 1890s AND SUBSEQUENT LAWS

A depression in 1891 spurred renewed efforts to restrict immigration. An even more severe depression in 1893 contributed to a natural falling-off in immigration. The decade of 1891 to 1900, for example, saw only 3,687,564 immigrants enter compared to the 5,246,613 persons who came during the previous decade (Bennett, M.: 24). These depressions also strengthened the spectrum of support and the arguments of the restrictionist movement.

In 1891, Congress created the position of Superintendent of Immigration (26 Stat. 1084), which was changed to Commissioner-General of

Immigration in 1895. The 1891 Act also prohibited the immigration of "paupers, polygamists, and those with contagious diseases." The act placed the supervision of immigration wholly under federal authority (Jones M., 1960: 263).

Senator McPherson of New Jersey had introduced a resolution to establish a station for immigration on Ellis Island. It was passed in the House after but brief debate, and signed into law by President Harrison on April 11, 1890. By January of 1892, it was being used for the reception of immigrants, replacing Castle Garden as the nation's major reception depot (Pitkin: 13-19). Until the 1891 act, there was no federal agency responsible for immigration. The Port of New York (Castle Garden) was the only one at which immigration was handled directly by the Treasury Department. At other ports—Boston, Baltimore, Galveston, Key West, Philadelphia, Portland, New Orleans and San Francisco—the federal government contracted with state authorities to administer immigration matters through those respective ports. The 1891 law, however, placed immigration matters solely under federal authority by creating the Office of Superintendent of Immigration within the Treasury Department, and charging the superintendent to report annually to the Secretary of the Treasury on the work of his office. The Bureau of Immigration was established within the department on July 12, 1891 (Pitkin: 15).

Organized labor blamed the Depression of 1893 on immigrants. A new restrictionist fervor was manifested in several ways. The Geary Act of 1892 (27 Stat. 25) extended the Chinese Exclusion Act another ten years. It has been described as the "most repressive legislation ever experienced by the Chinese in America. . . . [An act] which violated every single one of the articles of the Treaty of 1880" (Ringer: 658-59. See Also, Jones M., 1960: 263).

Critics of open immigration were no longer content to merely charge that the "new" immigrants had some shortcomings that prevented their adjustment to life in the U.S. They began to demand, with increasing vigor, that the entire process of immigration be greatly curtailed or, indeed, be brought to an immediate halt (Handlin 1959: 3). In 1892, Senator Henry Cabot Lodge advocated the use of a literacy test to bar immigrants, and, in 1894, a congressional committee on immigration first recommended a bill which proposed the use of a literacy test (Bernard: 13). By 1896, Congress actually passed a bill imposing such a test, but it was vetoed by President Cleveland.

In 1894, Congress enhanced the authority of the Treasury Department by making its decisions final, subject only to appeal to the Secretary of the Treasury. This action essentially prevented the Chinese immigrant (and later, others as well) from exercising a right to redress through the courts (Ringer: 665).

The restrictionist movement was aided in the 1890s by the development of "scholarly" studies supporting the need for restrictionism and developing the concept of racism. A number of eastern intellectuals joined the movement. In 1890, for example, General Francis A. Walker, President of M.I.T. and incoming President of the American Economic Association, delivered his presidential address to the association in which he called, on economic grounds, for the sharp reduction of immigration. In 1894, John Fiske, Nathaniel Shaler and Senator Lodge organized the Immigration Restriction League (Divine: 3). The League spearheaded the restrictionist movement for the next twenty-five years, stressing the need for a literacy test and emphasizing the differences between the "old" and the "new" immigrants as to their capabilities to assimilate.

The mid-1890s saw a vast increase in the strength of the American Protective Association, which peaked in its members in 1894, but declined after a few years due to internal factional splits (Jones M., 1960: 256). The Knights of Labor contributed their strength to the growing arguments against the "new" immigrants, although it refrained from advocating the use of a literacy test until 1897. Violent outbreaks against Italian and eastern European immigrants became almost commonplace from the mid-1890s to early 1900s. One scholar summarizes the trend:

> From the 1890s to the First World War, and in the succeeding decade, a large number of American scholars, journalists, and politicians devoted their talents to elaborating the doctrine of "racism" as the basis for immigration and population policy. In this country the varied and considerable literature which they produced had a profound effect in preparing the public for the National Origins Law before it passed and in creating a set of rationalizations to justify the law after it was passed. We might add that these writings not only molded American attitudes but proved extremely useful in the propaganda of the leaders of Nazi Germany in later years (Bernard: 16).

The creation of a federal immigration bureaucracy was especially important in that the Supreme Court tended to defer to those administrative officers all the power granted Congress over immigration matters. By the mid-1890s, those immigration officers could and did operate with a fairly wide latitude, and their actions reflected the growing racist ideas of the period. An immigration official, writing in 1917 but reflecting the norms of behavior of the officers from the earlier period as well, is cited below, in Box 1, at some length because his speech captures so well the racist ideas then current as well as illustrating the administrative powers of the immigration officers in the inspection process.

Another trend that added to the momentum of the restrictionist movement was the wave of Japanese immigration (see LeMay: 191–93). Japan

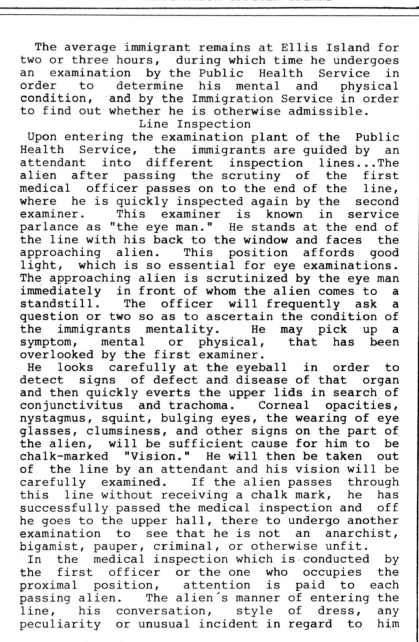

BOX 1: AN IMMIGRATION OFFICER SPEAKS

The average immigrant remains at Ellis Island for two or three hours, during which time he undergoes an examination by the Public Health Service in order to determine his mental and physical condition, and by the Immigration Service in order to find out whether he is otherwise admissible.

Line Inspection

Upon entering the examination plant of the Public Health Service, the immigrants are guided by an attendant into different inspection lines...The alien after passing the scrutiny of the first medical officer passes on to the end of the line, where he is quickly inspected again by the second examiner. This examiner is known in service parlance as "the eye man." He stands at the end of the line with his back to the window and faces the approaching alien. This position affords good light, which is so essential for eye examinations. The approaching alien is scrutinized by the eye man immediately in front of whom the alien comes to a standstill. The officer will frequently ask a question or two so as to ascertain the condition of the immigrants mentality. He may pick up a symptom, mental or physical, that has been overlooked by the first examiner.

He looks carefully at the eyeball in order to detect signs of defect and disease of that organ and then quickly everts the upper lids in search of conjunctivitus and trachoma. Corneal opacities, nystagmus, squint, bulging eyes, the wearing of eye glasses, clumsiness, and other signs on the part of the alien, will be sufficient cause for him to be chalk-marked "Vision." He will then be taken out of the line by an attendant and his vision will be carefully examined. If the alien passes through this line without receiving a chalk mark, he has successfully passed the medical inspection and off he goes to the upper hall, there to undergo another examination to see that he is not an anarchist, bigamist, pauper, criminal, or otherwise unfit.

In the medical inspection which is conducted by the first officer or the one who occupies the proximal position, attention is paid to each passing alien. The alien´s manner of entering the line, his conversation, style of dress, any peculiarity or unusual incident in regard to him are all observed. Knowledge of racial characteristics in physique, costume, and behavior are important in this primary sifting process.

Every effort is made to detect signs and symptoms of mental disease and defect. Any suggestion, no matter how trivial, that would point to abnormal mentality is sufficient cause to defer the immigrant for a thorough examination.

The following signs and symptoms occurring in immigrants at the line inspection might suggest active or maniacal psychoses: Striking peculiarities in dress, talkativeness, witticism, facetiousness, detailing, apparent shrewdness, keeness, excitement, impatience in word or manner, impudence, unruliness, flightiness, nervousness, restlessness, egotism, smiling, facial expression of mirth, laughing eroticism, boisterous conduct, meddling with the affairs of others, and uncommon activity.

Psychoses of a depressive nature would be indicated by: Slow speech, low voice, trembling articulation, sad faces, tearful eyes, perplexity, difficulty in thinking, delayed responses, psycho motor retardation.

Alcoholism, paresis, and organic dementias may exhibit any of the following signs: Surliness, apprehensiveness, untidiness, intoxication, apparent intoxication, confusion, aimlessness, dullness, stupidity, expressionless face, ataxia, stuttering and tremulous speech, great amount of calmness, jovial air, self-confident smile, talkativeness, fabrications, grandiousness, sullenness, fussiness, excessive friendliness, defective memory, misstatement of age, disorientation, difficulty in computation, pupil symptoms, and other physical signs.

Various kinds of dementia, mental deficiency, or epilepsy would be suggested by: Stigmata of degeneration, facial scars, acneform rashes, stupidity, confusion, inattention, lack of comprehension, facial expression of earnestness or preoccupation, inability to add simple digits, general untidiness, forgetfulness, verbigeration, neologisms, talking to one's self, incoherent talk, impulsive or stereotyped actions, constrained bearing, suspicious attitude, refusing to be examined, objecting to have eyelids turned, nonresponse to questions, evidences of negativism, silly laughing, hallucinating, awkward manner, biting nails, unnatural actions, mannerisms and other eccentricities.

BOX 1: CONTINUED

Experience enables the inspecting officer to tell at a glance the race of an alien. There are, however, exceptions to this rule. It occasionally happens that the inspecting officer thinking that an approaching alien is of a certain race brings him to a standstill and questions him. The alien's facial expression and manner are peculiar and just as the officer is about to decide that this alien is mentally unbalanced, he finds out that the alien in question belongs to an entirely different race. The peculiar attitude of the alien in question is no longer peculiar; it is readily accounted for by racial considerations. Accordingly the officer passes him on as a mentally normal person. Those who have inspected immigrants know that almost every race has its own type of reaction during the line of inspection. On the line if an Englishman reacts to questions in the manner of an Irishman, his lack of mental balance would be suspect. The converse is also true. If the Italian responded to questions as the Russian Finn responds, the former would in all probability be suffering with a depressive psychosis...(Mullan, as cited in Vecoli and Lintelman: 31-33).

---

passed its first emigration law in 1855, which allowed their first real influx into the United States (Ringer: 685). They came to the United States in 1868, when 148 contract laborers went to Hawaii where they were well-received as a source of cheap labor and an alternative to the Chinese "coolie" labor force (Peterson: 10). After an initial three-year period (the length of their contracts), some immigrated to the mainland. In 1870, there were only 56 Japanese immigrants on the mainland. By 1890 they exceeded 24,000; and they numbered just over 72,000 by the 1910 Census. In 1920, they exceeded 111,000, at which level they essentially stabilized because they were barred by the 1924 law.

The Japanese immigrant adapted well to working conditions here. The majority of them were young males (the ratio of male to female was about four to one) from the farming class. In Japan, that gave them middle-class status. They were highly literate—98.7 percent were able to read—distinguishing them from their western and eastern European counterparts. In Hawaii, most Japanese immigrants worked in farming, usually in all-male workgangs under the supervision of an agent. Those who immigrated to the mainland established a more diversified occupational pattern. Their most typical jobs came from working on the railroad, in canneries, in the mines, as domestic servants, cooks and waiters, and in groceries and dry goods. Their low-wage scale troubled them as they evidenced strong desires for upward mobility. They soon turned to agriculture, particularly truck farming, and became strong economic competitors. Prior to World War I, although the Japanese immigrants farmed less than 1 percent of the agricultural land in California, and often the most marginal land, they produced 10 percent of the crop.

Thomas Sowell refers to their success and to the reactions it brought about among the native population:

> No matter what their first jobs, most Japanese wanted to acquire a plot of land, and many accomplished this goal piecemeal through a succession of different types of tenure. By 1909, according to the Immigration Commission's estimate, throughout the West some 6,000 Japanese were farming a total area of more than 210,000 acres. The success of these farms derived in part from an unusual degree of specialization, but more fundamentally from the hard work and extraordinary efficiency of their owners or tenants. To block this advance, California enacted the first anti-Japanese land law in 1913. Even though President Wilson sent his Secretary of State to Sacramento to argue against it, the bill passed by 35 to 2 in the Senate and 72 to 3 in the House. Under its terms, persons ineligible for citizenship could not own agricultural land or lease it for more than three years (Sowell, 1978: 77–78).

The Japanese influx instigated a Supreme Court case that had significant impact for the power of immigration officials to allow or refuse entry into the country. In *Nishimura Ekiu* v. *the United States* (142 U.S. 651, 1891), the Court ruled that immigration officials had such power.

Similarly, the Court ruled on a case involving the power of the federal government to *expel* an alien. In *Fong Yue Ting* v. *United States* (149 U.S. 698, 1893), the petitioner, a Chinese laborer, challenged the immigration bureau's order to expel him for failing to have a "certificate of residence." Justice Gray again delivered the majority opinion, which determined such cases were a matter of *civil* law, not criminal law, and those operated with far fewer due process restrictions. The majority opinion also emphasized that immigration policy was a matter of *sovereignty*, not merely commerce.

> The right to exclude or to expel all aliens or any class of aliens, absolutely or upon certain conditions, in war or in peace, being an inherent right of every sovereign and independent nation, essential to its safety, its independence and its welfare, the question now before the court is whether the manner in which Congress has exercised this right in sections 6 and 7 of the act of 1892 is consistent with the Constitution . . . . Congress, having the right, as it may see fit, to expel aliens of a particular class, or to permit them to remain, has

undoubtedly the right to provide a system of registration and identification of the members of that class within the country, . . .

The proceeding before a United States judge . . . is in no proper sense a trial and sentence for a crime or offense. It is simply the ascertainment, by appropriate and lawful means, of the fact whether the conditions exist upon which Congress has enacted that an alien of this class may remain within the country. The order of deportation is not a punishment for crime. It is not a banishment, in the sense in which that word is often applied to the expulsion of a citizen from his country by way of punishment. It is but a method of enforcing the return to his own country of an alien who has not complied with the conditions upon the performance of which the government of the nation, acting within its constitutional authority and through the proper departments, has determined that his continuing to reside here shall depend. He has not, therefore, been deprived of life, liberty or property, without due process of law; and the provisions of the Constitution, securing the right of trial by jury, and prohibiting unreasonable searches and seizures, and cruel and unusual punishment, have no application.

Later Courts reaffirmed the majority position that Congress had sole and virtually absolute discretion in deciding whom to admit, ban, or allow to remain in this country and under whatever administrative conditions it desired. Three years later a majority opinion of the Court, again reflecting the prevailing racism of the time, stated

No limits can be put by the Court upon the power of Congress to protect, by summary methods, the country from the advent of aliens whose race or habits render them undesirable as citizens, or to expel such if they have already found their way into our land and unlawfully remain therein (*Wong Wing* v. *U.S.* 163 U.S. 228, 237, 1896).

The immigration bureaucracy became an increasingly important part of the process of admission or denial. Boards of Special Inquiry, established in 1893, began to hear tens of thousands of cases annually—in 1910 alone, for instance, they heard 70,829 cases (Pitkin: 45–46). Critics assailed the boards as being arbitrary, inefficient and often politically corrupt. In the spring of 1896, following a lingering depression in the United States, the immigration bureau used the special inquiry process to detain hundreds of Italian immigrants by invoking the "pauper" clause. Conditions on Ellis Island became so bad that the Italian emigrés rioted. Dr. Senner, then Commissioner on Ellis Island, had openly worked with Prescott Hall, Robert DeCourcey Ward, and Senator Henry Cabot Lodge of the Immigration Restriction League.

Inspectors were hired on the basis of a political spoils system and throughout the 1890s inspections were badly administered and politically corrupt. The money-exchange service, baggage handling and food concessions were a source of wealth and an inducement to corruption. The flood of immigrants taxed the system as well. Ellis Island processed some 6,500 immigrants daily.

In 1896, Terrance Powderly became the new head—then entitled Commissioner-General of Immigration—of the Bureau of Immigration in Washington, D.C. Factions in the Treasury Department developed between Powderly in D.C. and Fitchie and McSweeney in New York (Pitkin: 28). Reforms under President Theodore Roosevelt, after 1902, cleaned up the worst aspects of the political corruption of the bureau. The agency began to tighten administrative procedures as well from 1903 through 1907. Watchorn, a career immigration service officer handpicked by Roosevelt, took over Ellis Island in 1907. His administration was highly praised (Pitkin: 42).

FURTHER ATTEMPTS AT RESTRICTIONISM

During the early 1900s, the restrictionist movement pushed ahead, employing several approaches. It pushed for the exclusion of the Japanese as well as the Chinese, advocated the extension of excluded groups, and pushed for the adoption of a literacy test. The major proponents for these increased restrictionist provisions were the Immigration Restriction League, many officials of charitable and law enforcement agencies, leading sociologists and biologists, organized labor, and a variety of patriotic societies. Opposing them as well as any further restrictions were an assortment of ethnic societies, the steamship and railroad lines, manufacturers, and the National Liberal Immigration League, formed in 1906 to counter the Immigration Restriction League (Pitkin: 36).

In 1896, Senator Lodge sponsored a literacy bill that passed both Houses of Congress but was vetoed by President Cleveland during his last days in office. The restrictionist forces renewed attempts to pass a literacy bill in 1898, 1902 and 1906, all of which were defeated.

The pro-literacy efforts failed enactment prior to World War I because an effective coalition developed against that provision. Business groups remained in favor of an open-door policy as a means to ensure the continued supply of cheap labor. The National Union of Manufacturers and the National Association of Manufacturers helped defeat the literacy bills (Pitkin: 46; Jones M.: 260–62). A coalition of southern senators helped maintain Cleveland's veto in 1896, as representatives from those states also wanted the continued influx of cheap labor (Divine: 4). During the period between the Spanish-American War and World War I, overall nativism declined somewhat as the nation experienced a period of economic expansion and social buoyancy. The imperialistic outburst drained off some of the xenophobic impulses. Then, too, a growing number of ethnic associations were fighting the proposals to restrict immigration. The German-American Alliance, the Ancient Order of Hibernians, the B'nai B'rith, the Hebrew Immigrant Aid Society, and the Council of the Union of American Hebrew Congregations all fought the literacy proposals and other restrictionist attempts.

The Republican party platforms from 1904 through 1912 had no restrictionist planks, as they had in the preceding decade. Speaker Joe Cannon led the effort strenuously and successfully to defeat the literacy bills (Jones M., 1960: 261–62).

In 1903, two immigration bills were passed, however, which signaled a slight movement in the direction of restrictionism. One act (32 Stat. 1213) codified all existing immigration acts into a single statute. It expanded the excluded groups to include epileptics, prostitutes and professional beggars (Jones M., 1960: 263). The other (32 Stat. 828) moved the immigration service from the Treasury Department to the newly created Department of Commerce and Labor. The 1903 act also strengthened the organization and structure of the administrative authority by giving the Commissioner-General of Immigration greater control over the personnel and activities involved in the machinery of enforcement. By 1906, the new commissioner took pride in claiming that his bureau was being converted into an efficient and depersonalized bureaucratic instrument of social policy. Critics maintained, however, that the policy was inhumane, inequitable, and cruel in its treatment of hapless human beings.

> Aware of their strategic role as gatekeepers, a number of these officials soon took advantage of the situation in which so much was at stake for the Chinese, particularly the merchants. They extorted bribes and engaged in other corrupt practices. Compounding these problems . . . was the fact that many of these officials were drawn from California with its pathological dislike of the Chinese. As a result, they resorted to technicalities to reject the credentials of Chinese, detained many others unnecessarily while their credentials were being checked, and demanded payoffs from still others. (Ringer: 670)

The move of the bureau to the Department of Commerce and Labor did afford business interests greater access to the immigration bureaucracy in continuing their advocacy of a more open-door stance, thereby maintaining the tradition of a relatively free supply of cheap labor. The 1903 law also extended the classes of excluded aliens to anarchists, inspired no doubt by the assassination of President McKinley by the avowed anarchist Leon Czolgosz (Bennett M., 1963: 24).

During the decade from 1900 to 1910, the nation experienced the largest influx of immigrants ever—8,795,386 persons entered in those years.

This renewed massive influx, plus the concern over Japanese immigration, coupled with the Panic of 1907 and its subsequent economic depression, fueled the fires for a renewed effort at restrictionism.

The Japanese immigrants faced hostility and violence soon after their arrival on the mainland. Anti-Chinese feelings were extended to the Japanese. The shoemakers union attacked Japanese cobblers in 1890. Similar attacks by cooks' and waiters' union members followed in 1892. In 1904, the American Federation of Labor stated that the Japanese had succeeded the Chinese as the more threatening source of immigrants (Ringer: 687). Fears of the "Yellow Peril" grew markedly with the success of Japan in the Russo-Japanese War of 1905. In May of 1905, the Japanese and Korean Exclusion League was formed and claimed a membership of over 100,000 in California alone. It was renamed the Asiatic Exclusion League in 1907. It was comprised of 231 affiliated groups, 84 percent of which were labor organizations. The *San Francisco Chronicle* led a large anti-Japanese protest movement in 1905. It maintained that "two or more unassimilable races cannot exist peaceably in the same territory" (Ringer: 688). In 1906, the San Francisco School Board, despite President Roosevelt's vigorous opposition, ordered Japanese students to attend segregated schools (Jones M., 1960: 264). This ordinance compelled them to attend Chinese schools, affecting a total of 93 children. In 1907, responding to labor pressure and the politicians from California and the West Coast, President Roosevelt issued an executive order, which lasted until 1948, barring Japanese entry into the United States from a bordering country or a U.S. territory (that is, Canada, Mexico, and Hawaii, respectively). Opposition to Japanese immigration and calls for legal restrictions came from the full spectrum of political opinion. In 1907, for instance, even the American Socialist Party unanimously agreed to oppose the immigration of Asiatics. The Immigration Act of 1907 (34 Stat. 898) raised the head tax from 50 cents to four dollars and enabled the president to enter into agreements to regulate immigration, thus setting the stage for the Gentlemen's Agreement (Bennett M., 1963: 25). It also banned persons with tuberculosis, imbeciles, and "persons of moral turpitude." It also added more stringent enforcement machinery.

The sheer volume of immigration was taxing the ability of the immigration service to adequately process the influx. In 1905, Ellis Island processed 821,169 aliens alone. Each inspector had to examine 400–500 immigrants per day!

In 1907–1908, the Roosevelt Administration pressured, through economic and diplomatic means, the Japanese government to accept the Gentlemen's Agreement, by which Japan agreed to voluntarily restrict emigration.

The results of the Gentlemen's Agreement, once it began to run smoothly by June of 1908, were both dramatic and quick. During that month, for example, total immigration to the continental United States and Hawaii shrunk to only 35 percent of what it had been for that same month a year before. And, for the first complete fiscal year of operation, ending on June 30, 1909, the total figure had dropped to 3,275 from 16,418 for the year 1908; it had been 30,824 in 1907, and 14,243 in 1906. In 1910, it was less than 3,000, though in 1911 it rose to 4,000 (Ringer: 705).

The peak years of Japanese immigration were 1907 and 1908, after which it declined sharply except during the period of the "picture-bride marriage" system, which brought wives here (as with the Chinese, miscegenation laws forbade the Japanese from marrying caucasians). Between 1911 and 1920, some 87,000 Japanese were admitted, but 70,000 returned to Japan, for a net gain of a mere 17,000 for the entire decade (Peterson: 36; McLemore: 161–64; and Parrillo: 285).

Homer Lea, California's leading publicist of the "Yellow Peril," warned, in 1909, that the U.S. was loosing its "racial purity" to Asian and SCE European immigrants. The south began to join the anti-immigration movement as those racial arguments struck a responsive chord there. The American Federation of Labor endorsed calls for a literacy test. Samuel Gompers, stating the position of the AFL, said:

> The strength of this country is in the intelligence and prosperity of our working people. But both the intelligence and the prosperity of our working people are endangered by the present immigration. Cheap labor, ignorant labor, takes our jobs and cuts our wages.
>
> The fittest survive; that is, those that fit the conditions best. But it is the economically weak, not the economically strong, that fit the conditions of the labor market. They fit best because they can be got to work cheapest. Women and children drive out men, unless either law or labor organization stops it. In just the same way, the Chinaman and others drive out the American, the German, the Irishman.
>
> The tariff keeps out cheap foreign goods. It is employers, not workingmen, that have goods to sell. Workingmen sell labor, and cheap labor is not kept out by the tariff. The protection that would directly help the workers is protection against cheap labor itself.
>
> The Nashville convention of the American Federation of Labor, by a vote of 1,858 to 352, pronounced in favor of an educational test for immigrants. Such a measure would check immigration in a moderate degree, and those who would be kept out by it are those whose competition in the labor market is most injurious to American workers. No other measure which would have any important effect of this kind is seriously proposed (as cited in Handlin, 1959: 186).

Congress passed another literacy test bill in 1909, but it was vetoed by President Taft. His veto message was written by Secretary of Labor Nagel and argued that there still was a need for immigrant labor (Bernard: 13–14).

THE PRE-WAR YEARS

In 1910, Congress amended the 1907 law to remove all limitations on the deportation of alien prostitutes. Agitation for increased restrictions continued. From 1907 to 1911, a special immigration commission, the Dillingham Commission, met and studied immigration policy. It was composed of nine members—three senators, three representatives, and three presidential appointees. It was heavily stacked in favor of the restrictionist point of view. It issued its massive report—42 volumes—in 1911. The significance of the *report* was in the fact that it was proported to be an objective and scientific study, although the bias of its members is evident in its findings. The commission, not surprisingly, given its membership, recommended the adoption of a literacy test, stating that such a test was "demanded by economic, moral, and social considerations" (see Divine: 4).

It openly admitted that the purpose of the proposed law, which included the literacy test, was to decrease immigration by a quarter.

> Among its suggested means of obtaining restrictions were the following: a literacy test, the exclusion of unskilled laborers; an increase in the amount of money which the immigrant was required to have in his possession; and an increase in the head tax. The Commission also suggested the introduction of the principle of limiting the number of each "race" admitted during any given year, such limitation to be based on the numbers of that "race" which had entered the United States during a given period of years—a proposal which foreshadowed the quota law (Bernard: 13).

The commission accepted the Darwinian theories taken by the Immigration Restriction League from the writings of John Commons, Edward Ross, and especially from William Ripley's *The Races of Europe* (1899). The racial overtones of the commission's report were augmented at the time by Madison Grant's influential work, *The Passing of the Great Race in America* (1916).

Of course, the commission's study and the restrictionist movement's literature did not go unchallenged. Scholars and social workers disputed the findings of the study—particularly Jane Addams of the Hull House movement in Chicago and Grace Abbott of the Immigrants Protective League, who later served as head of the Children's Bureau. Sympathetic or pro-immigrant works by scholars and journalists included: *The Making of America*, by Jacob Riis, a journalist who went on to become especially influential with the Roosevelt Administration; Mary Antin's *The Promised Land*; Carl Schurz's *Reminiscences*; Edward Steiner's *On the Trail of the Immigrant*; and Louis Adamic's *Two-Way Passages* (Bernard: 17).

The restrictionist movement continued pushing for legal action against the Japanese. In 1913, the Webb-Henry Bill, known as the California Alien Land Act, was passed. This law restricted Japanese aliens from owning land, limited them to leasing land for three years, and forbade land already owned from being bequeathed (Jones M. 1960: 265). After the Supreme Court ruled the law constitutional, a spate of related laws were passed by several other states in the West. California Attorney General Webb frankly described the law he coauthored as follows:

> The fundamental basis of all legislation . . . has been and is, race undesirability. It seeks to limit their presence by curtailing the privileges which they may enjoy here, for they will not come in large numbers and long abide with us if they may not acquire land. And it seeks to limit the numbers who will come by limiting the opportunities for their activities here when they arrive (Kitano, 1969: 17).

Also in 1913, Congress, following the recommendations of the Dillingham Commission, passed a literacy test bill, which was vetoed by President Taft. In March of the same year, Congress enacted a law moving the immigration service to the newly created Department of Labor (37 Stat. 737, 1913). The act divided the service into two bureaus known as the Bureau of Immigration and the Bureau of Naturalization. The Bureau of Immigration was headed by a commissioner-general and the Bureau of Naturalization by a commissioner. These bureaus were placed under the immediate direction of the Secretary of Labor. The Department of Labor promptly reduced the immigration service staff.

THE POST-WAR YEARS

The World War I years were something of an interlude in immigration pressures. Whereas over 1,200,000 entered the United States in 1914, by 1915 that number had dropped off by 75 percent, to just over 300,000. In 1918, less than 30,000 were processed through Ellis Island. This slackening off in the immigration flow reduced the restrictionist pressures somewhat during the war-time interlude. A 1915 literacy test bill passed by Congress was vetoed by President Wilson, and his veto was sustained. He labeled it a test of opportunity, not of intelligence.

The Russian Bolshevik Revolution, however, aroused fears of radicalism in this country and renewed the efforts of the restrictionists. In the post-war years they were more effective. The American Legion, the National Grange, and the American Federation of Labor strongly supported the literacy test bill. This time a new law passed by Congress was enacted over President Wilson's veto (39 Stat. 874). The new law doubled the head tax from four to eight dollars, and added chronic alcoholics, vagrants, and those suffering from psychopathic inferiority to the list of excluded classes. In 1917, Congress also passed the Asiatic Barred-Zone, which more forcefully excluded the Chinese and Japanese, virtually excluding all Asian Immigration (Jones M., 1960: 270). By 1919, the Japanese practice of bringing in "picture brides" had become so acute that it became the center of a mounting anti-Japanese campaign in California (Ringer: 719).

As the 1920s were ushered in, then, the restrictionist movement crested. With a resumption of immigration after World War I that demonstrated the inefficiency of the literacy test as a means of wide-scale restriction, the movement shifted its support to the quota system as the best means to restrict immigration.

The Japanese Exclusion League, which operated mostly on the West Coast, and whose goals were pushed in California by State Senator Iman, and in Congress by California's senior senator, Hiram Johnson and lobbyist Valentine Stuart McCatchy, launched both state and national legislative drives. A series of alien land acts were passed in 1920 and 1923 to "remedy the defects" of the 1913 law. In 1922, the Supreme Court held that the Japanese were ineligible for naturalization in the Ozawa case.

Post-war periods have commonly been times of reaction, and the years after WWI fit the pattern. Radicals of all types were fiercely persecuted during the war and immediately thereafter. Wobblies, socialists, anarchists, and anyone suspected of holding such views were tarred and feathered, jailed, and sometimes even lynched. The Red Scare of 1919 led to the arrest of thousands and the deportation of about 500. The period seemed to unleash the darker forces of the American psyche. The Ku Klux Klan revived and grew alarmingly, taking on an anti-Catholic, anti-Jew, and increasingly anti-foreign outlook. "100-Percent Americanism" became the order of the day. The Klan joined forces with the American Protective League and the True Americans and launched an incendiary period of anti-Catholicism (Higham 1955: 286–98).

It was the triumph of racist ideas that provided the rationale for the restrictive immigration laws of the 1920s. "Eugenics," a pseudo-science that supposedly "proved" that certain races were endowed with an hereditary superiority or inferiority, provided the basis for the quota system (Vecoli and Lintelman: 93).

Campaigning on the theme, "Return to Normalcy," the Republicans elected President Harding with the avowed purpose of returning to conservatism, traditionalism, and a closed society. There was a climate of opinion that favored a reversal of the open-door policy on immigration. In the words of one scholar of immigration history:

Now for the first time important sections of Big Business, as a result of the fear that immigrants might propagate the ideas of the Russian Revolution, took a stand for the restriction of immigration. For the first time leaders of industry feared the alleged radicalism of the immigrant laborer more than they desired his services as a worker. Economic depression and unemployment again faced the country, and the immigrant, as had happened many times before in our history, was made a scapegoat for the hard times. More significant, however, were the intensified nationalism growing out of the war and the specter of Soviet Russia on the distant horizon (Bernard: 19).

NOTES

1. Thomas and Znaniecki put their number at 875,000; Dinnerstein and Reimers: 38, Dinnerstein and Jaher: 232, and Parrillo: 174 all put it at over one million. Lopata: 38 puts the maximum at 1,670,000 for the number who immigrated here from 1885 to 1972, and estimates the total Polish-American group, referred to as Polonia, at about 12 million. Levy and Kramer's estimates of "Slavic-Americans" range from 6 to 15 million: 141–42.

2. See, for instance, Thomas and Znaniecki: 238; Parrillo: 175; Lopata: 48; and Dinnerstein and Reimers: 53.

3. See Joseph: 69; Howe: 5; and Dinnerstein and Reimers: 37–38.

4
The Pet-Door Era, 1920–1950

THE IMMIGRATION ACT OF 1917

The ability of Congress to override President Wilson's second veto of the literacy bill passed in 1917 was a clear indication that the tide in favor for restrictionism was flowing to irresistible levels. The Red Scare of 1919, with its accompanying xenophobic fear of Bolshevick radicalism, set the stage for the 1920s that in turn ushered in a new era of immigration policy. A tradition of open-door policy over a century-old was to be overturned. In its stead, the United States was about to adopt a policy of avowed restrictionism. Moreover, it was about to enact a policy of *effective* restrictionism, one which would essentially close the door to all but a favored few.

When it became clear that the passage of the literacy bill, even if over the president's veto, was not enough to stem the large-scale influx of immigration, the proponents of restrictionism were forced to advocate a more stringent and effective measure: the imposition of an absolute number limiting the influx of immigrants. Some called for the total suspension of all immigration from anywhere from two to as long as fifty years. In terms of both absolute numbers and as a percent of the total population, the decade from 1900 to 1910 showed the largest influx of immigration in our history (see Figure 4.1). Despite the various restrictive measures passed during the 1880s and 1890s, and despite the literacy test imposed in 1917, the decade from 1910 to 1920 was second only to the preceding one in terms of absolute numbers entering the United States during a decennial period, and third in terms of annual immigration as a percentage of total population size. The proponents of restriction realized a more drastic step was needed than any previous measure passed if they were to successfully stem the flood of immigration. They rather quickly changed from advocating literacy to the imposition of quotas based upon national origins. As we shall see more fully below, they did so with rather remarkably dramatic results.

Figures 4.1 and 4.2 graphically portray the effects of that policy change. As Figure 4.1 demonstrates, absolute numbers declined sharply in the decade from 1920 to 1930. In the decade from 1930 to 1940, when the Great Depression was added as a factor greatly reducing immigration, the U.S. experienced the least-ever influx of immigration, both in absolute terms and as a percentage of total population. Indeed, the 1930–40 period was one in which emigration exceeded immigration by some 85,000, resulting in a *negative* decennial net migration as a percentage of population growth. But the change in numbers was not the only dramatic result of the new policy.

Figure 4.2 presents the origins of U.S. immigration by region for the decades of the Pet-Door Era. The pronounced movement away from south/central/eastern European immigration and towards that from northwestern Europe is clearly evident in Figure 4.2.

This chapter will briefly discuss how and why those dramatic shifts occurred. It begins that discussion by focusing upon the 1921 emergency immigration restriction law that first introduced the quota system. As we shall see below, it was very heavily weighted in favor of immigrants from northwestern Europe. The 1924 National Origins Act somewhat modified those weightings, showing an even greater bias against SCE European immigration and firmly setting the principle of the national origins system as the prevailing policy position for the next forty years!

THE QUOTA ACT OF 1921

The years from 1917 to 1920 saw the restrictionist fervor rise to its high point. An "Americanization" movement swept the nation in the aftermath of World War I. In the hysteria of the war era, people had called sauerkraut "liberty cabbage," and hamburgers became "Salisbury steaks." Many cities and towns renamed "foreign"-sounding streets, giving them "American" names. The state of Oregon passed a law requiring all children to attend public schools [obviously aimed against Catholic parochial schools], and California struck out at aliens by ordering every adult male alien to register and pay a special annual poll tax of ten dollars. Although both the Oregon and California laws were declared unconstitutional, their passage represented the zenith of the Americanization movement (Higham 1955:260). The *Dearborn Independent*, Henry Ford's notorious paper, launched a massive anti-Jewish campaign and stressed the need for immigration restriction. The revived Ku Klux Klan grew in membership and influence. It, too, advocated strict limits on immigration. The AFL continued its campaign, begun in the 1880s, to limit the influx of "cheap immigrant labor." Both the Democratic and the Republican party platforms called for effective limits on immigration.

FIGURE 4.1
Levels and Rates of U.S. Immigration, 1870–1979

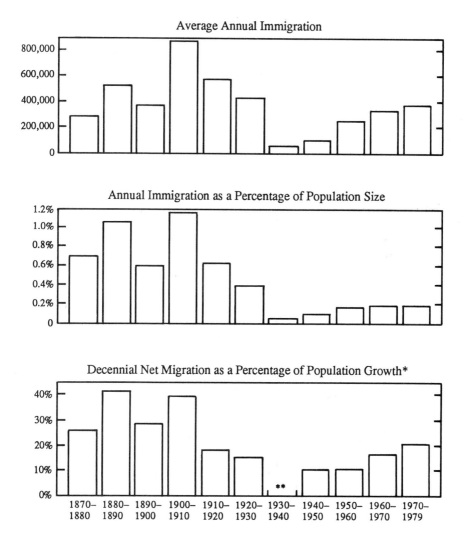

*Decennial migration as a percentage of population growth equals total decennial population increase minus natural population increase [births and deaths] divided by total population increase.

**Emigration exceeded immigration by 85,000.

Source: Select Commision on Immigration and Refugee Policy, *Staff Report*, Washington, D.C.: U.S. Government Printing Office, April, 1981: 28.

FIGURE 4.2
The Origins of U.S. Immigration, By Region, 1920–1950

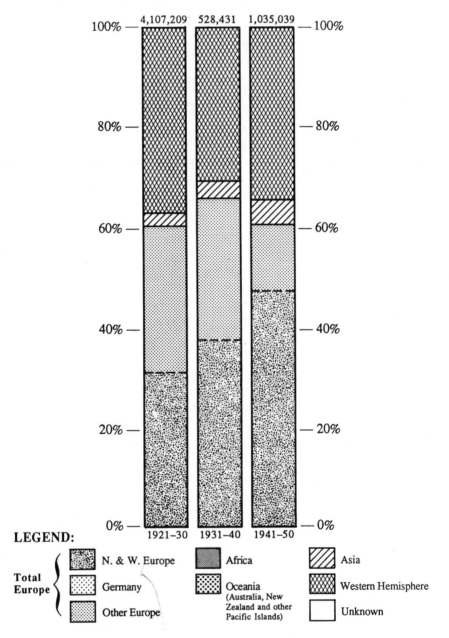

Source: U.S. Bureau of the Census, *Historical Statistics of the United States, Colonial Times to 1970*. Washington, D.C.: U.S. Government Printing Office, 1975: 28.

The fear that the economic chaos which gripped Europe in the immediate post-war years would lead to a flood of immigrants to the United States fed the restrictionist movement. When the United States experienced a slight depression in 1920, the passage of some restrictionist legislation seemed inevitable. In 1920, the House voted to end immigration altogether, although the Senate refused to go that far. A number of leading senators, however, advocated a strict restrictionist policy. Among the more prominent were: Senators Danford and Taylor of Ohio, Johnson and Shortridge of California, Lodge and Morse of Massachusetts, Johnson and Watson of Indiana, Reed of Pennsylvania, Corliss of Michigan, Hepburn of Iowa, Caffery of Louisiana and Wilson of South Carolina. Clearly the restrictionist sentiment was becoming evident in every region of the country. There were only a few defenders of immigration openly vocal in the Senate: Gibson of Maryland, Mahany of New York, Bartholdt of Missouri, and Buch of Louisiana (see Taylor: 244). In the House, Bourke Cochran and Adolph Sabath were the primary voices in favor of open immigration.

The restrictionist forces were gaining not only in numbers, but also in the influence of their positions in Congress. Senator Dillingham, who had chaired the Immigration Commission in 1907, was, by 1917, the chairman of the Immigration Committee of the Senate. Likewise, the chairman of the Republican-dominated House Immigration Committee was Albert Johnson of Washington, a leading restrictionist voice.

In 1919, after the famous "Palmer Raids", 500 immigrants suspected as radical anarchists were deported aboard a ship to Russia nicknamed "The Soviet Ark." Public sentiment, aroused by the Sacco-Vanzetti case and the collapse of Wilsonian idealism evident in our rejection of the League of Nations, gave a new edge to the restrictionist arguments. The post-war isolationist mood was easily tapped by the forces advocating limits on immigration. The new nationalism, distrustful of further entanglements with Europe, was committed to isolationism and disdainful of all foreigners. It echoed through the debates over our joining the League of Nations. It swayed the position taken by the American Legion. It rumbled in the "konklaves" of the Klan. It unleashed a torrent of state legislation excluding aliens from many occupations. Licensing acts barred them from practicing architecture, engineering, chiropractic, pharmacy, medicine, surgery, surveying, and executing wills. Such laws even forbade their operating motor buses (Higham, 1955: 271, 301).

The 1919 Red Scare, coupled with a depression, led to the adoption of a pro-restrictionist stance by forces one might otherwise expect to have been in favor of more open policy. The Progressive party voiced concern about the nation's ability to absorb and assimilate so many aliens. *The New Republic* mused that unrestricted immigration was an element of nineteenth-century liberalism fated to end and that a progressive society could not allow social ills to be aggrevated by excessive immigration (Higham 1955: 302).

Business and economic interests that previously had been strong advocates of continuing an open-door policy were either silent or changed to a restrictionist position. The 1920 Depression meant that there was no labor shortage. Many business leaders accepted the arguments of the "100 Percenters," the American Legion, and similar nationalist groups within the Americanization movement. Kenneth Roberts published a series of articles in *The Saturday Evening Post*, which became a leading proponent of the restrictionist crusade from 1920 to 1924. Roberts' series popularized a new element in the restrictionists' arsenal of arguments—an "ethnic theory" (Divine: 10). The halls of Congress soon echoed with calls to end the "alien flood," "barbarian horde," and "foreign tide." All the stereotypes common in the popular press were used in Congress. In the words of a congressman from Arkansas:

> We have admitted the dregs of Europe until America has been orientalized, Europeanized, Africanized and mongrelized to that insidious degree that our genius, stability, greatness, and promise of advancement and achievement are actually menaced. Accordingly, I should like to exclude all foreigners for years to come, at least until we can ascertain whether or not the foreign and discordant element now in what many are pleased to term "our great melting pot" will melt into real American citizens (in Ringer: 801).

Such sentiments were a far cry from those inscribed but a few decades earlier at the base of the Statue of Liberty.

When the business forces were either silent or switched to a pro-restrictionist position, the passage of some sort of limiting legislation became inevitable. It was virtually unopposed in Congress. As Professor Divine notes:

> Fundamentally, it was the transformations in American economic and political development that set the stage for restriction. The growth of the American economy and particularly the technological changes brought about by the industrial revolution had greatly reduced the need for the raw labor furnished by immigrants. A mature industrial system required a moderate number of trained workers, not great masses of manual labor (Divine: 9).

When the United States emerged from World War I as a true world power, it developed a more intense nationalism in which U.S. citizens increasingly demanded unity and conformity. The new position of the nation on the international scene became the base for the restrictionist policy.

The thrust of advocating the quota approach to restrictionism came from several sources. The return to economic prosperity in 1921 relegated the *economic* issues to a secondary role in the debates over passage of an immigration law. The National Association of Manufacturers led the pro-immigration forces. The AFL attacked them as being interested only in cheap labor. It argued strenuously that there already was an adequate supply of labor in the nation's work force. A leading sociologist, Henry Pratt Fairchild, advocated the position taken by organized labor. As a result, the economic arguments became largely deadlocked between opposing pressure groups. This development forced the restrictionists to concentrate their attacks on immigrants from the "ethnic theory" approach. Among the leading voices for these theories were Carl Brigham, a Princeton psychologist famous for devloping the "I.Q." test; William MacDougall of Harvard, who proposed a "Nordic Race" superiority theory; Dr. Harry Laughlin, the prominent and extreme "eugenist," who was the "biological expert" for the House Immigration Committee and who went so far as to advocate the sterilization of all inmates of mental institutions (Bernard: 29); and Gino Speranza, a native-born U.S. citizen of Italian descent who wrote a series of articles in *World's Work* that popularized the idea of the need for national unity and conformity by defending racial and cultural homogeneity. These sources helped forge a new concept of "racial nationalism." Undoubtedly, however, the most influential voice and central inspiration in these racial theory writings was that of Madison Grant. In his highly influential book, *The Passing of the Great Race*, Grant wrote that the nation was becoming inundated by

> a large and increasing number of the weak and broken and mentally crippled of all races drawn from the lowest stratum of the Mediterranean basin and the Balkans, together with the hordes of the wretched, submerged populations of the Polish ghettos. Our jails, insane asylums and almshouses are filled with this human flotsam and the whole tone of American life, social, moral and political, has been lowered and vulgarized by them. (89–90)

The book was first published in 1916, but new editions in 1921 and 1923 brought its total sales to nearly 16,000 copies. Grant also published a series of editorials in the *New York Times* and the *Saturday Evening Post*. He inspired a number of popular writers and influenced many scholarly ones. He was the leading popularizer of a theory that recognized within the "white race" a three-tiered hierarchy of Mediterraneans, Alpines, and Nordics. According to Grant, white Americans were Nordics, the highest, and should regard any mixture with the other two as a destructive process of "mongrelization" (Higham, 1955: 272).

By 1921, congressmen, reflecting this perspective, were arguing that the melting pot had failed and immigration was causing the nation to suffer from "alien indigestion." They feared the country was becoming an "intermingled and mongrelized people," and began substituting the idea of racial purity for the "melting pot." A Maryland senator called for a "racially pure" country so that we might achieve the greatness of England, France, or Germany. A congressmen from Maine stated:

> God intended, I believe, [the U.S.] to be the home of a great people. English-speaking—a white race with great ideals, the Christian religion, one race, one country, and one destiny . . . It [the U.S.] was a mighty land, settled by northern Europeans from the United Kingdom, the Norsemen, and the Saxons, the people of a mixed blood. The Africans, the orientals, the Mongolians, and all the yellow races of Europe, Asia, and Africa should never have been allowed to people this great land (cited in *"We the People" and Others*: 801–802).

The House Committee on Immigration was the most prominent voice in Congress for these racial theories. Indeed, by 1921, it was stressing a racial theory as *the fundamental* justification for restriction.

Nor was Congress alone susceptible to the new racist ideology. The Supreme Court, in *Ozawa* v. *U.S.* (260 U.S. 1922), upheld the constitutionality of a blatantly racist law that made the Japanese "aliens ineligible for citizenship" (Ringer: 790–91). And later, in 1927, the Court upheld an ordinance of Cincinnati which barred noncitizens from operating pool halls. Although the Court acknowledged the Fourteenth Amendment's prohibition against irrational discrimination, it ruled that the Cincinnati ordinance was not irrational. The Court agreed with Cincinnati's attorney, who depicted pool halls as vile places in need of strong police powers to curb them. Since "noncitizens" as a class were less familiar with the laws and customs of the nation (and in this case of the municipality) than were native-born or naturalized citizens, the city argued, it was a reasonable exercise of local police powers to exclude them. The Court agreed that "alien race and allegiance" may be a legitimate object of legislation so as to be made the basis of a permanent classification.

This same line of judicial reasoning later allowed a host of state licensing laws that limited aliens in practicing various professions (*Clarke* v. *Deckenback*, 274 U.S. 392, 1917).

The principle of allocating quotas on the basis of those already represented by the various nationalities among the U.S. foreign-born population was first introduced by Dr. Sidney Gulick in 1914. He intended it as a liberal alternative to positions being advocated by the strict restrictionists, some of whom had begun calling for total suspension of immigration. Dr. Gulick was a former missionary in Asia. In 1918, he formed the National Committee on Constructive Immigration Legislation. He suggested that each nationality be assigned a quota proportionate to the number of *naturalized* citizens and their U.S.-born children already drawn from that nationality. Annually, an immigration commission would fix a certain percentage—he suggested 10 percent or less—of those first-and second-generation *citizens*. As he put it: "The proved capacity for genuine Americanization on the part of those already here from any land should be the measure for the further immigration of that people" (cited in Higham, 1955:302).

The "percentage quota principle," as it became known, was soon the central piece of all immigration laws passed in the 1920s. What differed among its advocates was the notion of precisely how the quotas should be set up. After the 1921 law, however, the basic principle that there should be quotas was fairly well accepted.

The pivotal and basic function of the quota system was to limit immigration from Europe. The battles were largely over how to distribute such quotas among the various countries of Europe.

In the final Congressional debate over the bill, and in the later battles in 1923 and 1924, the primary organizational support in favor of the origins bill and concept included: the American Federation of Labor, the American Legion, the Immigration Restriction League, the National Grange, the Ku Klux Klan, the Junior Order of the United American Mechanics, as well as such patriotic associations as the Sons of the American Revolution, the Patriotic Order of the Sons of America and the Daughters of the American Revolution. The primary opposition to the bill included: the Anti-National Origins Clause League; a New York taxpayers association; several industrial and employer organizations, chiefly the National Association of Manufacturers, the American Mining Congress, the Associated General Contractors, the National Industrial Conference Board, and the U.S. Chamber of Commerce; some farm organizations concerned that agriculture would be denied sufficient manpower; spokesmen for various Jewish, foreign-language, and other "ethnic groups" that would be adversely affected by the 1890 base year, such as the Vasa Order of America (Swedish), the Steuben Society, the Danish Brotherhood of America, the Sons of Norway, and the German-American Citizens League (Bennett, M. 1963: 52–53; and Divine: 33–37).

The Senate passed a bill, sponsored by Senator Dillingham, which limited European immigration to 5 percent of the number of foreign-born of that nationality present in the U.S. as determined by the 1910 census. The bill exempted Canada and Latin America from the quota system. The Senate version would have limited total annual immigration to a quarter of a million. The bill easily passed the Senate—its only real opposition coming from southern and western senators who wanted total suspension of immigration. The House abandoned its various suspension plans in favor of the Senate quota system, but reduced the limits from 5 to 3 percent of the 1910 census (Higham: 310–11). It limited total immigration to 350,000 and assigned most of that to northwestern Europe. Congress adopted that version in a conference committee and sent the bill to President Wilson. He killed the bill with a pocket veto during his last days in office—a veto which was quickly to be in vain.

The in-coming president, Warren Harding, called a special session of Congress. In the House, Albert Johnson supported the bill rather than his own total suspension plan. It passed the House without a record vote. In the Senate, it passed 78 to 1 and was signed into law by the president in May of 1921.

The Johnson Act, the Emergency Immigration Restriction Act of 1921, thus first established the principle of the quota system. It was heavily weighted in favor of northwestern Europe. The 1921 law set the total quota at 357,803. It drastically cut down the influx of immigration and shifted the composition of that by limiting Asia, Africa, and Oceania to less than 1000 immigrants, northwestern Europe to basically 200,000 immigrants, and southeastern Europe to just over 155,000 immigrants. The act reaffirmed, moreover, all the previous restrictions on "excluded groups" by barring the mentally, physically, and morally "undesirable" classes, including those persons likely to become public charges, as was established in the 1917 Immigration Act. The central basis for determining each country's quota under the 1921 law was 3 percent of the foreign-born population as present in the U.S. according to the 1910 Census data.

THE IMMIGRATION ACT OF 1924

Passage of the emergency act in 1921 hardly settled the matter. The restrictionists were not fully satisfied that the law sufficiently limited the influx, and the quota system as temporarily set up imposed some harsh injustices. Ships arriving during the first months after passage of the law often carried more than the monthly quota from that country would allow entry. Polish, Rumanian, and Italian immigrants jammed Ellis Island and steamships in the harbors of Boston and New York. Administrative "exemptions" to the monthly quotas necessitated by these dire conditions angered the congressional restrictionist forces.

For two years, the Congress was deadlocked over attempts to set up a more permanent quota system. Albert Johnson's committee in the House, with the strong and vocal backing of the AFL and the American Legion, continued urging total suspension. Preston Hall, of the Immigration Restriction League, Madison Grant, Lothrop Stoddard, Kenneth Roberts and Harry Laughlin all supported the Johnson Committee and stirred up public debate on the issue.

A prominent New York attorney, John D. Trevor, began to work closely with the Johnson Committee. By the fall of 1922 they were advocating changing the base year for the Census from 1910 to 1890, and reducing the quota from 3 to 2 percent. The calculation of the quotas based on the 1890 census data, of course, meant that the total annual immigration would be less, and the continued influx from SCE European nations would be reduced from a flood to a trickle.

By 1922, the effects of the 1920 Depression were dissipating markedly. As unemployment shrank, business began experiencing a labor shortage. Manufacturers began advocating the easing of restrictions. The National

Association of Manufacturers lobbied strenuously for easing the limits. The U.S. Chamber of Commerce lobbied for *adding 2 percent* to the quotas. The president of U.S. Steel labeled the 1921 law "one of the worst things this country has ever done for itself economically" (cited in Higham, 1955: 315). Big farmers, losing their hired hands to the lure of the cities' better-paying jobs in the factories, joined business in protesting the law.

By 1923, the Senate Immigration Committee, at the urging of NAM, introduced a bill retaining the quota system, but allowing for additional immigrants in times of labor shortage. Senator Reed of Pennsylvania sponsored a compromise bill that increased total immigration but reduced the share of southeastern European nations. A period of stalemate ensued as the Republican leadership in both Houses decided to defer action until 1924.

From late 1923 to early 1924, sentiment began to shift. Increased mechanization in the economy was easing labor shortage pains and requiring more skilled workers rather than more unskilled ones. The National Industrial Conference Board, a research and public relations agency for thirty-one leading industrial associations, held a conference on immigration in New York in December of 1923. Business resolve for easing restrictions was wavering. NAM and the Chamber of Commerce recommended, early in 1924, that the quotas of 1921 be retained rather than being reduced, but neither organization was willing to strongly lobby the Congress on the matter.

The battleground shifted, then, to various ethnic associations pushing for or opposing quotas as they would affect the immigration status from those countries. A "Nordic theory" gained ground. The newly elected Calvin Coolidge gave the restrictionist cause his blessing by calling, in his first presidential address, for action that would assure that "America might be kept American" (Higham, 1955: 318). The Secretary of Labor, James Davis, after touring Europe, submitted an administrative proposal to the house committee. The Johnson Committee overhauled it, relying more on its unofficial advisor, John Trevor, who supplied what became the solution to the deadlock.

Trevor designed an attack on the quota scheme of the 1921 law. He argued that quotas based on the 1910 census data did not reflect the "racial status quo" of that nation. Use of the 1910 data base, he maintained, overly favored southeastern Europeans. Trevor used a "racial breakdown" of the U.S. population published earlier by Clinton Stoddard Burr in *America's Race Heritage*. Trevor's analysis "proved" that, as of 1920, about 12 percent of the U.S. population derived from southeastern European countries, but on the basis of the 1921 law they were allocated 44 percent of the total immigration quota. If, however, the 1890 census were used, they would have only 15 percent.

Johnson's Committee, relying on the Trevor brief, introduced a new bill. The Ku Klux Klan launched a massive letter-writing campaign supporting the bill designed to "preserve" America's racial purity. The AFL also backed the bill.

Representative Carl Vinson of Georgia stated the committee's majority perspective on the proposal in April of 1924 when he said:

> Those favoring unrestricted immigration are wont to harken back to the days of the discovery, colonization and settlement of our country. In respect of this argument, I want to be thoroughly understood. Were the immigrants now flooding our shores possessed of the same traits, characteristics and blood of our forefathers, I would have no concern upon this problem confronting us, because, in the main, they belonged to the same branch of the Aryan race. Americans and their forebears, the English, Scotch and Welsh, are the same people.
>
> These ancestors of the real American people were related one to the other and possessed, to a large degree, similar tastes, traits and characteristics. And in the amalgamation of these people and their transition into American life we find the persons who created and now maintain the greatest Nation on the globe.
>
> But it is the "new" immigrant who is restricted in emigrating to this country. The emigrants affected by this bill are those from Italy, Greece, Russia, Poland, Bulgaria, Armenia, Czechoslovakia, Yugoslavia, and Turkey. I respectfully submit, with all the power within me, that the people from these countries do not yield their national characteristics, but retain them practically unimpaired by contact with others (cited in Bennett M., 1963:48).

In its report on the bill to the full House, the committee stated:

> Since it is the axiom of political science that a government not imposed by external force is the visible expression of the ideals, standards and social viewpoint of the people over which it rules, it is obvious that a change in the character or composition of the population must inevitably result in the evolution of a form of government consonant with the base upon which it rests. If, therefore, the principles of individual liberty, guarded by constitutional government created on this continent nearly a century and a half ago are to endure, the basic strain of our population must be maintained and our economic standards preserved (Bennet M., 1963:49).

Congressional representatives from the West Coast, particularly those from California, and those from the south, emphasized similar racial sentiments in their concerted efforts at restrictionism. California's representatives bore down on the alleged inadequacies of the Gentlemen's Agreement: they stressed its questionable legal validity, its vagueness, and its ineffectiveness. They played on the "Yellow Peril" theme, warning that Japan's overpopulation and thirst for land might lead to a future "race war." A congressman from Maine, likewise, railed against past immigration policies by maintaining that they:

have thrown open wide our gates and through them have come . . . alien races, of alien blood, from Asia and southern Europe, the Malay, the Mongolian, the oriental with their strange and pagan rites, their babble of tongues—a people that we can not digest, that bear no similarity to our people, that never can become true Americans, that add nothing to civilization, but are a menace to our form of government. . . .

The hour has come. It may be even now too late for the white race in America, the English-speaking people, the laborer of high ideals, to assert his superiority in the work of civilization and to save America from the menace of further immigration of undesirable aliens. [Applause] . . . [to accomplish this] I wish it were possible to close our gates against any quota from southern Europe or from the orientals, the Mongolian countries and the yellow races of men. (as cited in *"We the People" and Others*: 802).

The anti-Japanese provisions was to exclude "those persons who could not become citizens and who must continue to owe allegiance to a foreign country." The debate centered on the theme on nonassimilability and linked Japanese exclusion and minimal quotas for those from southeastern European nations.

Only Representative Burton of Ohio argued for giving Japan a quota, and his views were considered to reflect the administration's position, particularly that of Secretary of State Hughes. In the Senate, Reed of Pennsylvania, the bill's co-author, originally fought against the provision to totally exclude the Japanese. Senators Shortridge of California and Lodge of Massachusetts fought vigorously to include their restriction. When opposition to the ban against the Japanese collapsed, even Senator Reed switched his position, supporting an amendment to the bill that would preclude them. The provision passed 71 to 4 (two opposed, two abstained). (See Ringer: 822). It clearly demonstrated the *racist ideas* behind the restrictionist law.

Senator Colt, however, the chairman of the Senate's Immigration Committee, adamantly opposed changing the census base year. He argued it was discriminatory. Secretary of State Hughes quietly supported the senator's position. The Senate committee reported a bill to keep the census year at 1910, but to lower the percentage from 3 percent to 2 percent of that base. Senator David Reed led the measure through the committee and Senate deliberations, as Senator Colt was in poor health and not enthusiastic about the bill (Divine: 35).

Senator Reed then pushed a proposal through the Senate committee that used the quota based on 1890 census data, receiving valuable support and encouragement from Senator Henry Cabot Lodge of Massachusetts. The full Senate, however, adopted the version retaining the 1910 census base and stipulated that the quota system would not go into effect until

1927, enabling the immigration service ample time to formulate exact quotas. For the interim (that is, until 1927—although it was actually 1929 before the issue was resolved), the Senate accepted the House version of 2 percent, based on the 1890 census. This compromise version won overwhelming Senate support: 62 to 6. In the House, it passed by a vote of 323 to 71 (Divine: 17). President Coolidge signed the bill on May 26, 1924.

The only opponents of the measure were representatives who served as advocates of the southeastern European groups so adversely effected by the law. Jewish leaders secured the vocal support of Senator Sabath of Illinois and Senator Colt of Rhode Island, who labeled the measure and its proponents as unAmerican and lackies of the Ku Klux Klan. Senator Underwood, of Alabama, however, responded that his opposition to immigration was economic, not racial.

The law had support from members of both parties: only 35 Republicans and 36 Democrats opposed it in the House. It had overwhelming support from virtually every section of the country, the only dissent coming from some senators and representatives of districts in the northeast where immigrants from SCE Europe were concentrated. The measure was politically popular. It reflected the triumph of the "Nordic majority" in the country over the southeastern minority.

The Immigration Act of 1924, or the Johnson-Reed Act, as it became popularly known, was a lengthy and technical one. Its central restrictive features are summarized in Box 2.

Perhaps as important to the quota system, the provision for requiring visas served as an effective regulating device. Indeed, the *overseas* issuance of visas charged against quotas became the most effective means devised to control the use of quotas and to allow for *administrative screening* of immigrants prior to their entry into the U.S. The 1917 provision prohibiting persons "who might become public charges" provided an effective administrative tool to enforce that prohibition. It was used to dramatically cut down the amount of total immigration during times of depression by setting strict standards for economic tests to demonstrate the applicant's admissibility.

THE NATIONAL ORIGINS ACT OF 1929

Passage of the 1924 Johnson-Reed Act did not end the battles, although it settled the major policy position firmly in favor of restriction. The national origins principle was by then accepted as the basis of our national immigration policy. Future battles concerned only the mechanics of how the quotas themselves would be fixed.

In an editorial in March of 1924, the *New York Times* summed up the fundamental perspective of the national origins system, advocating what it held to be the basic needs of a *permanent* quota system:

1) It preserved all of the qualitative restrictions of the 1917 Immigration Act. As we shall see more fully below, this aspect became increasingly important as administrative actions based upon the strict interpretation of the "public charge" clause of the 1917 Act came to be more frequently used to limit immigration during periods of economic recession or depression.

2) It maintained the principle of numerical limitation first established by the 1921 Act, although reducing the total numbers allowed to enter through the quota system by using a new formula. Essentially, it reduced the total European quota from the 350,000 allowed in under the 1921 Act to just under 165,000.

3) It shifted the base year of census data from 1910 to 1890. This substantially reduced the proportion of immigrants coming from S/C/E Europe. This provision was stipulated as an interim one with a permanent national origins formula to take effect in 1927 [although it was actually 1929 before such a formula was enacted].

4) It reduced the annual quota admissible from three percent to two percent, based on the 1890 census. Again, this provision was an interim measure to be in effect only until a national origins plan became operative.

5) Perhaps as significant as the quota system, the Act also set up a system whereby immigrants were required to obtain a visa from an American consulate abroad. This provision replaced the system letting immigrants land at immigration stations here only, perhaps, to be turned away after the considerable hardships and expense of the trip here had been incurred. This provision was designed to mitigate the human hardship and tragedy experienced immediately after the 1921 Act. By having the quotas being filled by counting the number of visas issued abroad instead of waiting until the steamships arrived at U.S. ports of entry such as Boston and New York, it increased, too, the administrative powers of the bureaucracy overseeing the visa system.

6) It reduced the classes of aliens exempted from exclusion. It did, however, allow for a number of family exemptions to the quotas which permitted wives and/or minor children of American citizens (that is, naturalized citizens, not aliens).

7) The Act provided that the immigrant bear the burden of proof to show admissibility rather than the United States. This provision again strengthened the administrative powers of the immigration service.

8) It excluded admission to aliens not eligible for naturalization except for certain specified classes of nonquota immigrants and so-called nonimmigrants. This provision was aimed specifically at excluding the Japanese and touched off a diplomatic crisis with Japan which felt insulted by the Act and which was incensed with its passage.

9) The law more specifically defined "immigrants," "quota," and "nonquota immigrants."

10) It specified that "nationality" was to be determined by country of birth, with few exceptions.

11) When the national origins formula went into effect [July 1, 1929], it reduced the annual quota still further, to 153, 714. The national origins formula was then to be apportioned to the total quota on the basis of their contribution to the population of the U.S. as enumerated by the 1920 census (see Bennett: 51-52).

> In formulating a permanent policy two considerations are of prime importance. The first is that the country has a right to say who shall and who shall not come in. It is not for any foreign country to determine our immigration policy. The second is that the basis of restriction must be chosen with a view not to the interest of any group or groups in the country, whether racial or religious, but rather with a view to the country's best interest as a whole. The great test is admissibility. Will the newcomers fit into the American life readily? Is their culture sufficiently akin to our own to make it possible for them easily to take their place among us? There is no question of "superior" or "inferior" races or of "Nordics" or of prejudice, or of racial egotism. Certain groups not only do not fuse easily, but consistently endeavor to keep alive their racial distinctions when they settle among us. They perpetuate the "hyphen," which is but another way of saying that they seek to create foreign blocs in our midst. (in Bennett M., 1963:53)

In the years immediately after passage of the 1924 act, Congress continued to debate about a method for determining a permanent quota system. Many of the same group battle lines that had formed prior to the 1924 act's passage reformed.

In the Senate, Reed of Pennsylvania and Heflin of Alabama were leading restrictionist proponents. In the House, Albert Johnson of Washington, author of the 1924 law, continued to be a leading restrictionist voice, even while he pressed for total suspension. Southern congressional support was led by Representative John Box of Texas, who advocated extending the quota system to Mexico and Latin America. Representatives Vaile of Colorado and Jenkins of Ohio were other leading restrictionists. Hearings on the matter held by the House Committee on Immigration received testimony in favor of the national origins system from thirty-five college biology professors, mainly from such Ivy League schools as Harvard, Princeton and Yale (Divine: 35).

By 1928, John Trevor had formed a new group, the American Coalition, which was comprised of a coalition of earlier "patriotic" groups (such as the Sons of the American Revolution, the Patriotic Order of Sons of America, the Daughters of the American Revolution, etc.). It proved to be eminently successful.

The "racial nationalism" theories were popularized in the press, adding to public opinion support for the restrictionists' cause. Madison Grant published a series of articles in *The Forum* in 1927-28. Lothrop Stoddard propounded many of Grant's ideas in his influential book, *Reforging America*, published in 1927. Similarly, a Chicago lawyer, Edward Lewis, authored *Nation or Confusion* in 1928. Kenneth Roberts, the historical novelist and a leading advocate of the quota system during the 1920-24 debates, wrote a series for the *Saturday Evening Post* that ran in 1928 and supported the national origins plan and proposed extension of the law to include Mexicans. Other publications advocating the national origins system included Charles Goethe's articles in *Eugenics* (1929), and historian Albert Bushnell Hart's in *Current History* (1929) (Divine: 61–63). As with all the proponents of restrictionism, in their advocacy they emphasized race and nationalism.

Of course, groups such as the AFL, the Junior Order of United American Mechanics and the American Legion continued their staunch support, favoring those versions of the plan which increased northwestern European quotas at the expense of southeastern European quotas. By 1928, the United States Chamber of Commerce came out in support of the national origins quota system.

The Anti-National Origins Clause League became the leading group critical of the plan. It worked with a coalition of various ethnic groups opposed to the plan altogether or favoring revisions of it that would at least lessen its adverse impact upon their nationality groups. In the House of Representatives, Kvale of Minnesota and Newton of Massachusetts became leading opponents. In the Senate, Copeland of New York became a leading anti-restrictionist during the post-1924 law debates.

The opponents of restrictionism generally emphasized economic arguments, stressing the need for labor, and the fact that such immigrant labor was willing to do the unpleasant jobs that had to be done and that the native workers were generally unwilling to do.

The debates, of course, were more than about racial theories versus an economic supply of cheap labor. The various "formulae" being debated led to significantly different quota limits for the various national groupings. Table 4.1, for example, presents a comparison of the variations in immigration quotas for selected—but typical—European countries under the 1890 census and various national origins plans. It shows the dramatic differences the various quota formula made in a country's limits, sometimes increasing or decreasing a limit by two or three times!

The consequences of the 1924 act were dramatic. European immigration slumped from over 800,000 in 1921 to less than 150,000 by the end of the decade. The restrictionist movement was still not satisfied. The 1924 act exempted countries in the Western Hemisphere and the Philippine Islands [then a U.S. territory]. The restrictionist forces soon were advocating a limitation on Latin America, particularly Mexico.

The movement to restrict Mexican immigration began in 1926. Representative Box of Texas, an ardent restrictionist and member of the House Immigration Committee, led a strongly southern contingent that included Hiram Johnson of Texas and Thomas Heflin of Alabama. Senator Harris of Georgia, as well as Senators Willis of Ohio and Reed of Pennsylvania, were leading proponents in the Senate. They found a convenient slogan for their proposals of a quota for Mexican immigration, "close the back door" (Divine: 53).

TABLE 4.1

Comparison of Immigration Quotas Under 1890 Census and the National Origins Plan for Representative European Nations

Representative European Nations	1890 Census Plan:	1927 Quota Board Report:	1928 Quota Board Report:	1929 Quota Board Report:
Germany	51,227	23,428	24,908	25,957
Great Britain	34,007	73,039	65,894	65,721
Irish Free State	28,567	13,862	17,429	17,853
Italy	3,845	6,091	5,989	5,802
Norway	6,453	2,267	2,403	2,377
Poland	5,982	4,978	6,090	6,524
Russia	2,248	4,781	3,540	2,784
Sweden	9,561	3,259	3,399	3,314

Source: Adapted from Divine: 30.

Mexican immigrants were depicted as peons who taxed the school systems beyond their capacities and lowered educational standards. The Mexican immigrant was portrayed as a social leper who would contaminate the U.S. way of life. Harry Laughlin, the "eugenics expert" of the House Immigration Committee, testified that immigration from the entire Western Hemisphere should be limited to "whites." Representative Box voiced the most violently antiracial prejudices against the Mexicans. He described them as:

> ... illiterate, unclean, peonized masses ... a mixture of Mediterranean-blooded Spanish peasants with low-grade Indians who did not fight extinction but submitted and multiplied as serfs. [The influx of Mexicans] creates the most insidious and general mixture of white, Indian, and negro blood strains ever produced in America (cited in Divine: 57).

The proposal to limit Mexican immigration, however, ran into strong and well-organized opposition from the southwest. There an economic coalition of farmers, cattlemen, miners, sugar manufacturers, and railroad interests all favored continued and unlimited Mexican immigration. The Mexican workers were valued as a source of common labor preferred for being docile, unaggressive people who would do what they were told and would accept jobs white workers refused.

In addition to these economic perspectives, opposition to limits on Mexican immigration was founded on "Pan-Americanism." Secretary of State Kellogg was ardently seeking to foster better relations with Latin America. Senator Hiram Bingham of Connecticut and Carl Hayden of

Arizona led the fight against Latin American quotas. When Senator Harris of Georgia introduced a bill, in 1929, that would amend the quota law to include a limit on Mexican immigration, President Hoover indicated that if the Harris Bill passed he would veto it (Divine: 67).

In 1929, the National Origins Plan was finally enacted and the quota system became fully, and permanently, operational. Table 4.2 presents a comparison of the quota limits for various countries under the three different versions of the quota system of the 1920s—the 1921 Emergency Act, the 1924 Johnson-Reed Act, and the National Origins Act of 1929.

TABLE 4.2

Comparison of Quotas Allotted to Selected Countries Under Three Different Versions of the Quota System

	1921 Act 3%-1910	1924 Act 2%-1890	1929 National Origins Plan
Total	357,803	164,667	153,714
Asia	492	1,424	1,423
Africa/Oceania	359	1,821	1,800
Europe	356,952	161,422	150,491
Northern/Western Europe			
Belgium	1,563	512	1,304
Denmark	5,619	2,789	1,181
France	5,729	3,954	3,086
Germany	67,607	51,227	25,957
Great Britain/ N. Ireland	77,342	34.007	65,721
Irish Free State	"	28,567	17,853
Netherlands	3,607	1,648	3,153
Norway	12,202	6,453	2,377
Sweden	20,042	9,561	3,314
Switzerland	3,752	2,081	1,707
Total NW Europe	197,630	140,999	127,266
Southern/Eastern Europe			
Austria	7,342	785	1,413
Czechoslovakia	14,357	3,073	2,874
Greece	3,063	100	307
Hungary	5,747	473	869
Italy	42,057	3,845	5,802
Poland	30,977	5,982	6,524
Portugal	2,465	503	440
Romania	7,419	603	295
U.S.S.R.	24,405	2,248	2,784
Turkey	2,654	100	226
Yugoslavia	6,426	671	845
Total SE Europe	155,585	20,423	23,235

Source: Bernard: 27. Reprinted by permission from Harper & Row.

THE GREAT DEPRESSION DECADE

The year 1929 saw not only the passage of the National Origins Act that set permanently the quota system; it was the year of the stock market crash that ushered in the Great Depression. This worldwide depression had a greater impact on restriction of immigration than did any law ever passed by Congress. The drop in immigration, already precipitous since the quota acts of the 1920s, was exceptional during the 1930s. While over 4,100,000 had entered during the 1920s, immigration fell to just slightly over .5 million for the entire decade of the 1930s. Total immigration to the United States was at the lowest level for a decade since 1820.

Periods of depression have always resulted in a slackening off of immigration, since the economic crisis means the U.S. will be perceived as offering less opportunity to perspective immigrants. When the depression is worldwide, moreover, it means the ability and opportunity to migrate is lessened. Periods of economic dislocation—recessions and depressions—have also been times when the restrictionist movement flowered, instigating new demands for the protection of the native worker against the encroachment of foreign labor. The 1930s were no exception.

In the decade of the 1930s, the major battles over restriction centered on whether to do so by administrative or legislative action, and on the extension of the quota limitations to the Philippines. The major restrictionist groups wanted Congress to decrease quotas (as set by the 1929 law) by 60 to 90 percent. Opponents of the restriction movement argued that more strict administrative enforcement of the existing laws would be adequate to reduce the influx.

In 1930, Senator Hugo Black of Alabama introduced a bill to suspend all immigration except for immediate family members of U.S. citizens for a period of five years. While the Senate rejected the Black proposal, the vote was fairly close, 37 to 29.

The State Department reacted to the Black proposal and related restrictionist debate in Congress by enforcing administratively a strict interpretation of the "public charge" clause before granting a visa. Within five months, it succeeded in cutting European immigration by 90 percent. Consular officers throughout the decade followed the president's orders to interpret strictly that provision, and the period from 1930 to 1931 saw a drop of 62 percent in quota immigration, and during the decade from 1931 to 1940 those immigrants coming into the United States exceeded repatriated immigrants for a net total of only 68,693 (Divine: 78).

Nonquota immigration (for example, from Canada, Mexico and the Philippines) throughout the decade was nearly as large as quota immigration, and it rose and fell in a manner closely paralleling that of quota immigration. Obviously, the depression conditions were lessening the incentives to migrate. The rigid screening process for visas and the unfavorable economic conditions depressed both quota and nonquota immigration alike. Table 4.3 shows the annual quota and nonquota immigration data for the 1930s decade by regions of origin.

Having successfully passed the National Origins Act in 1929, the restrictionists moved on during the 1930s to a campaign designed to "plug" what they felt were holes in the immigration barriers. One of the major targets was the immigration from the Philippines. Among the first attempts to limit Filipino immigration was a proposal introduced in 1928 by Representative Richard Welch of California. It had the staunch support of the West Coast labor unions and the AFL. When a deadly outbreak of spinal meningitis in 1929 was traced to a Filipino immigrant, the movement to impose a quota on the Philippines gained momentum.

TABLE 4.3
Quota and Nonquota Immigration, 1930–1940

Annual Immigration Quotas and Quota Immigrants Admitted by Region

Annual	All Countries:	N/W Europe:	S/W Europe:	Asia:	Africa:	Pacific:
Quotas:	153,714	125,853	24,648	1,805	1,200	700
1930	141,497	116,062	24,002	891	273	269
1931	54,118	38,706	14,498	490	206	218
1932	12,983	6,368	6,402	331	72	170
1933	8,220	3,831	4,091	189	20	89
1934	12,483	6,839	5,286	223	33	102
1935	17,207	8,849	7.971	202	41	144
1936	18,675	10,102	8,142	234	40	157
1937	27,762	16,481	10,754	295	64	168
1938	42,494	25,383	16,254	584	74	199
1939	62,402	41,135	20,400	587	78	202
1940	51,997	34,313	16,828	549	99	208

NonQuota Immigrants Admitted by Region for Years 1930-1940

	All Nations:	All Quota Nations:	N/W Europe:	S/E Europe:	Asia:	Africa:	Pacific:	All NonQuota Nations:
'30	100,203	36,895	3,805	30,350	2,474	117	149	63,308
'31	43,021	21,357	3,101	16,253	1,821	71	111	21,664
'32	22,593	12,884	2,566	8,748	1,390	62	118	9,709
'33	14,848	7,306	1,778	5,223	254	15	36	7,542
'34	16,987	8.307	2,000	6,038	228	8	33	8,680
'35	17,749	9,571	1,760	7,513	241	12	45	8,178
'36	17,654	9,049	1,687	7,068	229	19	46	8,605
'37	22,482	9,776	1,875	7,505	323	18	55	12,706
'38	25,401	10,397	1,891	8,099	334	9	64	15,004
'39	20,596	8,038	1,910	5,675	374	-13	66	12,558
'40	18,759	6,405	1,784	4,201	327	20	73	12,354

Source: Bennett M., 1963: 68–69; Divine: 90

The prorestrictionist forces used mostly the same hodgepodge of racial arguments and economic fears that had characterized earlier battles. Indeed, many of the same organizations were active, once again lobbying Congress. The major prorestrictionist organizations of the 1930s included the American Coalition, the California Joint Immigration Committee, the AFL, the National Grange, the American Legion, and the Native Sons of the Golden West (Divine: 69–70).

The forces opposing Filipino restriction included, of course, various Filipino political leaders, particularly Manuel Roxas, the Speaker of the Philippine Legislature, who argued eloquently that the right to migrate anywhere in the United States and its territories was a moral right of all residents under the U.S. flag. He was supported by the U.S. War Department, the Department of State, Hawaiian sugar planters, and the Pacific American Steamship Association. Senators Hawes of Missouri and Norris of Nebraska, both strong advocates of Philippine Independence, called the restriction proposal "dishonorable" and "amoral." In 1930, the proposal was defeated in the Senate by a vote of 41 to 23 (Divine: 70).

Southern and western state representatives continued to battle for restriction. In addition to Johnson of Washington and Reed of Pennsylvania, Representatives Moore, Johnson and Dies of Texas continued to push for limits. In 1931, they urged adoption of a "reduction of quotas" bill that was the high point of their legislative efforts in the early depression years. They were opposed by congressional representatives from the northeast. Leading antirestrictionists in the House were the New York City delegation, Representatives LaGuardia, O'Connor and Dickstein. In the Senate, Walsh of Massachusetts and Elmer Thomas of Oklahoma were prominent anti-restrictionist voices. In December of 1931, Samuel Dickstein of New York, an ardent antirestrictionist, replaced Albert Johnson as chairman of the powerful House Immigration Committee. The antirestrictionist forces generally had the support of the Roosevelt Administration, particularly that of the Secretary of Labor, Frances Perkins.

In 1932, Representative Moore of Kentucky introduced a new bill to restrict immigration by lowering the quotas and expanding their coverage. It was vigorously opposed by Jewish organizations [already attempting to increase the number of immigrants allowed in as the persecution of Jews increased in central and eastern Europe in the early 1930s], such as the Hebrew Sheltering and Immigration Aid Society. They also had the lobbying support of the YWCA. In 1932, a new source of antirestriction organization surfaced as well—the extreme left-wing groups such as the American Communist Party and the Young Communist League. Also active in the early 1930s was the National Council for Protection of the Foreign Born.

In 1933, the political forces advocating Philippine independence tried a new ploy. They attempted to gain the support of the restrictionist forces in Congress by offering a compromise bill. In essence, the bill provided that if Congress should enact a law fixing a specific date for Philippine independence, the Filipino representatives and their supporters would accept a provision restricting Filipino immigration during the transition period, as long as such restrictions was based on economic grounds rather than racial ones.

The bill passed in 1934, signed by President Roosevelt, and approved by the Philippine Legislature in May of 1934. The Philippine Islands were given an annual quota of 50, and the "problem" of Filipino restriction was settled (Divine 73–75).

With that issue settled, the mid-1930s were a time of relative inaction. From 1933 to 1938, Congress was more friendly in tone, at least, toward immigration. Representative Dickstein, as chair of the House Immigration Committee, introduced a series of proposals to liberalize the immigration laws on behalf of refugees from Germany. His proposals were supported by the lobbying efforts of the American Jewish Congress, the Hebrew Sheltering and Immigrant Aid Society, and some Catholic and Protestant groups concerned about the Refugee problem. In 1933, the League of Nations established a High Commission for Refugees Coming From Germany. It was headed by a U.S. citizen James MacDonald. In 1938, the league established a single High Commission for Refugees. These efforts added to the public relations push of forces advocating relaxation of the quota restrictions. By 1938, the Jewish refugee problem was becoming increasingly critical.

Such moves to ease restrictions were vigorously opposed by Trevor of the American Coalition; by the American Legion; and by the AFL. Representative Jenkins of Ohio and Rankin of Mississippi were leading opponents in the House. Public opinion was still on the side of the restrictionists, and the measures all died in the House.

In 1939, another attempt was made. Senator Wagner of New York introduced a bill to allow the nonquota entry of 20,000 German *refugee children*. A Nonsectarian Committee for German Refugee Children was formed which won over organized labor by getting the endorsement of the AFL-CIO. It even had southern proponents in the persons of Frank Graham, the president of the University of North Carolina, and Homer Rainey, president of the University of Texas. This proposal, too, had the traditional opposition of the American Legion, the American Coalition and the like (except organized labor), which had characterized so many of the earlier battles. Even this proposal died in Congress.

Finally, the administration acted, applying its own interpretation. It allowed in some 20,000 children in 1939. In total, some 250,000 refugees entered the U.S. during the 1934–1941 period, but all came in under the existing quota laws (Jones M., 1960:281).

The refugee problem pointed out a major weakness of the quota system—its inflexibility. Full use of the quota system was often prevented by its procedural rules. The 1929 law, for example, provided that, for quotas over 100, no more than 10 percent of a yearly quota could be used in a single month. When transportation conditions or refugee-related problems blocked the movement of persons to fill the 10 percent provision, no carryover was allowed. Also, there was no carryover provided for unused quotas from one year to the next. In addition, the red tape involved in getting the visas, especially during the turbulent 1930s, meant that many quotas were unused.

The quota laws had their intended effect, however, as can readily be seen in Table 4.4. It presents the sources of immigration to the U.S. from 1820 to 1947, showing the distribution by percentages and by decades for the major regional sources of origin. Northwestern European immigration, which had fallen from over 70 percent of the total in the 1880s to less than 20 percent during the 1910–20 decade, prior to the quota laws, shifted dramatically upwards to nearly 40 percent during the 1930s. Southeastern European immigration fell from nearly 71 percent in the 1910–20 decade to under 30 percent during the 1930s.

THE WORLD WAR II YEARS

As was the case with previous war periods, during World War II immigration dropped dramatically. The war-time era had an impact on immigration-related policy far beyond depressing the levels of the influx.

TABLE 4.4
Sources of Immigration to the U.S., 1820–1947
(Distribution by Percentages, By Decades)

Decades:	All Europe:	N/W Europe:	S/W Europe:	Canada:	Mexico:	All Others:
1820-1830	70.2%	68.0%	2.2%	1.6%	3.2%	25.0%
1831-1840	82.8	81.7	1.0	2.3	1.1	13.9
1841-1850	93.3	93.0	0.3	2.4	0.2	4.1
1851-1860	94.4	93.6	0.8	2.3	0.1	3.2
1861-1870	89.3	87.8	1.5	6.6	0.1	4.0
1871-1880	80.7	73.6	7.2	13.6	0.2	5.4
1881-1890	90.3	72.0	18.3	7.5	---	2.2
1890-1900	96.5	44.6	51.9	0.1	---	3.4
1900-1910	92.5	21.7	70.8	2.0	0.6	4.9
1910-1920	76.4	17.4	59.0	12.9	3.8	6.9
1920-1930	60.3	31.2	29.0	22.5	11.2	6.0
1930-1940	66.0	37.4	28.6	20.5	4.2	9.3
1941-1947	44.4	34.9	9.5	23.2	8.7	23.6

Source: Bernard: 40. Reprinted by permission from Harper & Row.

When the Japanese attacked Pearl Harbor on December 7, 1941, they brought on a virtual nightmare experience to the Japanese-Americans living on the mainland. A total of 112,000 persons of Japanese ancestry, some 70,000 of whom were native-born U.S. citizens, were sent to "relocation camps" in the interior because of what was termed "military necessity." The relocation camps were, in fact, concentration camps. Conditions, especially in the beginning, were grim. Men and women, grandparents and infants, young children and young adults, simple gardeners and fishermen, were herded behind fifteen-foot-high barbed-wire fences. The camps were guarded by tommygun-armed troops stationed around the perimeter and on spotlight towers. Residents lived in crude barracks, in which stalls a mere 18 feet by 21 feet housed families of six or seven. They were partitioned off with seven-foot-high partitions with four-foot openings—affording virtually no privacy. A barrack building 90 feet by 20 feet typically held six families. Residents had to use outside latrines. They were locked in by 9:00 p.m. and had a 10:00 p.m. lights-out curfew. The camps were governed by a War Relocation Authority and the War Relocation Work Corps. One scholar describes the conditions at Poston in Arizona, whose peak population reached 17,867 by August of 1942, as follows:

> The barracks were flimsily constructed. Sometimes as many as eight people lived in one room. Mattresses were made by stuffing cloth bags with straw. There was hardly any furniture. The heat was intense in the summer, and the minimum temperature during the winter occasionally fell below the freezing mark. And then there was the barbed wire and the guards. It is little wonder that some people felt betrayed at having been sent to such a place and either actively resisted or failed to cooperate fully with the administration's plans (McClemore: 179).

Since we treated even enemy aliens from Germany and Italy far better than we did those native-born U.S. citizens, and since no other ethnic or racial group residing in America during World War II suffered comparable indignities nor was treated in such a cavalier and categorical manner, only *racial prejudice* can account for this policy.[1] Indeed, the chief author of the plan, Lt. General John L. DeWitt, commanding general of the Western Defense Command, offered a blatantly racist rationale:

> In the war in which we are now engaged racial affinities are not severed by migration. The *Japanese race is an enemy race* and while many second- and third-generation Japanese born on the United States soil and possessed of United States citizenship, have become "Americanized," *the racial strains are undiluted* . . . (in McClemore: 174; my italics).

Although General Mark Clark had earlier informed General George Marshall that there really was no military necessity for these camps, and although this assessment was concurred in by the head of th FBI, General DeWitt was not dissuaded. Earl Warren, then Attorney General of California, and General DeWitt responded to the fact that no acts of sabotage had taken place with the ingenious reasoning that the very absence of sabotage or any other evidence of fifth column activity "merely showed how disciplined the resident Japanese were . . . they were merely biding their time to strike a well-planned and devastating blow synchronized with attacks by the armed forces of Japan" (cited in Ringer: 863). And DeWitt said elsewhere: "A Jap is a Jap. It makes no difference whether he's an American or not."[2]

The FBI and naval intelligence officers had quickly rounded up everyone who might be regarded as the slightest threat. Nonetheless, General DeWitt and the congressional delegation from the coast pressed on with the evacuation plans. Secretary of War Stimson and Attorney General Biddle agreed to go along with the plan, and Roosevelt issued executive order 9066 on February 12, 1942. The president sought and received congressional approval. It passed overwhelmingly; in the Senate only Taft spoke against it. By October of 1942, approximately 110,000 were relocated.

The Japanese-Americans suffered a huge financial loss. And of course, no price can be placed on the emotional trauma, the broken hearts or the sorrows of the separated families. The overall cost to the U.S. taxpayers was about $250,000,000 for a program that history has demonstrated was simply not justified by military or any other necessity. In the succinct words of one scholar of the topic: "One hundred thousand persons were sent to concentration camps on a record which wouldn't support a conviction for stealing a dog" (McClemore: 184).

Paradoxically, the territory of Hawaii, in a much more vulnerable position, did not attempt a mass evacuation of its 120,552 Japanese-American citizens. The war passed without a proven act of espionage or sabotage by a Japanese-American there or on the mainland. The army announced that "the shipping situation and labor shortage make it a matter of military necessity to keep the people of Japanese blood on the Island." Yet the army had also used the words "military necessity" to justify the West Coast evacuation plan (Hosokawa: 457–67).

The Japanese-Americans accepted the evacuation and internment surprisingly peacefully. There was one riot at Poston, and a riot at Manzanar during the early period when conditions were exceptionally bad. Once the period of hysteria passed, Japanese-American evacuees of proven loyalty were allowed to leave the camp and join the United States Army. Some 20,000 did so, 6,000 of whom served in the Pacific, but most of whom were in the famed 100th Battalion, 442nd Regimental Combat Team which went on to become the most highly decorated unit in the European theatre.[3]

In *Hirobayashi* v. *the United States*, in 1943, and in *Korematsu* v. *the United States*, in 1944, the Supreme Court upheld the constitutionality of the evacuation program. In the latter decision, approved by a 6–3 vote, the dissenting justices rendered sharp dissents. Justice Francis Murphy labeled the evacuation as "the legislation of racism." Justice Robert Jackson wrote:

> Once a judicial opinion rationalizes an order to show it conforms to the Constitution, or rather, rationalizes the Constitution to show that the Constitution sanctions such an order, the Court for all time has validated the principle of racial discrimination in criminal procedure, and of transplanting American citizens. The principle then lies about like a loaded weapon ready for the hand of any authority that can bring forward a plausible claim of an urgent need. Every repetition imbeds that principle more deeply in our law and thinking and expands it to new purposes.[4]

Fortunately, the principle did not lie about for long. In *Endo* v. *the United States*, in 1944, the Supreme Court revoked the West Coast Exclusion Order. Effective January 2, 1945, the Japanese-Americans were no longer under forcible detention. By June of 1946, all camps were closed.

The wartime sentiments which so plagued the Japanese-Americans aided another Asian racial group and led to a slight modification of immigration policy. Our alliance with China in the war with Japan was the main factor leading to the repeal of the Chinese Exclusion Act. Madame Chiang Kai-shek visited the United States in 1943. A citizen's committee was formed to advocate for repeal. It was passed virtually without opposition on December 13, 1943, and a small quota was established for China.

The immediate postwar years and several war-induced "problems" increasingly highlighted the difficulties and inflexibilities of the quota system. In 1946, Congress passed the War Brides Act, which allowed for up to 150,000 wives, fiancees, and some 25,000 children and a few hundred husbands of U.S. citizens serving in the armed forces to be brought in outside the quota limits. A similar act in 1947 allowed in some 5,000 Chinese and 800 Japanese wives of U.S. servicemen outside of the quota system (Jones M., 1960:284).

It was the problem of refugees and displaced persons, however, which really showed the greatest need for some modification of the quota system. At wars end, there were an estimated 8 million displaced persons in Austria, Italy and Germany, over 1 million of whom were in displaced-persons camps. President Truman's first response to this problem was to issue a presidential directive, in 1945, which admitted some 2,500 that year. They were aliens admitted *under* the quota system, brought in as permanent residents at government expense. Preferences were given to orphans and relatives of U.S. citizens. About half were from Poland and nearly 1,000 were from Italy (Bennett M.: 89). For the next two and one-half years, this presidential directive was used to bring in over 41,000 persons, some 38,000 of whom were quota immigrants, over 2,000 of whom were nonquota, and just over 1,000 of whom were nonimmigrants (mostly students). About 12 percent of the DPs admitted as quota immigrants had a preference within the quota as blood relatives of U.S. citizens or of admitted resident aliens (Bennett M., 1963: 89).

The millions of refugees in the DP camps in Europe, however, demonstrated the need for further action. In June of 1948, Congress passed the Displaced Persons Act. This act set up a preference category and established a Displaced Persons Commission to administer the act. Besides giving preference within the quotas to certain categories of displaced persons, it allowed some persons from some countries to immigrate beyond that country's quotas by "mortgaging" against future quotas. Existing health, literacy and related requirements of the quota act, however, were *not* set aside for the displaced persons.

President Truman reluctantly signed the act, stating he did so "with very great reluctance" because he believed the act did not go far enough, that it discriminated against Catholics and Jews, and that in his view displaced persons should be permitted to enter as nonquota immigrants. Congress amended the bill in 1950, admitting higher percentages of Catholics and Jews. Ultimately, the Displaced Persons Act provided for the admission of 400,000 refugees over a four-year period (Jones M., 1960: 285; and Bennett M., 1963: 76–77).

The growing need for agricultural workers, especially in the west, led to the Agricultural Labor and Illegal Entry Act of 1948. This act established an agreement between the United States, Canada, Mexico, and the British West Indies to allow immigrants to come in as temporary agricultural workers. It was needed since, under the 1917 Immigration Act, such workers would have been inadmissible under the contract labor prohibitions. The act also strengthened the border patrol, since the problem of illegal entrants along the thousands of miles of border with Mexico became increasingly apparent.

In 1949, Congress amended the Philippine Act of 1946 by extending its benefits to June of 1951. It also passed another agricultural act providing for the recruitment of agricultural labor in short supply.

In June of 1950, Congress made a special provision for 250 special immigration visas for alien sheepherders for a one-year period. In August of that year, Congress declared Guamanians born after April 11, 1899, to be citizens, and thus eliminated any immigration restrictions upon them. That same month, it also passed an act that permitted the admission of racially inadmissible alien spouses and minor children of citizen members of the armed forces.

TABLE 4.5

Annual Immigrant Arrivals and Departures, United States, 1924–1948

Year:	Immigrant Aliens Admitted:	Emigrant Aliens Departed:	Net Immigration:
	PROSPERITY YEARS		
1924-1925	294,314	92,728	201,586
1925-1926	304,488	76,992	227,496
1926-1927	335,175	73,366	261,809
1927-1928	307,255	77,457	229,798
1928-1929	279,678	69,203	210,475
1929-1930	241,700	50,661	191,039
	DEPRESSION YEARS		
1930-1931	97,139	61,882	35,257
1931-1932	35,576	103,295	-67,719
1932-1933	23,068	80,081	-57,013
1933-1934	29,470	39,771	-10,301
1934-1935	34,956	38,834	- 3,878
1935-1936	36,329	35,817	512
	PEAK OF REFUGEE MOVEMENT		
1936-1937	50,244	26,736	23,508
1937-1938	67,895	25,210	42,685
1938-1939	82,998	26,631	56,347
1939-1940	70,756	21,461	49,295
1940-1941	51,776	17,115	34,661
	THE WAR YEARS		
1941-1942	28,781	7,363	21,418
1942-1943	23,725	5,107	18,618
1943-1944	28,551	5,669	22,882
1944-1945	38,119	7,442	30,677
	POST-WAR YEARS		
1945-1946	108,721	18,143	90,578
1946-1947	147,292	22,501	124,791
1947-1948	170,570	20,875	149,695

Source: Bernard: 323. Reprinted by permission from Harper & Row.

Finally, in September of 1950, Congress passed the Internal Security Act (64 Stat. 987). This act increased the grounds for exclusion and deportation of alleged alien subversives. Reflecting the cold-war tenor of the times, it required Communist organizations and officers to be registered and refined, as well as clarifying and augmenting the classes of persons considered to be risks to internal security. It banned their admission and strengthened the administrative and enforcement work of the Immigration Service, while strengthening the deportation authority and procedures of the Immigration Act of 1917. It also required all resident aliens to annually report their address.

The special problems of dealing with refugees, the human hardship obviously caused by the inflexibility of the quota system, and the growing hysteria and fear of communism associated with the Cold War all pointed to the need for a major revision of our basic immigration policy. The result was the passage of the Immigration and Naturalization Act of 1952, ushering in the next phase of the nation's immigration policy, the "Dutch-Door Era." The subsequent chapter discusses that phase. We close this chapter with Table 4.5 which presents an overview of the "Pet-Door Era" by detailing the annual immigrant arrivals and departures for the years 1924–48.

NOTES

1. See, for instance, Eugene Rostow, "Our Worst Wartime Mistake," *Harper's Magazine*, (September, 1945): 193–201; Ken Ringle, "What Did You Do Before the War, Dad?," *The Washington Post Magazine*, (December 6, 1981): 54–62; Ringer: 884, and LeMay: 191–206.

2. "One Time Internee Returns to Camp," *Cumberland Evening Times*, Thursday, August 15, 1985:38.

3. See Hosokawa: 366; McClemore: 180–81; and Peterson: 84.

4. Justice Robert Jackson, dissenting opinion in *Korematsu* v. *States*, 65 *Supreme Court Reporter*, 1944: 206–208.

5

The Dutch-Door Era,
1950–1980

INTRODUCTION

The Displaced Persons Act of 1948 highlighted the need for a revision in U.S. immigration policy and served as the precursor for later policy that much more substantially changed the direction of policy. While the 1948 Displaced Persons Act and its 1950 amendment did not significantly alter the basic policy, it did mark a turning point in that for the first time in the twentieth century the U.S. Congress enacted policy that *relaxed* the restrictions on immigration. It signaled the opening of the door a bit and the beginning of a new phase in immigration policy, the Dutch-Door Era.

This phase opened with the McCarran-Walter Act of 1952 which essentially reaffirmed the restrictionism of the national origins system. The years of the Eisenhower Administration saw a very gradual chipping away at restrictionism, as the cold war and foreign policy considerations worked towards allowing in special "refugees" and "anti-Communist freedom fighters." By the mid-1960s the forces advocating relaxation of the restrictionist policy were on the offensive, and the restrictionist forces were increasingly fighting a holding action. By the end of the era, the need for another substantial revision of immigration policy was rather widely accepted.[1]

This phase is also characterized by some significant changes in the flow of immigration. Total immigration expanded during the era. Nonquota and nondocumented immigration rose dramatically. The composition of the legal immigration also shifted markedly during the phase.

Figure 5.1 shows the origins of U.S. immigration by region for the decades from 1950 to 1980. The substantial increase in immigration from

Asian and Western Hemisphere nations (principally Mexico and other Latin-American countries) is apparent in the graph, as is the corresponding decline in immigration from northwestern and other European nations. Mexico, Cuba, China and Taiwan, Korea and the Philippines emerge during this phase as the principle sources of immigration.

The late 1940s witnessed the development of a general consensus about the need for a comprehensive review of U.S. immigration policy. In 1950, a special Senate committee, established in 1947 under the chairmanship of Senator Rivercomb and then continuing under Senator McCarran, issued its lengthy report. This report was the most comprehensive study of immigration since the Dillingham Commission Report of 1911. It served as the basis for the debate and proposed legislation that marked the beginning of the Dutch-Door Era—the McCarran-Walter Act of 1952.

THE IMMIGRATION AND NATURALIZATION ACT OF 1952

The McCarran-Walter Act of 1952 was but a very modest step in the direction of relaxing the restrictionism of the U.S. national origins quota system. It basically codified existing legislation, in some cases making the quota system even more rigid, although it granted a token quota to those nations in what is defined as the "Asian-Pacific Triangle."

While avoiding the more racist arguments characterizing the original implementation of the quota system, the Senate committee's report, which formed the basis of the proposal for the act, did reaffirm that U.S. immigration policy should favor northwestern over southeastern European immigrants since, in the subcommittee's words, ". . . the peoples who had made the greatest contribution to the development of this nation were fully justified in determining that the country was no longer a field for further colonization, and henceforth further immigration would not only be restricted but directed to admit immigrants considered to be more readily assimilable because of the similarity of their cultural background to those of the principle components of our population."[2]

The antirestrictionist forces were led by Representative Emmanual Celler in the House, and Senators Lehman and Humphrey in the Senate. They attacked the continuation of the quota system as an incorporation of a philosophy of racism not unlike that of Nazi Germany, the espousal of which had led to such tragic consequences for the entire world. Major ethnic associations generally supported the liberalizing efforts of the Lehman-Humphrey forces.

Proponents argued that the postwar economy could not absorb a large-scale immigration, which would surely follow any substantial easing of restriction limits. They also raised the specter of the cold war, stressing the

FIGURE 5.1

The Origins of U.S. Immigration, by Region, 1950–1980

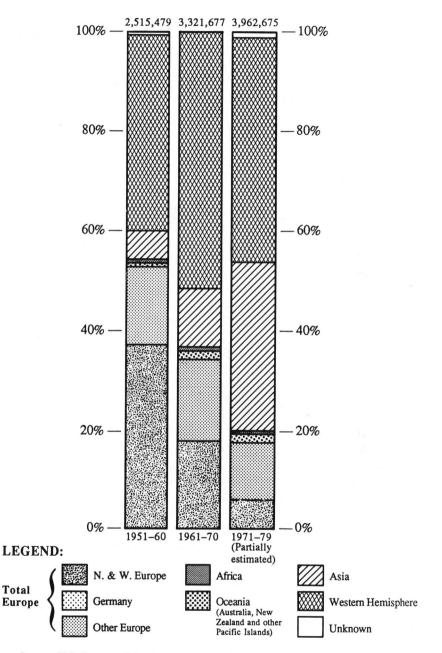

LEGEND:

Total Europe {
 N. & W. Europe
 Germany
 Other Europe
}

Africa
Oceania (Australia, New Zealand and other Pacific Islands)

Asia
Western Hemisphere
Unknown

Source: U.S. Bureau of the Census, *Historical Statistics of the United States, Colonial Times to 1970*. Washington, D.C.: U.S. Government Printing Office, 1975.

dangers of Communist subversion and defending the tight security provision of the proposal.

The forces advocating the easing of restrictionism lacked the votes to block its passage or uphold President Truman's threatened veto. They tried a compromise proposal: pooling unused quotas, which could then be used by countries with small quotas, and increasing the total volume slightly by using census data from 1950 rather than 1920.

Congress rejected these attempts to block or modify the bill. It passed the McCarran-Walter Act by a voice vote in May of 1952.

The act listed 31 classes of aliens inadmissible to receive visas, and thus excluded from admission to the United States. Most of those were simply reaffirmations of those excluded in the 1917 act and those already incorporated in the national origins quota law.

The law limited the quota of colonies and dependent areas to 100, thus sharply reducing immigration from the West Indies. While defenders of the bill claimed all colonies were subject to the same restriction, critics noted that *black* West Indians were the most affected by that change [prior to this bill's enactment, West Indians had entered under the large British quota, but as colonists they were limited to 100 per year].³

The act also included a preference system within the quotas, based on relatives of U.S. citizens and economic considerations. While these provision were of minor importance in the 1952 debates, they foreshadowed the 1965 act that liberalized immigration policy.

A modest but most liberalizing provision of the bill concerned Asian immigration. The bill repealed the racial ban on citizenship, thereby winning over the lobbying support of the Japanese-American Citizens League (JACL). While most ethnic associations opposed the bill, the JACL supported it, since its passage would make thousands of elderly Japanese (the Issei) eligible for citizenship. The repeal of the racial ban was not too controversial. In 1949, the House had passed a similar measure. Congressman Judd's bill, suggesting the creation of an Asian-Pacific Triangle, each nation of which would be granted an annual quota of 100 for a total triangle quota of 2,000, was incorporated into the 1952 act.

Even restrictionist forces agreed with the removal of the racial ban. The Asian Triangle provision, however, did maintain an aspect of racial discrimination within it. While in all cases the quotas were charged to the country of birth, this provision stipulated that persons of half or more Asian ancestry were to be charged to that Asian quota. Thus, a person born in Colombia of Japanese ancestry would not enter as a Colombian, i.e, as though from a Western Hemisphere nation that had no quota, but as part of the much smaller Japanese allotment. The intent of the law was clearly directed at the hundreds of thousands of persons of Asian backgrounds living in Latin America and Canada who would otherwise have been eligible to come in as *nonquota* immigrants from the Western Hemisphere (Chiswick: 27).

The 1952 act did not impose a quota for the Western Hemisphere. It relied on the general categories of exclusion—such as the "public charge" clause—to limit immigration from that region. The act also largely ignored the bracero program and the problems of illegal immigration.

The act defined nonimmigrants, elaborating upon previous law regarding nonimmigrants with respect to treaty traders, students, temporary workers and the like. It developed the most elaborate provisions concerning the definition of and process for naturalization. It strengthened the powers of the Attorney General in deciding upon borderline or questionable cases.

President Truman vetoed the bill. While he agreed that the immigration laws were in need of a general revision and he approved of the elimination of racial barriers as provided for in the act, he objected to the law on several grounds. He opposed the continuation of the national origins quota system, holding that the quotas were unfair to nationalities from southeastern Europe. He pointedly noted that it had increasingly been necessary to pass special legislation to admit many of the SE Europeans who were refugees from totalitarian regimes. He objected to the unfair racial provision regarding the Asian Triangle quotas. He objected to provision in the act that restricted immigration of aliens who had been convicted of crimes and who had made misrepresentations to obtain visas, suggesting that the standards of justice in some foreign countries were far different from ours and that the desperation of individuals who had a great desire to come here and therefore sometimes made some fraudulent representation should be forgiven. His veto message objected to the grounds for inadmission of drug addicts. He objected to the reenactment of provisions contained in the Internal Security Act of 1950. He objected to the provisions regarding the process of denaturalization and deportation of persons suspected to have engaged in subversive activities, arguing the provision gave too much power to the attorney general.

Congress overrode President Truman's veto by a vote of 278 to 113 in the House. In the Senate, the anti-restrictionists failed by but two votes to uphold the veto. The vote to overturn passed in the upper chamber by a margin of 57 to 26 (Chiswick: 28).

Despite his loss of the veto battle, and over objections of Congress, President Truman established a special commission to study the whole issue of immigration, Its report, issued in 1953, advocated Truman's positions on immigration. While the report, entitled *Whom Shall We Welcome*, was ignored by Congress, it did lay the groundwork for much of the subsequent revisions made in 1965.

President Truman tried to interject the immigration issue into the 1952 Presidential election [the Senate vote to overturn the veto had depended on overwhelming Republican support, 32 to 8 to override, plus a few southern Democrats]. The issue never caught on, however, and, with President Eisenhower's election, the report and the issue were left to die.

While Congress chose to ignore the report, the compelling refugee problems alluded to in the report did not go away. President Eisenhower soon called for revisions in the immigration laws to admit escapees from behind the iron curtain. One of his first proposals to Congress stipulated such, numbering the allowance for them *outside the quota system* at 120,000 annually for two years. The president stressed the need to allow them in on both humanitarian grounds and to further U.S. foreign policy.

A House minority report objected to even this modest attempt at liberalizing the immigration law since it would "destroy the principle of national origins upon which our immigration system is based" (in Chiswick: 30). Representative Francis Walter led the House opposition to the proposal, and Senator McCarran not surprisingly led the Senate forces to amend the administration's plan. The Congress finally agreed to accept 214,000 special immigrants in the Refugee Act of 1953 (Jones M., 1960: 286). The group contained large numbers of German ethnic expellees, and Poles, Italians, Greeks, and some Arabs and Asians. These prospective immigrants were required to obtain U.S. citizen sponsors assuring them of jobs and housing, unless they were close relatives. It also involved elaborate screening to assure that no subversives would sneak in through the act.

Debate on this proposal typified the immigration policy conflicts that went on throughout the 1950s. Proposals to amend or radically change the national origins system died in committee. Proposals, however, which were tied in to foreign policy and national security and/or which stressed humanitarian grounds fared better. The actual effect of the "special legislation," however, was indeed to undercut the national origins system. Immigrants from southeastern European countries who came in under these various special provision often resulted in doubling or tripling the numbers from that country allowed in under the quota system.

In 1956, Congress rejected another proposal to overhaul the national origins system. It did, however, allow for another "special" act to deal with a particular refugee problem. The failed Hungarian revolution of that year produced a mass exodus of "freedom fighters," whom President Eisenhower wanted to be admitted to the United States. Initially he brought in around 5,000 under the Refugee Relief Act of 1953. That was still too inadequate a number to handle the problem. In early 1957, the president asked for special legislation and some broader changes in the immigration laws. Congress rejected the broad changes, but did grant the president greater latitude in bringing in the freedom fighters. A special parole status enabled over 30,000 more Hungarian refugees to enter that year (Chiswick: 32; and Jones M.: 286). This was the first large-scale use of the "parole" status. Roughly 12,000 of the 38,000 Hungarian refugees entered under the "parole status." The remainder were admitted under the regular quota system. Voluntary agencies met the cost of their resettlement, assisting them in finding sponsors, jobs and housing (see McClellan: 21; and Chiswick: 32).

In 1957, Congress cancelled the mortgage quotas of the Displaced Persons Act. This marked a further breakdown in the restrictionist policy of the quota system. While Congress continued to chip away at the system, it became clearer that a broader revision was becoming necessary.

Late in the Eisenhower presidency, the Castro revolution in Cuba generated another large wave of refugees from communism seeking entry to the United States. President Eisenhower again used the parole status, this time to admit the Cuban refugees. Ultimately, some 800,000 Cuban refugees entered the United States, making it the largest long-term refugee movement in United States history (Chiswick: 32; and McClellan: 22). President Eisenhower also used the parole status for Chinese arriving from Hong Kong. In all, from the end of World War II until 1980, over 1.4 million refugees from all over the world have immigrated to the United States (McClellan: 45).

Another method of getting around the quota system was the use of the private bill. Under this procedure, an alien sought exception to the quota system through private legislation. A member of Congress introduced a bill for his/her relief. The use of this procedure expanded during the 1950s, again serving to undercut the quota system. Table 5.1 shows the number of such bills introduced and those actually enacted for the years 1937 through 1972. While the total numbers of immigrants who actually entered the United States by this method has not been large, totaling only in the thousands, it further indicates the inflexibility of the quota system.

In 1962, after the election of President Kennedy and a somewhat more liberal Congress, Congress passed the Migration and Refugee Assistance Act. In part a response to the Cuban refugee problem, this law strengthened the role of the executive branch in the formulation and implementation of immigration policy, paving the way for the act of 1965.

THE IMMIGRATION AND NATIONALITY ACT OF 1965

The election of President Kennedy in 1960 eased the way for a frontal attack on the quota system. It placed in the White House an executive who strongly desired a major revision. As senator, Kennedy had written *A nation of Immigrants* (1958), in which he showed his obviously favorable attitude towards more open immigration. During his first two years in office, so dominated by foreign policy crises, he failed to propose any specific action.

TABLE 5.1
Private Immigration and Nationality Bills

YEAR:	INTRODUCED:	ENACTED:
1937–1938	293	30
1939–1940	601	65
1941–1942	430	22
1943–1944	163	12
1945–1946	429	14
1947–1948	1,141	121
1949–1950	2,811	505
1951–1952	3,669	729
1953–1954	4,797	755
1955–1956	4,474	1,227
1957–1958	4,364	927
1959–1960	3,069	488
1961–1962	3,592	544
1963–1964	3,647	196
1965–1966	5,285	279
1967–1968	7,293	218
1969–1970	6,266	113
1971–1972	2,866	62

Source: Adapted from data in Harper: 652.

But the growing agitation over civil rights turned the administration's and the nation's attention inward. The civil rights movement marked a changing national attitude towards racism that undercut the restrictionist policy. The sort of bigotry contributing to the lopsided majorities in favor of the quota system in 1952 were no longer publically acceptable by the mid-1960s.

The success of the Kennedy Administration's economic policies, moreover, resulted in the end of the recessions that plagued so much of the Eisenhower period and again worked to undercut opposition to immigration reform. The healthy economy of the early through mid-1960s enabled even organized labor to favor a more liberal policy. By the mid-1960s, the traditional supporters of the national origins quota system were unorganized and largely inactive. Senator Edward Kennedy, the youngest brother of the president, led the Senate forces seeking to change the law. He met with leaders from the American Coalition, the American Legion, the Daughters of the American Revolution, and the National Association of Evangelicals. In his words, "No significant opposition to eliminating the national origins quota system was organized by any of their organizations" (cited in Chiswick: 33).

In July of 1963, President Kennedy sent to Congress his immigration reform proposal. Senator Hart of Michigan and Representative Celler introduced companion bills. President Kennedy's assassination and some congressional opposition delayed passage of the bill. Senator Sam Ervin fought a rear guard battle to preserve the quota system and won some eventual revisions to the proposal which the administration had not particularly wanted. In the House, Representative Michael Feighan of Ohio, chairman of the House Subcommittee on Immigration, was also effective in the use of delaying tactics in 1963–64. In July of 1963, he was appointed chairman of the Joint Committee on Immigration and Nationality Policy (Harper: 38).

President Kennedy's assassination, viewed almost immediately as a "martyrdom," plus the landslide election of President Johnson in 1964, meant the end of the quota system and its replacement by a preference system was virtually inevitable. President Johnson, as a former Senate Majority leader, was one of the best "nose counters" in the business. And his landslide victory swept into office a large number of liberal Democrats. He suddenly had more noses to count then ever before. By 1964–65, a significant number of congressmen were climbing on the immigration-reform bandwagon. Dozens of bills were introduced abolishing the national origins quota system.

The administration's proposal was resubmitted by President Johnson on January 13, 1965. It was introduced in the House by Representative Emmanuel Celler, chairman of the House Judiciary Committee. It was introduced into the Senate on January 15th by Senator Philip Hart of Michigan, cosponsored by thirty-two others, including both Senators Edward and Robert Kennedy. It sought to balance five major goals: 1) to preserve the family unit and reunite separated families; 2) to meet the need for some highly skilled aliens; 3) to help ease population problems created by emergencies, such as political upheavals, Communist aggression, and natural disasters; 4) to better the understanding of people cross-nationally through exchange programs; and 5) to bar from the United States aliens who would likely represent problems of adjustment due to their physical or mental health, criminal history, dependency, or for national security reasons (Harper: 56). The major provisions of the act are shown in the following Box.

The preference system established by the act for the allocation of immigrant visas within each foreign state was as follows:

1) First preference: unmarried sons and daughters of U.S. citizens;

2) Second preference: spouses and unmarried sons and daughters of permanent resident aliens;

3) Third preference: members of the professions and scientists and artists of exceptional ability;

4) Fourth preference: married sons and daughters of United States citizens;

BOX 3: MAJOR PROVISIONS OF THE IMMIGRATION ACT OF 1965

---

1) It abolished the national origins quota system, after a transition period to June of 1968.

2) It abolished the Asian-Pacific Triangle provision.

3) It allowed use of quota numbers unused in the previous year as a pool of additional numbers for each year of the transition period, for preference applicants chargeable to oversubscribed quotas.

4) It revised previous preference categories into a new system of preferences strongly favoring [74 percent] relatives of citizens and permanent resident aliens.

5) It required that an alien coming to work in the U.S. and not entitled to a preference obtain certification from the Secretary of Labor that he/she would not displace nor adversely affect the wages and working conditions of workers in the same field in the United States.

6) It included refugees as one of the preference categories.

7) It set an annual ceiling of 170,000 on immigration of aliens in the preference and nonpreference classifications with a 20,000 limit for any single foreign state.

8) It established an "immediate relative" [previously called "nonquota"] status for parents of adult United States citizens.

9) It increased the dependent area immigration [previously "subquota"] to one percent of the 20,000 maximum allowable numbers available to the governing country, that is, from 100 to 200 annually.

10) It set the filing date of the petition to determine the chronological order of preference applicants.

11) It required that applicants be considered in the order of their preference class.

12) It created a Select Commission on Western Hemisphere Immigration to study economic, political, and demographic factors affecting immigration.

13) It set a ceiling of 120,000 on immigration from the Western Hemisphere nations after July, 1968.

14) It included all independent countries of the Western Hemisphere in "special immigrant" status [previously called "nonquota" status]. (See Harper: 38-39).

---

5) Fifth preference: brothers and sisters of United States citizens;

6) Sixth preference: skilled and unskilled workers in short supply; and

7) Seventy preference: refugees (See Harper: 132-33).

President Johnson signed the law on October 3, 1965, in front of the Statue of Liberty in New York harbor. His remarks upon signing the bill into law are presented in Box 4.

Senator Everett Dirksen of Illinois, and Senator Sam Ervin had forced the administration to compromise on its original version of the bill by accepting an overall ceiling of 120,000 for the Western Hemisphere, rather than continuing the unlimited status of that influx. That figure was a compromise

...This bill that we sign today is not a revolutionary bill. It does not affect the lives of millions. It will not shape the structure of our daily lives, or really add importantly to our wealth or our power. Yet it is still one of the most important acts of this Congress and of this Administration. For it does repair a very deep and painful flaw in the fabric of American justice. It corrects a cruel and enduring wrong in the conduct of the American nation.

...This bill says simply that from this day forth those wishing to emigrate to America shall be admitted on the basis of their skills and their **close relationship to those already** here.

This is a simple test, and it is a fair test. Those who can contribute most to this country--to its growth, to its strength, to its spirit--will be the first that are admitted to this land.

The fairness of this standard is so self-evident that we may well wonder that it has not always been applied. Yet the fact is that for over four decades the immigration policy of the United States has been distorted by the harsh injustice of the National Origins Quota System...

We can now believe that it will never again shadow the gate to the American nation with the twin barriers of prejudice and privilege.

Our beautiful America was built by a nation of strangers. From a hundred different places or more, they have poured forth into an empty land-- joining and blending in one mighty and irresistible tide.

The land flourished because it was fed from so many sources--because it was nourished by so many cultures and traditions and peoples...

Now, under the monument which has welcomed so many to our shores, the American nation returns to the finest of its traditions today. The days of unlimited immigration are past. But those who do come will come because of what they are, and not because of the land from which they sprang...

Over my shoulder here you can see Ellis Island, whose vacant corridors echo today the joyous sounds of long-ago voices.

And today we can all believe that the lamp of this grand old lady is brighter today--and the golden door that she guards gleams more brilliantly in the light of an increased liberty for the peoples from all the countries of the globe (Lyndon Johnson, "Remarks on Immigration Law," Congressional Quarterly ,October, 1965: 2063-64.).

representing roughly the flow of Western Hemisphere immigration for the few years immediately preceding the act. With that compromise, the act passed easily. The Senate passed the measure 76 to 18. The House agreed to it by a vote of 320 to 69 (Chiswick: 37).

Some significant changes in the immigration flow resulted from the 1965 act. In the decade after its passage total immigration increased by nearly 60 percent. Immigrants from some countries experienced a really dramatic increase: Greek immigration rose by 162 percent; Portuguese by 382 percent; Asian immigration overall rose by 663 percent, with some countries showing remarkable gains; Indian by over 3,000 percent; Korean by 1,328 percent; Pakistan by 1,600 percent; the Philippines by nearly 1,200 percent; Thailand by over 1,700 percent; and Vietnam by over 1,900 percent. Among the countries of Europe, immigration from which declined by over 38 percent overall, those which registered the largest negative percent change were: Austria, with a decline of over 76 percent; Ireland by over 77 percent; Norway by over 85 percent; and the United Kingdom by nearly 120 percent (see Table 1, Chiswick: 39).

The 1965 act's provision for professionals was especially helpful for opening up immigration from Asia. Korean and the Philippine health professionals entered in large numbers, who then could use the family preference category to later bring in their family members. By the late 1970s over 70,000 medical doctors alone had immigrated. By that time there were more Filipino physicians in the U.S. than native-born black doctors.[4]

The 1965 act was also soon outmoded in its provisions for refugees. That act set what at the time seemed the generous provision of an annual preference limit for refugees at 10,200. Events in Cuba, Vietnam and Haiti soon outstripped the ability of that limit to begin to cope with the demand for entrance on the basis of refugee status.

THE 1976 AMENDMENT TO THE IMMIGRATION AND NATIONALITY ACT AND THE 1980 REFUGEE ACT

By the mid-1970s, the number of refugees seeking entrance far exceeded the 6 percent set aside for them in the 1965 Act's preference category for refugees. From Cuba alone, from 1960 to 1980, 800,000 refugees came. Since the 1965 law defined refugees as those fleeing communism or from the mideast, it did not even consider the case of those fleeing right-wing dictatorships in the Western Hemisphere, e.g. the Haitians. The collapse of the South Vietnamese government in 1975 created another large pool of refugees fleeing communism. From 1975 to 1979, over 200,000 Vietnamese came to the U.S.

When the boat people began to arrive in 1979, the administration committed itself to allow in another 168,000 in 1980. In the spring of that year another dramatic influx of Cubans arrived by boat. In all, from 1975 to 1980 some 500,000 refugees from Southeast Asia alone arrived. Soviet Jews fleeing the Soviet Union contributed another 70,000 from 1969 to 1980. The foreign policy exigencies of the cold war compelled some further changes in the immigration law.

In 1976, Congress amended the Immigration and Naturalization Act of 1965 by modifying the preference system to include migration from the Western Hemisphere, along with a 20,000 annual limit for each nation.

The Asian and Hispanic influx of the late 1970s sharply changed the mix of legal immigration. European immigration had fallen to 13 percent of the total. Most legal immigrants came from Mexico, the Philippines, Cuba, Korea, and China/Taiwan.

At first, the president and attorney general responded to these refugee pressures by using the executive parole power to permit Cubans, Vietnamese and others to enter beyond the refugee category limits. Congress joined in by allocating funds to support the parolees and passed legislation to adjust their status—such as the Indochinese Refugee Resettlement Program in 1975.[5]

These refugee pressures and the growing anxiety over the estimated .5 million to 1 million undocumented aliens entering the United States illegally by the end of the decade prompted Congress to establish a Select Commission on Immigration and Refugee Policy in 1978. It issued its report in 1981.

By the end of the decade, Congress, the president, and the various relief agencies all realized that the limit on the refugee preference category was simply too low and too rigidly defined. In 1980, Congress reacted by passing the Refugee Act of 1980. This amended the 1965 act by redefining "refugee" to incude those from anywhere in the world, not just Communist countries or the Middle Eastern nations. It expanded the annual limit for refugees to 50,000 and raised total immigration from 290,000 to 320,000. It strengthened the refugee procedures and gave the president greater powers to deal with emergency situations.

The plight and the problems of the Haitian influx, who as "economic refugees" and who, not incidently, were black, raised other perplexing issues. The Vietnamese refugees were political allies to whom we felt a moral obligation, and the nation was generally willing to help them. They were also largely well-educated, middle-class persons. Two-thirds of them held white-collar jobs in Vietnam. Twenty-four percent were from professional, technical and managerial occupational backgrounds. Only 5 percent were farmers and fishermen (Montero: 23). The Vietnamese have acculturated more rapidly than any previous Asian group, undoubtedly due in part to their middle-class status and to the assistance programs. The Haitians, by contrast, were first treated as illegal immigrants. As "economic refugees" held to be fleeing dire economic conditions, not political repression, they were not allowed in under the refugee category. They began steadily arriving in large numbers in 1972. For years, their legal status was clouded as the State Department and the country grappled with what to do with them.

Being economic refugees, they were not accorded the aid or public support given to the Cubans, the Vietnamese, the Hungarians or the Soviet Jews. They were overwhelmingly unskilled and illiterate. They were held in detention camps for years. Since being released from those camps, they have not been aided, as were the other refugees, in finding jobs and housing or otherwise acculturating to U.S. life. Their illiteracy, low job skills and language problems have made them easily exploitable, and they have lived in near slavelike conditions as migrant workers. They have been viewed as a special threat to the labor market.

The problems of such "economic refugees" and the undocumented aliens have mounted considerably since the late 1970s. Their numbers have been estimated at some 3 to 6 million.[6]

The coming-to-power of a conservative Republican Administration with the election of President Reagan in 1980, plus the most severe economic recession since the end of World War II during the first years of that administration, have heightened public awareness of and concern over the "illegal immigration issue." The Report of the Select Commission on Immigration and Refugee Policy, which constituted the broadest inquiry into the immigration process and policy problems since the Dillingham Commission Report in 1911, suggested the broad outlines for the newest revision of immigration policy. It is to a discussion of recent trends in immigration and the passage and likely impact of that law that the final chapter is devoted.

NOTES

1. This chapter relies heavily upon the succinct but excellent discussion of immigration policy since World War II by David Reimers, "Recent Immigration Policy: An Analysis" in Barry Chiswick (ed.), *The Gateway*. (Washington, D.C.: American Enterprise Institute, 1982): 13-53. Two other sound discussions of immigration policy during the 1950s are Marion Bennett, *American Immigration Policies: A History*. (Washington, D.C.: Public Affairs Press, 1963), and U.S. Congress, Senate, *U.S. Immigration Law and Policy, 1952-1972*, Report of the Select Commission on Immigration and Refugee Policy, 96th Congress, (Washington, D.C.: U.S. Government Printing Office, 1979).

2. U.S. Congress, Senate, Committee on the Judiciary, *The Immigration and Naturalization Systems of the United States*, 81st Congress, 2nd Session, 1950, Senate Report 1515: 455.

3. See Marius Dimmitt, "The Enactment of the McCarran-Walter Act of 1952," (Ph.D. dissertation, University of Kansas, 1970): 136, 240. See too, M. Bennett, Chapters 10-13, and Divine: Chapter 9 for a more complete discussion of the bill and its criticisms.

4. Cited in Chiswick: 41. See also Rosemary Stevens, *The Alien Doctors* (New York: Wiley and Sons, 1978), and Patricia R. Mamot, *Foreign Medical Graduates in America* (Springfield, Illinois: Charles Thomas, 1974).

5. See LeMay: 358–359. See also Darrell Montero, *Vietnamese Americans* (Boulder, Col.: Westview Press, 1979), and Gail Kelly, *From Vietnam to America* (Boulder, Col.: Westview Press, 1977). For a broader discussion of the entire "refugee" aid programs, see Grant S. McClellan, *Immigrants, Refugees and U.S. Policy* (New York: H. W. Wilson, 1981). For aid to Soviet Jews, see William Orback, *The American Movement to Aid Soviet Jews*. (Amherst: University of Massachusetts Press, 1979).

6. LeMay: 359–362. See also, McClellan, op. cit.; and John Crewdson, *The Tarnished Door: The New Immigrants and the Transformation of America* (New York: Time Books, 1983); Harry Cross and James Sandos, *Across the Border* (Berkeley: Institute of Government Studies, 1981); and Nathan Glazer (ed.), *Clamor at the Gates: The New American Immigration* (San Francisco: ICS Press, 1985).

6
Current Law and Future Trends

INTRODUCTION

The 1980s have witnessed a renewed interest in immigration policy. A major Congressional Commission has reviewed United States immigration and refugee policy. In October, 1986 Congress finally passed the Immigration Reform and Control Act. It constitutes the most substantial revision of immigration law since 1965. The reader might well ask, "Are we entering a new phase or era in U.S. immigration policy?" Certainly this brief historical review of U.S. immigration policy suggests that the times and conditions are ripe for such major revision and a shift in policy with respect to immigration. That historical review highlights several commonalities evident in each previous period marked by a major change in immigration policy. All such elements are evident again today.

1. Each major shift was preceded by a major recession or a depression: 1873, 1893, 1920, the Great Depression, the early 1950s; and the early 1960s. The recession of 1980–1981 was the most severe since World War II.
2. Each period was marked by social unrest and anxiety. The labor unrest and strife of the 1870s led to the first restrictions imposed in 1882. The Red Scare of 1919 immediately preceded the imposition of the quota system in the 1920s. The Cold War and hysteria of McCarthyism ushered in the Immigration Act of 1952. The social turmoil of the civil rights era and the Vietnam War were reflected in the changes in the Immigration Act of 1965. In each post-war period—be it after the Civil War, World War I, World War II, the Korean War, or the Vietnam War—agitation led to substantial changes in our immigration policy. The Iranian hostage crisis and the national anxiety spawned by the recent resurgence of international terrorism has engendered a rise in nationalistic fervor that has contributed markedly to the movement to revise immigration policy. So too, the huge trade deficits and the specter of

increased economic competition from Japan has spurred a protectionist fervor in Congress that, at least in part, is reflected in the proposals to tighten immigration laws by imposing employer sanctions.

3. Each major shift in immigration policy was enacted shortly after a major shift in the composition of the influx of immigrants. The influx of a new "Asian race" led to the first immigration restrictions. The change from Protestants from northwestern Europe to Catholics and Jews from southeastern Europe solidified support for the imposition of the national origins quota system. The need to deal with the "refugees" after World War II compelled another significant change in policy. More recently, the massive influx of Chicanos, Haitians, Cubans, Vietnamese, and other Asians has led to new demands to modify our current immigration law.

4. Each major shift in policy came after one or more of the major political parties advocated such change as an important plank of that party's platform. Immigration reform became a significant political campaign issue before each major shift occurred.

5. Likewise, each major shift followed the development of specific ad hoc interest groups formed to advocate such change. In the 1840s it was the Know–Nothing Party. The Asian Exclusion League was the principal proponent of such change in the 1880s and 1890s. In the 1920s, the Ku Klux Klan, the American Coalition, the Immigration Restriction League, and the American Protective League of True Americans battled the Hebrew Sheltering and Immigration Aid Society and the Anti-National Origins Clause League. Today we see the emergence of the Federation for American Immigration Reform [FAIR] and the Zero Population Growth as strong advocates of the need for change.

The historical review highlights some recurrent themes, which are echoed and reechoed by the proponents for a change in policy. Each major shift saw agitation over the impact of immigration on wages and working conditions. During each period one heard cries bewailing the adverse effects of immigration on U.S. culture; fears that the newcomers would damage U.S. culture, social mores, and politics were vehemently expressed. The recurrent theme of whether or not each new wave of immigrants could be or should be assimilated is a motif heard more distinctly during the period of each major shift—just as in the 1980s one hears grave concern raised over bilingualism and the supposed "unassimilability" of the Chicanos or the Asians.

Each period of change saw its advocates touting some new method for restriction. Public policy shifted from a reliance upon "excluded categories" to the "literacy test" and to the imposition of the "quota system." That was followed by an elaborate "system of preferences." Today's proponents advocate the use of "employer sanctions." While the method modified, a consistent pattern throughout is that each major shift in policy is associated with the advocacy of some "new method."

The historical overview shows that in each period the same stable coalition of interest groups generally supported the relatively unrestricted influx of newcomers while another such coalition of organized interests were pressing for increased restrictions on immigration. Time and again various business and ethnic coalitions in favor of unrestricted immigration battled a coalition of organized labor, the American Legion, and various patriotic associations who pressed the adoption of some new approach to restrict the influx.

So too, the period of each major shift saw a spate of scholarly books, a mass-media campaign, and a major government sponsored committee or commission that reviewed the "current problem" of immigration. Each such major movement to mold public opinion preceded a significant shift in public sentiment toward the direction of the new change in immigration policy.

The long-term historical overview of U.S. immigration policy demonstrates that four main elements figure prominently in the formulation of such policy: economic, racial, nationalistic, and foreign policy considerations. These four main elements of immigration policy sometimes worked in harmony with one another, reinforcing each other in their impact on policy. At other times they worked in conflict with each other as contending forces seeking to determine the primary thrust of immigration policy each stressed differing elements. But, in each case, the policy enacted reflected the then current "balance" between and among these four key elements.

This chapter will focus first upon recent trends in the size and composition of the immigration influx. It will discuss what are viewed as the major "problems" with current immigration policy as it attempts to cope with those changing conditions in the immigration process. The chapter will then focus on the major proposals for change in immigration policy that have emerged since 1981, stressing the thrust in the policy shift such proposals advocate. It will close with a critique of the new law, attempting to underscore likely future trends in immigration and immigration policy as we enter a new phase in the nation's immigration policy.

RECENT TRENDS IN IMMIGRATION

The 1965 Immigration Act, which as we have seen, ended the quota system, opened the way for forces that have dramatically altered the immigration influx, enabling the largest wave of immigration to arrive here since the turn of the century, and altering the makeup of that wave. Under the quota system, for roughly half a century, the immigrants entering the United States were overwhelmingly European. Today they come from the third-world nations--largely from Asia and Latin America. Of the 544,000 legal immigrants who entered in 1984, more than 10 percent (57,000) were from Mexico; followed by the Philippines (42,000) and Vietnam (37,000). British immigration, by contrast, at only 14,000 ranked ninth (*Time*, July 8, 1985: 26).

Our newest immigrants are highly visible. A single cluster of 14 stores in New York City has a Korean beauty parlor, a Chinese hardware store, a South Asian Spice shop, a Chinese watch store, and a Korean barber. A single high school in Chicago teaches algebra in English, Spanish, Cantonese, Vietnamese, and Asyrian. One can travel more than a mile along Bolsa Avenue in Santa Ana, California, and see nothing but Vietnamese store signs. Supermarkets, bookstores, pharmacies, and rare herb shops have replaced strawberry fields. These newest immigrants have converged on the major cities of a half-dozen states. California shows the most self-evident change: it is now home to 64 percent of the nation's Asians and 35 percent of its Hispanics. It is followed by New York, Texas, Florida, Illinois, and New Jersey. Miami is now 64 percent Hispanic; San Antonio is 55 percent. The City of Los Angeles today has—at over two million—more Mexicans than any other city except Mexico City, and nearly half as many Salvadorans (300,000) as San Salvadore (*Ibid*: 29).

The immigrants of today are more heavily white-collar (over 30 percent of legal immigrants held professional or managerial positions prior to their immigration), more urban in background, and include more females (approximately 53 precent are female) than those who came at the turn of the century (McClellan: 28).

A prominent scholar of immigration policy has noted three recent developments that have increased the significance of immigration policy. The first trend is a sustained increase in the number of potential migrants. The second trend is the related shift in focus from legal to illegal immigration. The third trend involves the politics of mass asylum. Each of these trends, and their combination, enhances the importance of immigration and refugee policy from both a domestic and foreign policy standpoint. And the humanitarian and human rights aspects of immigration and refugee policy give a new urgency to the issue (see Knichrehm: APSA Paper). We will here briefly examine each of those trends.

Professor Leibowitz argues that the 1980 Refugee Act's change in the definition of the status of "refugee" has increased the number of persons thus eligible from 3 million to nearly 13 million people (Leibowitz: 167). Although the definitional question of refugee status is a complicated one, involving political, social, economic as well as legal ramifications, the trends in third-world nations particularly have led to what is often called "the global refugee crisis" (Kritz: 157). Best estimates place the number of refugees in the world today at between 12 and 13 million [the *1981 World Refugee Survey* puts it at 12.5 million]. The vast majority of them are from third-world countries seeking refuge in another third-world country.

The United States, as well as some other industrialized countries, will continue to grant asylum to those refugees with whom they have historic ties. For example, from 1975 to 1980 the United States took in 677,000 refugees—including Soviet Jews, the Indochinese, and people from the Caribbean region. That was over three times as many as were taken in by any other country, and nearly as many as for all the other major receiving nations combined, as can be seen in Table 6.1.

The dramatic rise during the past decade in the number of potential immigrants has raised the pressure on immigration policy. The growing global interdependence and advances in transportation and communication make the United States more accessible than ever before. These pressures, moreover, result from causes largely outside the control of the United States government or policy. The worldwide population explosion, poverty, rising unemployment and the political turmoil experienced in much of the third world have been added to ethnic and religious tensions and natural disasters as powerful push factors. The United States is unique among the industrialized nations of the world in having nearly 2,000 miles of its borders face an adjoining third world nation. These forces have led to increased economic migration and occasional mass refugee flows that have been large enough and sufficiently concentrated in a few localities so that the domestic impact of the refugee flow is of increasing concern to the United States public and to Congress (Knickrehm, APSA Paper, 1985: 14; and Peters and Vega, 1986).

TABLE 6.1
Resettlement of Refugees, 1975–1980

Country	Number	Country	Number
U.S.	677,000	Austria	4,300
China	265,000	New Zealand	4,100
Israel	105,700	Belgium	3,900
Malaysia	102,100	Argentina	2,800
Canada	84,100	Norway	2,700
France	72,000	Denmark	2,300
Australia	51,200	Romania	1,200
Germany (FRG)	32,100	Spain	1,100
U.K.	27,600	Italy	900
Tanzania	26,000	Chile	800
Hong Kong	9,400	Japan	800
Switzerland	7,500	Cuba	700
Sweden	7,300	Mexico	700
Netherlands	4,700		

Source: *1981 World Refugee Survey*, ed. Michael J. Sherbinin (New York: U.S. Committee for Refugees, 1981). Cited in Papademetriou and Miller: 264.

The massive wave of legal and illegal immigration in response to these outside pressures raises some troubling questions. One such question concerns how many persons are actually entering our borders. In addition to the half-million annual legal immigrants, a substantial number of illegals are also entering. Estimates as to their number vary widely. In 1984, the INS apprehended 1.3 million undocumented aliens [many of them more than once] and the agency estimates that two to three times as many slipped through. In 1978, the Census Bureau estimated the total illegal immigration population in the country to be between 3.5 and 6 million. A National Academy of Sciences study released in August, 1985, however, denounced the INS figures as "woefully inadequate." It put the total number of undocumented aliens at between 2 and 4 million. These included anyone from persons deliberately overstaying their visas to the Haitian boat people who wash ashore in South Florida. But by everyone's standards, the majority of illegal immigrants are Hispanics, about two-thirds of whom are Mexicans driven by poverty and unemployment across the highly porous 2,000-mile Mexican/U.S. border (*Time*, July 8, 1985: 27).

Other questions raised by this trend are how many of these new aliens can we absorb and at what rate; how many unskilled laborers do we need in our increasingly high-tech society; do illegal immigrants drain the economy or enrich it; do the newcomers gain their foothold at the expense of the poor and the black; how possible and/or desirable is it to assimilate such large numbers and such diverse racial, language, and cultural backgrounds; and will the advantages of such diversity outweigh the dangers of separatism and conflict?

The Refugee Act of 1980 allowed for as many as 70,000 people annually who have a "well-founded fear of persecution" on account of race, religion, nationality, membership in a social group, or political opinion. In 1984, the country admitted 61,750 such refugees (*Time*, July 8, 1985: 27).

Refugees, moreover, tend to arrive in substantial numbers from given countries at given times—in mass asylum movements. Since 1960, for instance, nearly 400,000 came from Cuba; approximately 340,000 from Vietnam; 110,000 from Laos; nearly 70,000 from the U.S.S.R., and an equal number from Kampuchea; 30,000 from Yugoslavia; about 25,000 from mainland China and from Taiwan; nearly 20,000 each from Rumania and Poland; and about 10,000 each from Czechoslovakia, Spain, and Hungary. The current shift in the total influx, both legal and illegal, has been away from European and towards Asian and Latin American sources. Such events severely strained the 20,000 per-country limit of the 1965 Act.

During the last decade, Asian-Americans have become the fastest growing minority, at least as measured by births and legal immigration. At 4.1 million, they constitute 1.8 percent of the total population and show promise of having an influence far out of proportion to their numbers (*Parade*, June 2, 1985:2). In 1984 alone, more than 282,000 came to the United States. That number exceeded those who came during the three decades from 1930 to 1960! More than half settled in California, which has the nation's largest Asian population [64 percent]. More than 1 million other Asians have already applied and received preliminary clearance to immigrate to the United States. The Asian-American population is expected to more than double by 2010. Today, nearly 20,000 Asians arrive per month. In the next decade, the number is expected to rise 90 percent—almost double the rate of legal Hispanic immigration.

The new influx is altering the mix of Asian-Americans. Japanese-Americans, for example, who had been the most populous group since 1910, dropped to third place as of the 1980 census. According to that census, Chinese-Americans are now the largest group, at over 806,000. Filipinos, at 775,000, are now in second place. Their immigration has recently been running at over 35,000 annually, and one 1985 estimate places their number now at more than 1 million and projects them to overtake Chinese-Americans as the nation's largest Asian group around 1990.

Asian-Americans are not only the fastest growing, they are impressively the better-educated of the new immigrants. Among persons 25 or older, 32.5 percent completed college—as compared to 17.2 percent among white U.S. citizens; 75 percent of Asian-Americans are high school graduates compared to 69 percent of whites (*Parade*: 4).

In large measure because of such impressive educational accomplishments, Asian-Americans are climbing the economic ladder with remarkable speed. According to the 1980 census, the median income for Asian-American families was $22,713 in comparison to $20,835 for white families, and $19,900 for U.S. families in general. Asians are well-represented among managers and professionals—at roughly twice the rates for whites (*Parade*: 4; *Time*, July 8, 1985).

But the Asian-American success story, while impressive, is by no means universal. One group experiencing an especially difficult transition is the Hmong hill tribe of Laos, a large percentage of whom are still on welfare. The Vietnamese and Cambodian communities evidence unusually high (among Asians) rates of depression and marital discord.

Many Asians complain of experiencing racial prejudice. During the rapid influx of Chinese into California's Monterey Park bumper stickers reflecting such sentiment appeared, reading "Will the Last American to Leave Monterey Park Please Bring the Flag" (*Time*, Ibid.).

Hispanic Americans, now estimated between 17 and 20 million in population, are a highly diverse minority. Indeed, the term "Hispanic" is a catchall phrase that majority society uses to refer to all Spanish-speaking groups. Whereas Anglo society tends to treat all of these groups alike, there are some considerable and important differences among them. According to 1980 census data, Hispanics are comprised as follows: Mexicans, 59 percent; Puerto Ricans, 15 percent; Cubans, 6 percent; Central/South Americans, 7 percent; and all other Spanish-speaking, 13 percent. In 1980, all Hispanics shared one aspect in common besides their language—they are highly urbanized. Nearly 90 percent reside in metropolitan areas. About one-fourth of them [an estimated 3.5 million] live in the Los Angeles and New York areas alone. They are highly concentrated in six states: California, Florida, Texas, New York, New York and Arizona (LeMay: 145).

A recent study released by the Population Reference Bureau estimates that the Hispanic population will reach 47 million by the year 2020, displacing blacks as the nation's largest minority group. A recent Census Bureau study shows Hispanics averaged 97.9 births per 1,000 women in 1981, compared to 83.6 per 1,000 for blacks and 68.1 per 1,000 for white women (*Parade*, September 4, 1983).

Hispanics have been moving "down" the economic ladder rather than up. In 1972, their income was at 71 percent of the average Anglo family income. By 1982, that figure had fallen to 68 percent. Hispanic poverty increased by one-third during that decade, so that by 1982 30 percent of all Hispanics were officially below the poverty line.

Hispanics tend to cluster together more strongly than many other immigrant groups. Their emphasis upon bilingual education has raised fears as to their separatist tendencies. And, indeed, some Hispanics do question whether full assimilation is desirable. Their voter registration and turnout remains low.

The border between the United States and Mexico is one of extraordinary contrast—perhaps equaled or exceeded in its starkness only by that of the Berlin Wall. On the one side of a border—stretching 1,936 miles from the Pacific Ocean through coastal mountains, across the Sonora Desert and on up to the high plains by the Gulf of Mexico—is the world's greatest economic superpower. On the other side is a third-world country of widespread poverty and an enormous national debt. Across that border there occurs annually hundreds of millions of legal crossings. In addition, in 1984 over 1 million undocumented aliens were seized [up 50 percent from a decade ago], and no one can even firmly estimate the number who made it across illegally.

SOME MAJOR PROBLEMS

The increased size of the newest influx and its changing composition, coupled with the massive scale of the illegal flow, have raised particular concern as to a number of related problems. This chapter will briefly touch upon five. Can the U.S. control its borders? What about increased problems of morale and corrruption within the INS? Can the U.S. maintain rights and liberties yet search out and control the undocumented alien influx? Is bilingualism successful or will it contribute to separatism? What is the economic impact of the new wave of immigration?

The recent wave of immigration and the sizable illegal flow have demonstrated with sharp clarity one aspect of current immigration policy: the U.S. is no longer able to control its borders. Depiction of the border as a "tortilla curtain" or a "revolving door" illustrate a degree of frustration about our lack of ability to keep out those who wish to enter illegally, keep close count and track of those allowed in legally but temporarily to ensure that they leave when their visas expire, and keep up with the tide of illegals who daily pour in and out of the country.

The INS lacks sufficient border guards and equipment to stop the influx of illegals entering at an estimated rate of four per minute. There are fewer border patrol officers on duty along the 2,000 miles of Mexican-U.S. border than there are policemen on the day shift in Philadelphia. The agency's enforcement budget for 1985 comes to only $366 million for a staff of 7,599—less than a third the number of officers in New York City's police force (*Time*, July 8, 1985). Its ponderous and archaic operations result in foreigners who wish to enter legally having to wait years for approval. This state of affairs induces attempts at illegal entry. Members of Congress have characterized the INS as the "worst agency in government" (*The Wall Street Journal*, May 9, 1985: 1-2).

The INS has been treated with worse than benign neglect. Its agents have been left without enough gasoline to carry out routine patrols. Its record-keeping remains so outdated and outmoded as to be literally useless. What other agency of government would be allowed to drift along for two and one-half years without a permanent director?

Milton Morris, the director of research for the Joint Center for Political Studies in Washington, D.C., recently pointed out the anomaly implicit in our national attitude towards immigration policy: "We are opposed to illegal immigration in principle, but we really object to the idea of the INS arresting some hard-working guy and taking away his chance to make a living" (*The Wall Street Journal*, May 9, 1985: 1). The war against illegal immigration often makes the INS an unpopular agency in a nation that proudly sees itself as a melting pot. By keeping the INS weak we are simultaneously able to pursue two contradictory immigration policies: a stated policy of selective immigration, and an actual one of quite liberal immigration. As we shall see more fully below, the very vagueness of some of the language contained in the newly enacted Immigration Reform and Control Act of 1986, which seems to have been essential for its successful passage, retains the status of ambiguity in immigration policy.

Nor are Mexicans and Central Americans the only ones penetrating the soft underbelly of the nation's uncontrolled borders. In 1984 the border patrol in Texas arrested undocumented aliens from 43 countries, including China, Korea, and Poland. In Los Angeles, INS agents broke up a network that smuggled in India Sikhs through Tijuana. And in 1984, the INS cracked a South American smuggling ring nicknamed the "Andes Express" which brought illegals across two continents from Ecuador to Chicago. (*The Wall Street Journal*, May 9, 1985: 2).

The agency's ongoing battle against smugglers is also largely a losing one. In 1980, for example the INS charged 15,000 persons with alien smuggling. Of those, only 6,000 were tried and only 2,000 were ultimately convicted (Crewdson: 30).

And, as for those who do enter legally, the INS has been unable to ensure that they obey the terms of their visas. The U.S. was embarrassed greatly by the deficiencies of the INS's recordkeeping during the Iranian hostage crisis in 1979. At that time, President Carter ordered the INS to expel Iranian college students living here illegally. The president, and the nation, were shocked to learn that the INS didn't even know how many such students were living here, let alone how many were doing so illegally. A good number of the Iranians that the INS finally identified as subject to deportation simply failed to attend deportation hearings or to leave the country when told to do so (*The Wall Street Journal*, May 9, 1985: 7; Crewdson: 117).

That problem was by no means peculiar to the Iranian student situation. As one critic of the INS observed:

> The INS spends most of its time and money looking for illegal border crossers, not "visa abusers," as such bogus visitors are known. In 1980 it found only 64,000 foreigners who had overstayed their visas. Nobody knows how many it did not find, but indications are that their numbers are enormous; the same year 12 million foreigners entered the United States with nonimmigrant visas, but only 10.5 million left. Some of the 1.5 million shortfall is doubtless due to careless record keeping by the INS and airlines that bring the visitors here and take them home—but not all of it. Daniel Vining of the University of Pennsylvania, who has calculated net migration to this country by air, estimates the number of overstayers at around 200,000 and others think it may be twice that (Crewdson: 31).

A related book-keeping problem with the INS concerns the number of documents it issues. There are so many that even the agency has trouble keeping them straight. Since 1946, it has issued more than 15 different versions of the "green card" (which is currently white) that allows foreign workers to reside in the U.S.

Another problem is the ease with which INS documents can be counterfeited. Undocumented aliens exploit the confusion of INS green cards by counterfeiting them. California's "Silicon Valley" is awash in such cards, which sell openly on the streets for $50 to $100 and have been used as far north as Milwaukee, Wisconsin where officials have seen dozens of such fake green cards used by illegal workers.

Nor do all such undocumented aliens need fake green cards to get across. Many use perfectly legal "crossing cards." Mexicans who wish to remain in the U.S. for up to seventy-two hours to shop or visit a friend must have a border-crossing card. Needless to say, the demand for them is high, and those seeking them often begin lining up outside the INS offices at the border the day before they make their applications.

The Iranian student debacle and the Haitian and Cuban boat people flooding ashore demonstrated the inability of the U.S. to control its borders. And the thousands who do enter legally daily leave behind a paper trail of about 50 million files with which the INS is simply incapable of coping. It has no idea of who comes, leaves or overstays. Its disasterous record-keeping results from use of 19th century tools and approaches to the data handling and processing aspects of the agency's tasks. It is, indeed, remarkable and ironic that an immensely rich and technologically advanced nation like the United States is no longer able to keep out those from other countries who wish to come here. Anyone with the desire to cross and the physical stamina to do so is apparently able to do so with impunity.

Associated with the INS's inability to control our borders are the problems of the agency's low level of morale and high degree of corruption.

The agency suffers from a severe reputation problem. It is often perceived as more of an enemy than the illegal aliens it attempts to arrest and send back. Its officers are sometimes made to feel like social outcasts. This understandably depresses morale. And when agents catch the same persons over and over again, it makes the job frustrating and seemingly meaningless. Agents complain of feeling like "we're just truant officers going after people playing hooky from Mexico," others "like the Dutch boy with his thumb in the dike." (*The Wall Street Journal*, May 9, 1985: 6-7).

The morale problem is exacerbated by the ease with which illegal aliens can be smuggled in and obtain counterfeit documents. Smuggling in aliens is a big business along the Mexican border—rivaling in size and profitability even drug smuggling. Alien smuggling arrests in recent years have tripled.

In 1969, the U.S. Border Patrol apprehended 4,457 persons for smuggling illegal aliens; by 1984, they were arresting more than that every week! Alien smuggling is safer than narcotics smuggling. The aliens pay in advance. If a narcotics smuggler is caught he loses his load and the investment made to get it; if an alien smuggler is caught the smuggler has already been paid his fees. Then too, the courts are far more lenient on alien smugglers than on drug smugglers. Only one in ten arrested is convicted, and probated sentences are common. The average time an alien smuggler serves in prison, even without probation, is only nineteen months (Crewdson: 25–26).

Similarly, the counterfeiting of false documents—from green cards to border-crossing passes to driver's licenses, Social Security cards, selective service certificates, and voter registration cards—is a huge business. The INS has on file more than 6,000 suspected sellers of false documents and 150 known sources of false green cards and border crossing passes. In 1973, one agent stumbled upon 60,000 fake green cards in a bus depot locker in Los Angeles. These cards were of such high quality, even containing secret identifying marks known only to immigration inspectors, that they could have been sold for $500 apiece. Cheaper cards are readily available along the Mexican side of the border. Vendors sell their wares in bars and restaurants, and often include lesser "credentials" that lend credence to the major ones, such as student ID cards, library cards, business and membership cards (Crewdson: 40).

State Department consulate officials, even low-level secretaries, are routinely offered bribes to obtain visas or even genuine, but fraudulently obtained passports. The department's security agents estimate some 30,000 passports annually are issued to ineligible recipients. Passports can be obtained for a few hundred dollars on the black market.

The ease with which such documents can be obtained contributes to the low morale of the INS agents. Large numbers of them complain that they feel that they alone care about controlling illegal immigration, and they soon begin to wonder why they should do so when no one else does, or when they see the Coast Guard rushing to assist foundering boats filled with Cubans or Haitians and assisting them to Florida. To INS agents, the nation's immigration policy seems absurd: a Mexican caught walking across the border is sent home, but a Haitian coming ashore in Florida is a "Cuban/Haitian entrant." Immigration inspectors across the country are simply giving up on the job, waiting out their time to retirement.

Problems of corruption flow naturally from the tremendous pressures for immigration coupled with the restrictions of legal immigration and the inefficiency of the INS. Nor is the problem limited to the INS. The State Department and immigration lawyers share in the extensive nature of corruption associated with the whole immigration process. Immigrants seeking the legal right to live here are often desperate to do so. Compliance with the legal process involved often necessitates using an immigration lawyer—a legal specialty currently booming. High demand for entry has led to practices that are openly fraudulent or questionably legal, and a situation wherein the field of immigration law has a tarnished reputation. INS officials estimate that about 30 percent of all permanent-resident petitions are fraudulent, with corrupt or incompetent lawyers often to blame. To legally gain a green card, an immigrant must be qualified to fill a job for which there is a shortage of U.S. workers, to be a refugee facing persecution at home, or be related to a U.S. citizen or permanent resident. Each category breeds its own schemes or scams. Among the easiest and most popular is the phony marriage. In one year, of 111,653 who applied for resident status through marriage, 30 percent were found to be fraudulent. One district director estimates that half such marriages would turn out to be phony if investigators had enough time to check them all thoroughly ("Quiz Traps Fraudulent Immigrants," *The Cumberland Sunday Times*, November 3, 1985: A3).

Labor certificates are sometimes fraudulent or nearly so, often involving the use of a lawyer designing a job description so specific that no one except the client is likely to qualify. Some schemes involve wholesale lying—including the setting up of bogus corporations whose sole purpose is to substantiate the credentials of visa seekers (*Time*, July 8, 1985).

Ambiguities in the new law and the lack of a secure and settled system of "documentation" for those who can be here legally and who can work are likely to exacerbate, at least temporarily, such problems of document fraud.

The State Department's visa issuing procedures have also contributed to the problem and have involved allegations of widespread corruption. In 1980, temporary visas were issued to 12 million persons. INS records substantiate only 10 million left. Visa overstayers are an undoubtedly increasing problem largely beyond the resources of the INS to control. In part, this is due to the fact that the State Department is granting such temporary visas to more "bad risk" applicants. This practice contributes to the low morale of the INS. It is also costly. David North, a noted immigration researcher, noted that for the foreign service officer to check whether or not to issue or deny a visa costs the government an average of $3.37. The cost of the INS to inspect arriving passengers was only 42 cents. But for the border patrol to catch a visa overstayer once in the country, North estimated that it cost $43.38—if indeed it ever did catch them. Some State Department officials estimate that between 20,000 and 50,000 visas are sold annually (Crewdson: 136-37).

Similar problems of extensive corruption plague the INS. A notorious case in 1971 established that an INS inspector took bribes to let undocumented aliens in. In four years time, the government's attorneys concluded, he had supplemented his annual salary of $24,000 with more than $250,000 in bribes and proceeds from selling visitor's visas, green cards, border crossing cards, and the like. In the early 1970s an in-house investigation called "Operation Clean Sweep" opened criminal cases on 217 past and present INS officers, involving the taking of bribes, violations of civil rights, fraud against the government, with devastating evidence of alien and narcotics smuggling, perjury, rape, robbery, extortion of money and sex, influence peddling, and the misappropriation of government funds and property (Crewdson: 150–71).

Just as the tremendous number of undocumented aliens flooding into the country and the restrictive formal policy almost inevitably contributes to the problems of morale and corruption, so too they lead to abuses of civil rights and civil liberties.

In a discussion of the "crisis of enforcement" of immigration policy, one scholar recently noted that

> the enforcement of immigration law is punctuated with episodes of un-necessarily imposed hardship, corruption, and cruelty. U.S. citizens are detained, even deported, despite their protestations of legal status. Farmworkers caught in a field are bullied into signing voluntary depar-ture forms, herded into a bus and returned to Mexico, while their children are left behind in the United States in the care of an impromptu day-care center. Undocumented workers are shot crossing the border. In one horrifying case this past April [1984], a 12 year old Mexican boy was shot by U.S. INS officers because he was throwing rocks at them. In short, the current enforcement of our present immigration statutes neither effectively regulates entry into the United States nor respects the rights of citizens or non-citizens (Bennett, D., 1985: 1).

The underfunding of the INS compels it to engage in various secondary enforcement activities to locate illegal entrants: stopping traffic at check-points, watching air, bus and rail terminals, inspecting farms, ranches and areas of employment, and following up on specific leads. Such activities, however, pose more problems regarding the civil rights of individuals and numerous instances occur where such rights are likely to be abused. En-forcement begins to take on a perverse quality—we tend to apprehend and return those aliens who are truthful; the ones who avoid apprehension and remain among us are the ones most likely to be those who can successfully dissemble (Bennett, D., 1985: 8). The 1986 law does increase funding and staffing for the Border Patrol but probably still insufficiently so to substan-tially reduce this aspect of the problem.

The inability of the INS to effectively control the borders means that the later enforcement is necessarily somewhat arbitrary. *Time* reported recently on an almost humorous case which illustrates the point. A farm near El Mirage, Arizona, grew a vegetable called "broccoli de rapa" which needed a lot of irrigation, so the fields were always muddy. This dismayed the border patrol officers who came tramping through the fields about once a week to search for illegals, of whom they usually found about five. The farm crew boss suggested to the border patrol officer that "I give you five of them every week and you don't have to do any running or get your boots muddy.'' The border patrol went along, and the crew boss explained to his workers that everyone would make more if work were not interrupted by raids. So the workers drew lots once a week to pick the five who would be shipped back to Mexico. Before the victims left, however, the hat was passed for funds to help the unlucky five sneak back north, a trip that usually started the next day (*Time*, July 8, 1985). While the new law's provision requiring search warrants before the border patrol can "sweep" such agricultural operations may reduce instances of civil rights abuses, it will not likely change the inherently arbitrary nature of such enforcement.

The initial treatment of Haitians was particularly problematic. The government locked them up in detention centers—first at Krome Avenue outside Miami, then at Fort Allen in Puerto Rico. By the end of 1981, the Haitians were being kept in seventeen different camps and facilities around the country, including a federal prison at Lexington, Kentucky, while the INS, thoroughly unequipped for the job, tried to process their claims for asylum. During all of 1981, the INS managed to render a decision in 50 asylum cases, leaving a backlog of more than 5,000.

A federal judge in June of 1982 ruled their lock-up was unconstitutional, that the incarceration policy was both inhumane and racially motivated. The court ordered 1,900 Haitians under detention released. A few months later another federal judge ordered the INS to stop threatening and abusing refugees from El Salvador and to begin advising them of their legal right to seek political asylum. The judge ruled the INS had been using "verbal and physical abuse" to coerce them into waiving their rights to such asylum (Crewdson: 88–89).

The Tarnished Door describes numerous incidents involving the border patrol officers' abuse of people's civil rights and liberties, including cases of beating aliens; of forcing alien women to strip; of shootings [several of which led to deaths]; of using excessive and gratuitous brutality, administered out of frustration or to extort confessions; of extorting sex; and of illegally deporting U.S. citizens (173–217).

Another problem the current heavy influx in immigration raises is the fear that the newcomers will be increasingly unassimilable. A central aspect of that concern is the growing program of bilingualism. More than 1.3 million students are currently enrolled in U.S. schools in federal, state and local programs that provide instruction in their native tongues. These programs spring from the federal Bilingual Education Act of 1968. The original purpose of the bilingual education program was to help Hispanic children learn English quickly, while moving them ahead in their other schoolwork by letting them use their own language as much as necessary. Today, bilingual programs are conducted in 80 languages, ranging from Spanish to Lithuanian to Micronesian Yapese, at a cost of well over $350 million annually. Critics argue that such programs are distorted into a vehicle for bicultural education. There are estimates that as many as 3.6 million children are LEPs (limited English proficiency].

By far the most controversial problem—the one that has stirred the greatest debate—has been the economic impact of immigration, particularly of the illegal influx. There are scholars and interests aligned on both sides of this hotly debated issue.[1]

Virtually all of the experts agree that illegal immigration—as is true for legal immigration as well—is a boon for employers and consumers. Lower labor costs enable business to be more competitive, earn healthier profits, and pass along some of those benefits to the consumer in the form of lower prices. All agree that illegal immigrants also compete for many jobs with unskilled native labor—hurting some while benefiting others. The heated debate is over how many are hurt and how badly, against how much others are benefited.

The flood of illegal immigrant labor has helped hold down wages in a wide range of lower-level occupations, from computer assembly to sewing clothes. The pay of California's lemon harvest workers, for example, has held steady at about $6.00 per hour since 1980 because of the competition of illegal and nonunionized crews. In 1984, hotel workers in Los Angeles were forced to accept a pay cut from $4.20 to $3.60 per hour because of such competition.

David North argues that illegal laborers hurt the poor, benefiting a narrow but powerful and greedy band of interests to the detriment of the large but mostly silent majority (North, 1978 and 1980). Donald Huddle contends that the illegal immigrant impact reaches far higher into the job range. His study of illegal aliens working in the Houston-Galveston area found 53 percent made above $5.00 per hour, and 12 percent over $6.00 per hour; 60 percent were in jobs that were at least semi-skilled occupations, including cement laying, carpentry, and plumbing (*Time*, July 8, 1985: 75).

Thomas Muller counters that his study of illegals in Los Angeles shows that they create jobs—an estimated 52,000 in Los Angeles alone, principally as white-collar workers such as teachers, salesclerks, and health-care workers. California's blacks did not suffer an increase in unemployment because of immigration, according to his analysis (*Ibid*). Similarly, a 1986 Rand Corporation study examining the impact of Mexican immigrants on California concluded that up to now it has benefited the state's economy. The study found such immigration had stimulated low wage, labor intensive manufacturing while comparable manufacturing elsewhere across the nation had languished. For example, total manufacturing employment in Los Angeles grew by 13.6 percent between 1970 and 1980, and 28.4 percent statewide compared to a 4.8 percent increase nationwide. Jobs in the garment and furniture industries, which employ a high percentage of Mexican immigrants, grew by 47 percent during that same period compared to a 7.4 percent drop in jobs in those industries nationwide (McCarthy and Valdez, May, 1986).

Studies of the net impact of immigration on government finance are both sketchy and contradictory. A 1980 study by the Urban Institute found that California spent an average $3,254 on each Mexican immigrant household, both legal and illegal, in Los Angeles, and received only $1,515 in tax revenues in return. But a 1982–1983 study by Weintraub indicated that Texas receives about three times as much revenue from illegal aliens as it spends on them. The Rand study found that fewer than 5 percent of California's Mexican immigrants were receiving any form of public assistance in 1980. This compares to an all adult statewide figure of 12 percent. Mexican immigrants' contribution to public revenues exceeds the cost of their service usage, with the sole exception of education. The study concluded that they contributed less than the $2,900 it costs per year to educate a public school student largely because of their low income levels and the relative youth of the immigrants and their children (*Ibid*).

Some of the confusion in this assessment is the result of using different methodologies and economic assumptions in the various analytical studies. The picture that emerges from actual jobs uncovered by INS sweeps substantiates that the impact is at the lower level of jobs and probably is concentrated in largely "undesirable" jobs. Such sweeps are, however, no doubt skewed samples of the total job displacement picture.

"Project Jobs," a week-long operation of sweeping raids by the INS, instigated considerable criticism about the use of "gestapo-like" actions, and the arrest of "aliens who turned out to be legal residents (among them a twelve-year old boy who was a U.S. citizen). Although the INS hailed "Project Jobs" a success, the evidence seemed to be to the contrary. Only a few highly paid illegals were found—an occasional railroad or construction worker earning $9 or $10 dollars per hour. The average salary of the 5,440 employed aliens arrested during the sweep barely reached $190 per week, or less than $10,000 per year—below the poverty level for an average urban family. Of 356 alien workers arrested in New York, three-fourths of whom were not Mexican immigrants, the average weekly income was $174. The Bureau of Labor Statistics stated at the time that it took $251 a week to provide the most basic requirements for a family of four in New York City that year. In Chicago, the average income of all those arrested in the sweep was less than half the city's average hourly wage in manufacturing. The majority of all those arrested throughout the nation during Project Jobs was less than the minimum wage of $3.35 an hour. Most were working in essentially menial jobs (Crewdson: 243).

And few jobs opened by the raids were filled by U.S. citizens thereafter. The Texas Employment Commission found only 42 unemployed citizens who wanted to apply for the 1,105 jobs in that state opened up by the raids, and only 3 of the jobs were actually filled, largely because the wages being offered for the jobs were frequently $1 or $1.50 per hour less than what the INS claimed the arrested aliens were being paid. A similar pattern emerged at a fish-cleaning plant in northern California. The Midwest Steel Company, which lost 114 workers to the INS, was only able to hire 25 replacements. Another steel mill hired 92 workers to replace ones lost to the INS raids and 68 of those quit the first week (Crewdson: 244–45).

Those sweeps, as well as similar studies, have shown that illegal alien workers concentrate in several industries: the garment industry, electronic companies, domestic labor, construction, and agriculture. The Rand Study cited above found Mexican immigrants in California with the following percentages in occupation: 28 percent operatives, 16 percent personal service, 15 percent farm work, 15 percent white collar work, 14 percent skilled labor, and 12 percent general laborers. In terms of industry, 38 percent were in manufacturing, 16 percent were in agriculture, 12 percent in personal service and restaurants, 12 percent in other service jobs, 11 percent in wholesale and retail sales, 5 percent in construction, and 6 percent in "others" (McCarthy and Valdez: 1986).

Nor is it so clear that illegals "drive down" wages. In those industries where alien workers are most heavily concentrated wages may already be about as high as they can realistically go. Some economists, like John Kenneth Galbraith and Marvin Smith, argue that such jobs are being filled at what is an "economical wage"—that is, a wage low enough to allow the employer to make a profit. When an employer is faced with the loss of cheap labor, there are other options besides raising wages to be considered: replacing workers with machines, moving the operation overseas, or simply going out of business. When the Bracero Program ended in California, only the lettuce and citrus growers raised their wages in an attempt to attract domestic workers. The tomato growers began using mechanical harvesters, the asparagus growers moved to Mexico, and marginal growers in all crops simply closed down and sold their farms (Crewdson: 266–267).

Economist Walter Fogel counters, however, that the current flows of undocumented aliens exacerbates the job and income problems of blacks, Hispanics, and other secondary-market workers by reducing the number of jobs available to them, depressing wages for those jobs they do hold, and generally undercutting working conditions as well (*The Unavoidable Issue*: 88). The Rand Study also concludes that the changing job market and projected increases in immigration forecast trouble for many poorly educated Latinos before the turn of the century. They anticipate 3 million new jobs in California by 1995, for example, over half of which will be in white-collar and skilled, high-tech service jobs. Such jobs require skills beyond either immigrants or first-generation native born. Unskilled jobs are expected to grow at a rate far slower than the increase in the Mexican-American population which is expected to triple by the year 2000.

RECENT PROPOSALS TO REVISE IMMIGRATION LAWS

These problems, real or perceived, led to several proposals to reform immigration law. Heightened concern over immigration-related problems was evident by the late 1970s, seen in the media coverage and the number of federal task forces, committees, and commissions. During the 1970s immigration policy was the subject of five interagency task forces or cabinet committees in the executive branch. By the late 1970s the Carter Administration introduced a version of a bill initiated by Representative Peter Rodino that contained a provision for employer sanctions and legalization. Both pro- and anti-immigration forces opposed the bill, however, and it never reached the floor (*National Journal*, March 7, 1981: 390). In 1978, President Carter and Congress reacted by creating the Select Commission on Immigration and Refugee Policy to study the issue (Peters and Vega, 1986: 9; and Cornelius and Montoya, 1983: 33–34).

The Select Commission on Immigration and Refugee Policy opened in May of 1979. Its members were as follows: from the Senate, Charles Mathias (R., Md.), Alan Simpson (R., Wyo.), Edward Kennedy (D., Mass.), and Dennis De Concini (D., Ariz.); from the House, Peter Rodino (D., N.J.), Elizabeth Holtzman (D., N.Y.), Robert McClory (R., Ill.), and Hamilton Fish (R., N.Y.). The executive branch was represented by the secretary of state, Cyrus Vance, the attorney general, Benjamin Civiletti, the secretary of labor, Ray Marshall, and the secretary of HEW, Patricia Harris. Members of the public included Joaquin Otero of the Brotherhood of Railway and Airline Clerks, Judge Cruz Reynoso of the California Court of Appeals, Rose Ochi of the Office of the Mayor of Los Angeles, and Reubin Askew, former governor of Florida, designated as chairman. Before the commission was underway, however, President Carter appointed Askew to another position, and appointed the Reverend Theodore Hesburgh, President of Notre Dame University and former Chairman of the Civil Rights Commission as chair. The staff director of the Commission was Dr. Lawrence Fuchs, a professor of Political Science at Brandeis University and an acknowledged ethnic and immigration scholar. The commission began its work in October of 1979 and issued its report in January of 1981.

The commission essentially recommended "closing the back door" to undocumented immigration while opening slightly the front door to accommodate more legal immigration; defining our immigration goals more clearly; and providing a more effective structure to implement them by setting forth procedures that would lead to fair and efficient adjudication and administration of U.S. immigration laws (*Final Report*, SCIRP). It maintained that immigration unquestionably served humanitarian needs, and that continued immigration was in the national interest. While the commission stated that immigration entailed many benefits to U.S. society, it recognized our limited ability to absorb large numbers effectively. They held that "it is not the time for large-scale expansion in legal immigration, for resident aliens or temporary workers, because the first order of priority is in bringing undocumented/illegal immigration under control, while setting up a rational system for legal immigration." The commission recommended a "modest increase in legal immigration sufficient to expedite the clearance of backlogs--mainly to reunify families" (Introduction to the Final Report, SCIRP).

The commission argued that illegal immigration could also be reduced by strengthening and increasing the "family reunification" preference category, by putting immigrants whose entry into the U.S. would reunite families on a separate track from other immigrants, and by putting spouses and minor children of lawful permanent resident aliens under a separate, numerically limited category without country ceilings, thereby helping to assure the reunification of families on a first-come, first-serve basis within a fixed worldwide ceiling. It further advocated the creation of a separate category for nonfamily immigrants—an independent category—to provide immigration opportunities to those persons who came from countries where immigration here has not been recent or from countries that have no immigration base here. It called for upgrading our system for administering the laws, stressed streamlining deportation procedures, and the importance of English-language acquisition.

On March 6, 1981, President Reagan established a Task Force on Immigration and Refugee Policy. Chaired by the attorney General, the task force presented its recommendations to the president at three meetings in July, 1981. The major points in the immigration legislation proposal by President Reagan are presented, below, in Box Five.

By late 1981 the House and Senate Judiciary Subcommittees on Immigration had finished their respective hearings on the Reagan proposal [S1765, HR4832]. The chairmen of these subcommittees, Senator Alan Simpson (R.-Wy) and Congressman Romano Mazzoli (D.-Ky) emerged as the major proponents of the immigration reform issue. Virtually all the proposals Congress grappled with since then have been variations of their bill-- the Immigration Reform and Control Act of 1982.[2] That bill died in Congress in 1982, was reintroduced in 1983 and passed—in somewhat different versions in each House—in 1984. The following presents, in broad summary, the major provisions of the bill.

BOX 5: REAGAN´S PROPOSED IMMIGRATION REFORM BILL

1.) Amnesty. Aliens living in the U.S. illegally since January 1, 1980 would be permitted to remain, being made eligible for resident-alien status after being here ten years, and would also be free to seek U.S. citizenship [estimated number, 5 million persons].

2.) Guest Workers. A program allowing 50,000 Mexicans annually to come to work temporarily, gradually increasing in numbers over several years until up to hundreds-of-thousands annually.

3.) Employer Sanctions. Employers with more than four employees who "knowingly hire" illegal aliens would be subject to fines for up to $1,000 per violation.

4.) Boat People. Boats carrying Haitians would be intercepted. Detention camps would be established to hold as many as 6,000 people pending hearings on their deportation.

5.) Enforcement. Increase the budget of the INS by 50% and add 1,500 officers to the Border Patrol to enhance enforcement of immigration and labor laws.

6.) Immigration Limits. Allow 610,000 new immigrants to the U.S. annually, with a special preference to persons from Canada and Mexico.

(Source: "U.S. Immigration and Refugee Policy," Department of State, Thursday, July 30, 1981. See also "Reagan´s Plan for Illegal Aliens--the Impact" U.S. News and World Report, August 3, 1981: 42-43.)

---

1) Amnesty. The Senate version provided for temporary resident status to all illegal aliens who can prove they have been living in the U.S. since 1980 and would provide permanent resident status to all who could prove they have lived here since January 1, 1977. The House version offered permanent resident status to all who have lived here since January 1, 1982.

2) Employer Sanctions. Each House's version differed slightly, but both provided for civil and/or criminal penalties for employers who *knowingly* hire illegal aliens. First-offenders faced civil penalties; repeat offenders were subject to criminal penalties for up to a $3,000 fine per offense and up to a year in jail for conviction of each offense. In the Senate version, employers risked penalties if they did not try to verify the work status of all prospective employees by checking such things as passports, birth certificates, alien identification or green cards, driver's licenses or some similar documents.

Neither version of the bill called for a "national identity card." The Senate version, however, directed the executive branch to develop, within three years of the bill's enactment, a more secure or "tamper proof" method of worker-verification. It stipulated that no national identity card could be adopted without specific prior congressional approval.

3) Legal Immigration. The Senate placed a ceiling on legal immigration at 425,000 persons annually, not including refugees or immediate family members of U.S. citizens. The House version retained the 1965 law's ceiling of 20,000 persons per country.

4) Expense. Both bills authorized an increase in the budget of the border patrol of $200 million for hiring more agents for patrol and for more immigration officials to administer the amnesty and employer sanction programs.

5) Asylum. Both bills sought to speed up the asylum adjudication process by cutting the number of appeals available.

During the original debates on the bill (in 1982), two major amendments were offered. Senator Huddleston (D., Ky) proposed one that would have included refugees within the overall total for immigrants; Senator Bumpers (D., Ark) proposed one that would have set the normal flow of refugees at 75,000 but permitted no increase over that amount without congressional approval. Senator Simpson argued against the amendments, stressing the danger of emasculating the refugee program was high if it were forced to compete with regular immigrants, and defending the effectiveness of the congressional consultation process as contained in his bill. The Huddleston amendment failed by a vote of 35 to 63 (*Congressional Record*, August 12, 1982, S.10361). The Bumpers amendment was viewed by many as being fatally flawed by the inflexibility of its statutory limit. It failed by a vote of 41-45 (*Congressional Record*, August 13, 1982, S.10453).

The Simpson-Mazzoli Bill departed from several of the select commission recommendations. The commission's recommendation dropping the crown colony ceilings that apply to Hong Kong was not even touched upon in the legislative hearings on Simpson-Mazzoli. The commission's recommendations to increase the ceilings from 270,000 to 350,000 and to provide additionally 100,000 visas for the next five years to clear up backlogs were likewise never given serious consideration in the congressional hearings. Although these proposals have been considered by the Reagan Administration's interagency task force, they were not included because of the anti-immigration atmosphere that prevailed during the early 1980s when unemployment was still so high. The House bill more closely followed the Commission's recommendations, for example, with respect to due process issues, H-2 certification, the exemption of spouses, minor children and parents of U.S. citizens from the numerical restrictions, and its general emphasis on family reunification. Both versions of the bill followed the select commission in asserting the need to keep the front door open at least at present levels, to retain special admission of refugees separate from that of immigrants, and to provide for a substantial program to legalize illegal aliens already here (See Cornelius and Montoya: 49–50).

The asylum adjudication problems were addressed in the Simpson-Mazzoli Bill by setting up new procedures. The bill established an asylum adjudication officer specifically trained in international law, and prohibited any existing INS officer from holding the position. A U.S. Immigration Board, resembling the current Parole Commission, would hear appeals. Its members would be presidential appointees, and were independent of the attorney general. No judicial appeal from the decisions of these independent administrative tribunals would be permitted. Congress was seeking a fair process, but a sharply curtailed one. The State Department was given no role in the process.

These adjudication procedures were objected to by both the administration and by asylum advocates, although everyone agreed on the need to address the asylum problem. The Reagan Administration advocated greater control over the process by placing it under the authority of the attorney general, and by affording formal recognition of the State Department's foreign policy expertise. This approach was followed by the Senate-passed version of the bill. By contrast, the asylum advocates wanted to have judicial review placed over a truly independent administrative structure. This approach was adopted by the House Judiciary Committee (see Leibowitz: 169).

Senator Kennedy offered several amendments which would have deleted those provisions from the Simpson-Mazzoli Bill that were of most concern to Hispanic Americans: easing family reunification and doing away with the H-2 temporary worker expansion program. Groups like the Mexican American Legal Defense Education Fund (MALDEF), and SIN, the national Spanish-language network, lobbied strongly against the Simpson-Mazzoli Bill. SIN blasted the proposal as "the most blatantly anti-Hispanic bill ever." It called upon the Hispanic community to make their views known in Congress by writing or contacting Senator Kennedy about the issue. More than 8,000 letters and mailgrams from outraged Hispanics were delivered to Kennedy's office in less than a week, in addition to a nearly constant barrage of telephone calls (Crewdson: 323).

The Simpson-Mazzoli bill itself compromised an earlier Reagan proposal by including no provision for a guest worker program, substituting instead an expanded and streamlined version of the H-2 program with which it was deemed easier for employers to import temporary agricultural workers from Mexico. The 1982 version of the bill incorporated the administrative rules that the Department of Labor used in the H-2 program during the years following the termination of the Bracero Program. In committee, however, congressmen sympathetic to employer interests succeeded in incorporating changes designed to open up the flow of legal temporary labor through the H-2 channel should other provisions in the proposed law effectively cut off the supply of undocumented workers. The Senate rejected an amendment proposed by Senator Hayakawa that would have included a large-scale guest-worker program as well as one by Senator

Kennedy that would have retained the H-2 program as it was. The bill that ultimately passed the Senate contained several provisions that would have affected the number and type of H-2 workers entering the U.S. for temporary employment, enabling a greatly expanded temporary worker program. The Senate version of the bill would also have greatly restricted the role of the Department of Labor in the certification process. The 1982 bill would have converted the DOL certification from its current advisory status to a mandatory requirement. By eliminating this aspect, the Senate version allowed for the possibility that the INS, an agency less sensitive to domestic labor conditions, could ignore or overrule the DOL recommendations (see Cornelius and Montoya: 133).

The Simpson-Mazzoli Bill also eliminated the president's request for emergency powers to deal with the Mariel crisis. Its "employer sanctions" provision was revised to exclude any illegal aliens employed before the bill was enacted and called upon the administration to produce within three years some form of secure "worker-identification" card (*Ibid*: 318-19).

The bill passed in the House in 1983 but was killed in the Senate. In 1984, it was reintroduced, although finally passed in different versions in the House and the Senate as described above. The House-passed version, responding to pressure from growers of perishable crops, allowed for a vastly expanded temporary worker program reminiscent of the bracero program of World War II. The amendment's sponsor, Representative Leon Panetta, argued that the imported workers program would not allow their exploitation because of its provision that their wage and working conditions could not "adversely affect" those of domestic workers, and because the workers, once here, were free to leave the grower who brought them in. Critics argued that since the growers are able to import workers by name, they could quickly "blacklist" from future jobs anyone considered to be a troublemaker. Such critics also noted that although the amendment contained requirements for active recruitment of domestics workers to prevent displacement, growers have been routinely able to evade such requirements under the much smaller current H-2 program, and would be able to continue to do so under the new law. The vastly larger size of the new program, moreover, which was estimated by the Agriculture Committee to include as many as .5 million workers annually, would greatly increase the already difficult job of enforcing those labor standards that do apply to the guest workers.

The House version also was passed with an amendment by majority leader Jim Wright that provided for a two-year period of legal residence for immigrants, after which they could apply to become permanent residents, but to qualify they had to be employable, trying to learn English, and enrolling any children they had in school. The Wright amendment passed 247-170, and also elicited concern among Hispanic groups. In 1984, election-year pressure resulted in the Congress failing to find a compromise version for the two bills, and the measure died in conference committee, principally being stalled by Democratic opposition.[3]

The heart of the Simpson-Mazzoli approach are the "employer sanction/ amnesty" provisions. This aspect of their proposal has been assessed as follows:

> The authors of the pending legislation, Senator Simpson and Congressman Mazzoli, have at least practiced the virtue of candor. They have described their bill as a "leap into the dark," but stand by the proposal because, they allege, previous employer sanction laws have failed to reduce the hiring of illegal immigrants due to a lack of proper enforcement. They argue that with enough money, personnel, and a strong will to enforce, employer penalties can be an effective means of immigration control. Unfortunately, there is not a shred of evidence to support this claim (Cornelius and Montoya, 1985: 147).

In May of 1985, Senator Simpson introduced a new version of his bill, this time without the cosponsorship of Representative Mazzoli, who declined to sponsor the bill without support from the Democratic House leadership and from the black and Hispanic legislative caucuses which opposed it.

Simpson's newest bill had some details changed from the earlier versions, but the centerpiece remained the imposition of employer sanctions—including fines up to $10,000 per violation—against employers who knowingly hire illegal immigrants, and the eventual amnesty of those undocumented aliens who arrived prior to January 1, 1980 and have been living in the U.S. continuously since then. The new bill still required no responsibility of employers to authenticate the documents shown by potential employees. He again called for a new "tamper-proof" Social Security card, and stiffer penalties [up to two years in prison] for ID counterfeiters and traffickers. His new bill substantially weakened the "amnesty" or "legalization" provision. Where in the 1984 bill he called for amnesty provisions to start automatically 90 days after his bill became law, the 1985 proposal had amnesty take effect only after a presidential commission had certified that the new law's provisions had produced a "substantial" reduction of illegal immigration, estimating such effect would take place within a year's time. Critics argued such an effect would be difficult to document. His 1985 bill placed a $1.8 billion limit on federal reimbursements to states for services extended to those who benefit from the program. Congressional critics maintained that the figure was much too low. Simpson's stated major goal for the new bill was to produce a compromise which would finally pass Congress (*Time*, July 8, 1985; see also "Simpson Tackles Immigration Reform Again," *Minneapolis Star and Tribune*, Monday, June 24, 1985: 10 A).

Such compromise was not yet forthcoming. Senator Kennedy introduced an amendment which proposed to grant amnesty at the same time employee sanctions take effect. It was rejected by a vote of 65–26. Similarly, Senator Pete Wilson (R., Cal.) offered an amendment which would give growers of perishable crops a large, mobile, temporary work force of foreign workers to pick fruit and vegetables. The measure lost by a 50–48 vote ("Immigration Legislation Voted Down," *The Cumberland News*, September 14, 1985: A1).

Congressman Peter Rodino (D., N.J.), the influential chairman of the House Judiciary Committee, introduced legislation cosponsored by Representative Romano Mazzoli (D., Ky.) in July of 1985 which was similar to the compromise version that died in the final days of the 1984 conference committee. The Rodino-Mazzoli measure provided civil and criminal penalties for employees who knowingly hire illegal aliens and amnesty for illegals who arrived before 1982. To discourage discrimination against Hispanics, the bill created an Office of Special Counsel in the Justice Department empowered to investigate and prosecute civil rights violators. Like the Simpson bill in the Senate, the Rodino-Mazzoli bill also strengthened the enforcement of immigration laws by increasing funding for the Immigration and Naturalization Service ("Immigration Issue Heats Up Again," *The Washington Post*, July 28, 1985: A 15).

Hispanic groups and the American Civil Liberties Union opposed both the House and the Senate versions of the bill. Working through the Hispanic Congressional Caucus and the Black Congressional Caucus, they opposed the employer-sanction approach and feared it would inevitably lead to increased discrimination against all Hispanics. They opposed the guest worker program, arguing such workers have historically been exploited. Growers, by contrast, insist on such a program, and generally opposed both versions of the bill as being inadequate in size on this issue. The House Judiciary Committee insisted that an amnesty provision had to be tied to any employer sanctions provision. The White House strongly backed the Senate version, which would grant amnesty only after a presidential commission had been established and only when employer sanctions were seen to have succeeded in reducing the number of illegal aliens entering the country. In 1985, the Senate Judiciary Committee rejected all attempts by Senate Democrats to make the Senate version of the bill more like the House version.[4]

THE PASSAGE OF THE 1986 ACT

After the conference committee was unable to agree upon a compromise version of the bill, it seemed to be an issue on which the bill was "a corpse going to the morgue.'''⁵ Simpson re-introduced his bill, which the Senate passed for a third time in September, 1985. The House once again left the bill open to tinkering by submitting its version of the bill to six committees (see Peters and Vega).

The judiciary committee seemed deadlocked over the farm worker provision. It did not complete its drafting of the bill until the end of June, and then five other committees worked on it throughout the summer. When the House, late in September of 1986 rejected a rule for considering a bill [HR3810], immigration reform seemed once again a dead issue (*The New York Times*, October 13, 1986: A-16).

A small group of House members long involved with the issue, however, refused to let it die. Led by Representative Charles E. Schumer (D.-NY), they put the pieces back together again. Representative Rodino, chairman of the judiciary committee, and Hamilton Fish, Jr., its ranking Republican, aided Schumer in working out a compromise. Schumer met with Representative Howard Berman (D.-Cal.) and Leon Panetta (D.-Cal.) and the three hammered out a key aspect of the new compromise--the temporary farm workers provision. Extensive discussions with Representative Dan Lungren (R.-Cal.), the ranking Republican, and Romano Mazzoli, the chairman of the Judiciary Immigration, Refugees and International Law Subcommittee, resulted in further fine-tuning of the bill's provisions. After the House members agreed on the new package of provisions—including numerous points designed to protect the rights of the temporary workers—they secured Senator Simpson's support as well.

Congress was in a better mood to pass some sort of immigration law than in any previous year. As the Mexican economy deteriorated late in 1985 and early 1986 and the peso plunged in value, the INS caught a record number of illegal aliens attempting to cross. Their apprehensions rose by 31 percent during the fiscal year--to 1.8 million. The growing conservative mood of the country seemed to convince liberal opponents of the bill that continued resistance would only lead to even stricter legislation in 1987.

A key shift came when the Hispanic Caucus split on the bill--with five members supporting the new package and six opposing it. That split also enabled the Black Congressional Caucus to split on the bill. Representative Robert Garcia (D.-NY) and Edward Roybal (D.-Cal.) continued to lead the opposition to the bill. Representative Esteban Torress (D.-Cal.), chairman of the Hispanic Caucus, and Albert Bustamente (D.-Tex.), its vice-chairman, both voted for it.

Representative Schumer's negotiated compromise on the temporary farm worker provisions also split the opposition to the bill among the growers. His compromise served to meet the demands among western fruit and vegetable growers for foreign workers, while allowing for sufficient protection of the workers against likely exploitation so as to win over enough of the Hispanic/liberal/union votes in Congress for passage of the bill. Representative Schumer described the new bill as "a left-center bill," in contrast to the "right-center" version killed by the House Democrats in 1984, when they opposed it by a margin of 138 to 125. In the October of 1986 vote, Democrats supported it by a vote of 168 to 61. The House passed the new compromise version on October 10, 1986 by a margin of 238 to 173.

Passage by the House once again necessitated a conference committee to make adjustments between the two differing versions. Six issues remained in significant conflict. 1) The House version terminated employer penalties automatically after six and one-half years. The Senate version and the administration vigorously opposed that provision. 2) The House version contained an amendment sponsored by Representative Joseph Moakley (D.-Mass.) that granted temporary legal status to Salvadorans and Nicaraguans who were here illegally. The White House and the State Department strongly objected to that provision. 3) The House version had a provision by Barney Frank (D.-Mass.) that barred an employer from discriminating in hiring on the basis of citizenship and created a special counsel in the Justice Department to investigate such alleged discrimination. This provision was opposed by both the Senate and the administration. 4) The two versions differed in the dates for starting the "legalization" program. The House version set the eligibility date at January 1, 1982. The Senate version granted amnesty to those aliens here prior to January 1, 1980. 5) The two versions differed over how the federal government would reimburse states for costs associated with the complex legalization program. The House version provided for 100 percent federal reimbursement. The Senate bill provided for $3 billion over the six years after enactment. 6) Finally, the House bill included a provision sponsored by Howard Berman (D.-Cal.) which provided free legal services to farm workers entering the country under the H-2 temporary worker program.

The 1986 conference committee agreed upon a series of compromises to settle those six issues. The House agreed to the Senate version without the automatic end to sanctions in exchange for Senate provisions requiring Congress to review the program within three years, at which time the program could be terminated by joint resolution if the comptroller general determined that the employer sanction program had resulted in discrimination. The House also agreed to give up the Moakley provisions on Salvadorans and Nicaraguans in return for an administration pledge not to deport any Salvadorans to areas stricken by an October earthquake. In addition, Chairman Rodino promised to consider a bill on the subject early in the 100th Congress, and Senator Simpson promised that he would not prevent Senate consideration of such a bill if it passed the House. The Senate agreed to accept the Frank anti-discrimination provisions, and accepted in slightly modified form the free legal representation for H-2 workers—such legal work applying only to job-related problems such as wages, hours, and work conditions. The funding issue was resolved by a compromise involving a $1 billion dollar appropriation for the next four years, with unspent money in one year being available in the following year. Any unused money at the end of fiscal 1990 could be carried over through fiscal 1994. The compromise funding version further involved the amount of government payments for Social Security supplements and Medicaid to be deducted from the $1 billion dollar appropriation. Finally, the Senate agreed to the House version of the amnesty program's starting date of January 1, 1982.

The bill's tangled history helped make these compromises possible in 1986. Increased concern with the immigration problem meant that nearly everyone involved wanted a bill of some kind to pass. Previous fights meant there was less need for continued political posturing this time. Congress desperately wanted to recess for the upcoming elections. The Conferees "didn't want to do this again" (*C.Q. Weekly Report*, October 18, 1986: 2596). In the words of Representative Mazzoli who urged its final passage: "It's not a perfect bill, but its the least imperfect bill we will ever have before us" (*The Washington Post*, Thursday, October 16, 1986: A-5).

The House passed the measure by a vote of 238-173 on Wednesday, October 15, 1986. The Senate approved it by a vote of 63-24 on Friday, October 17, 1986. President Reagan signed the bill into law on November 6, 1986.

CONCLUSION

What conclusions and assessments can be drawn, then, from this historical review and analysis of U.S. immigration policy? As in the past, the new immigration law involved achieving a new balance on the four main elements of immigration policy: economic, racial, nationalistic, and foreign policy.

Answering the questions as to how effective the 1986 law is likely to be is a difficult task.[6] As a *Time* magazine feature on immigration noted, the debate over the immigration bills was drawn out, convoluted, and acrimonious. *Time* succinctly said:

> That is perhaps as it should be. Seldom has so important an issue come so far so often in the legislative process with those concerned with it having so little idea of its potential effects. No one can say for sure whether immigration reform can be made to work, what it might cost and, most important, whether it would ultimately help or hurt the country. In that information vacuum, politicians, businessmen, labor leaders, minority representatives and social scientists have taken positions on all sides of the issue. President Reagan is maintaining a discreet profile, hoping only for a policy that is "fair and nondiscriminatory" (*Time*, July 8, 1985).

Certainly this review of the history of immigration policy enables one to predict one thing with a fair degree of certainty: that this major revision, as have all those enacted in the past, will surely have some unforeseen consequences that will create new problems and will sow the seeds for the next revision.

Critics note that what is being sold as a measure to punish employers will in fact more likely end up punishing workers. The bulk of research on employer sanctions indicates that they are at best ineffective, and at worst exacerbate the exploitability of both documented and undocumented workers (Cornelius and Montoya: 71–73).

The optimistic assessment of the ability of the "employer sanction" method for cutting down on illegal immigration, such as the one expressed by INS Commissioner Nelson, holds that such employer sanctions are essential to cutting off the immigration flow. Proponents of the approach argue that such a law may be relatively self-enforcing, much like the 55 MPH speed limit wherein, they maintain, most motorists comply. They feel such a provision will significantly reduce the job magnet that now draws so many across the border.

Such a view is *unrealistically optimistic*. To use their analogy, those who economically gain from breaking the 55 MPH speed limit (e.g., truckers) notoriously fail to obey it. The employer sanctions provision is much more likely to just give a boost to the phony-document industry.[7] It is, indeed, "no more likely to be effective than tough penalties have been in curbing the U.S. market for cocaine" (*Time*, July 8, 1985).

The employer sanctions provision exemplifies the failure of a policy to spell out procedures. The employer sanctions approach is weakened by the fact that its mechanism for enforcement, some sort of a secure worker-identification system, is left largely unspecified. The decision that we need to have a secure system for worker-identification is not enough. A clear method must be spelled out. We have a consensus on the need to reduce unemployment too, but we still often suffer from unacceptably high unemployment. The method chosen to ensure a secure worker-identification system will have major implications for various aspects of our national life. The method chosen will affect employment discrimination, the extent of document fraud, and even the integrity of various official documents issued, such as birth certificates and passports. It will affect the cost of the system to employers. Many fear it will likely adversely affect civil liberties.

A review of how employer-sanctions laws have fared at the state level, or how successful or not they have been used by other nations that have adopted them would indicate that pessimistic assessments are more readily drawn from these experiences than are optimistic ones.

Eleven states and one city have passed employer-sanction statutes since 1971: California, Connecticut, Delaware, Florida, Kansas, Maine,

Massachusetts, Montana, New Hampshire, Vermont, Virginia, and the city of Las Vega, Nevada.[8] The main pattern that emerges from a study of the results of these state and local statutes is of an almost perfectly consistent failure to enforce sanctions. In large measure, the failure to enforce the law stems from the legal constraints imposed by the courts. Various courts have consistently enjoined or discouraged agencies from administering the statutes for a wide variety of constitutional and statutory reasons, including the employment rights of undocumented workers, the lack of proof that employers "knowingly" hired such workers, violations of Fourth Amendment protections against unreasonable search and seizure, and discrimination against aliens "authorized to work" by federal regulations even though they may not be "lawful residents" of the United States. Whether or not the new law's rather copious attempts to specify guarantees against discrimination will be sufficient to avoid such legal challenge remains to be seen. Most probably, they will engender a good bit of judicial proceedings.

The employer-sanctions provision essentially makes the employer an immigration agent. But the lack of a clear method to ensure proper documentation leaves the employer on the horns of a dilemma. Under-zealous compliance could lead to fines and penalties being imposed. Yet over-zealousness could lead to massive civil rights violations of due process and citizens' rights to privacy. The new law is likely to develop a whole new line of case and administrative law from complaints by racial and ethnic groups of discrimination against employers instead of the INS.

State and local prosecuters most often attribute nonenforcement of such laws to judicial rulings—of evidence of employer intent, on potential racial discrimination against job applicants and on due process violations during INS raids. They are also reluctant to prosecute because they perceive the prevention of employment of illegal aliens as a low-priority task. State attorneys often feel that the problem of prosecuting employers belongs to someone else—local district attorneys, the INS, or even state legislatures.

Even though states that have large concentrations of undocumented aliens have passed such laws, employer penalties have not reduced the hiring of illegal immigrants and have often created additional problems. In California, not a single person has ever been convicted under the employer sanctions law first passed in 1971. Nationwide, such state laws have only resulted in five convictions:

> One in Kansas, where a convicted employer got a $250 fine; two in Virginia, where the convicted employers received fines of $80 and $55, plus a 30-day suspended jail sentence; and two in Montana against the same corporation, which decided not to contest the $3,200 fine because the legal expenses of an appeal would have exceeded the amount of the penalty (Cornelius and Montoya, 1983: 143).

A major General Accounting Office report found that in all 20 countries it surveyed that had national employer-sanctions laws such laws were not an effective deterrent to illegal employment since employers were either able to evade responsibility, or, when apprehended, were penalized too lightly to be deterred. Judges did not seem to treat employment of undocumented workers as a serious crime and were reluctant to impose penalties, and the study found that the more severe the penalty, the less likely it was to be applied, especially criminal fines and jail sentences (G.A.O., 1982; see also Cornelius and Montoya, 1983: 91).

Such review of state, local, and other nation's experiences with the employer sanctions approach on balance seems to indicate the following expectations. They are far easier to legislate than to enforce. They are not likely to work. They are likely to be expensive to administer and enforce. They may subject the undocumented worker to even more exploitation. They may result in discrimination against certain ethnic groups. They create a significant potential for abuse.

Insofar as employer sanctions are likely to fail as a deterrent to the employer, they are not likely to reduce illegal immigration. Far from reducing the number of such illegal aliens, the new law may ironically create a double criminalization of undocumented workers. To get a job now the immigrant will have to cross the border without papers and will also have to present the employer with bogus documents. Such workers will thus be even more vulnerable, potentially more susceptible to implicit or explicit blackmail by their employers. It is, indeed, predictable that the undocumented workers, and in some cases even the documented ones, will pay a price for the new legislation. Initially they will likely pay by layoffs, wage reductions, and up-front payment at the time of employment. The employees will pay for the greater "risk" their employers assume in hiring them.

The new law, by relying upon the employer-sanctions approach, represents a compromise that allows for the political reinforcement of anti-immigrant sentiment while avoiding any real change in the economic reality of immigrant employment.

> The fundamental problem is that the American economy works like a huge siphon, drawing desperate thousands of job seekers illegally across the Mexican border. The question is whether to try to plug the siphon on the Mexican side (by helping Mexico and other Central American countries to develop their economies), to cut it in the middle (by vastly increasing border patrols), or stop it on the U.S. side (by imposing sanctions to make it less likely that the illegals could find work here). (Rasberry: 10 A).

The Mexican population is growing exponentially—at an annual rate of 3.2 percent compared to the 0.9 percent annual growth rate of the U.S. Mexican per capita income is $740, while the U.S. per capita income is over $6,000. Demographic projections estimate that Mexico will double its population every 20 years, reaching 150 million by the turn of the century. The political instability in Central America is likely to push migration northward, further increasing pressure on Mexico. Clearly, it will become increasingly attractive to cross the Rio Grande, legally or illegally, and work for whatever wages are available, as even the lowest U.S. wages will be far above those in Mexico. Mexican legislators predict the new law will fail to stem the flow and may further strain U.S.-Mexican relations.[9]

The special seasonal agricultural workers provision provides for up to 350,000 aliens who could prove that they have lived in the United States for at least three years and who could prove they had worked at least 90 days in American agriculture in each of those years to qualify for temporary resident alien status. They could become permanent residents after two years. They would not have to remain in such agricultural jobs after they have received their temporary status. This essentially creates a whole new category of legal immigration, and a sizable one at that. Children born of such immigrants here in the U.S. will, of course, be citizens. The potential impact of this provision is far reaching and was little studied. Inasmuch as the provision allows for a replenishment of such farm labor for up to seven years, it will prove to be one of the most significant aspects of the new law in its impact on the nation's economy, immigration policy, and the relationship between this new way to legally migrate to the U.S. and other past ways. It certainly raises questions of justice or equity in the immigration policy in as much as other persons seeking entry who have patiently waited for many years to receive legal permission to do so are essentially now being "end-runned" by those temporary workers who came here illegally and within the last three years and have only worked for 90 days in agriculture.

Other critics fault the law on its legalization provisions. The amnesty provision is yet another example of a policy goal with vague specifications as to the mechanisms to implement the goal. The amnesty proposal had strong political support. But the new law's legalization effort will necessarily require considerable intergovernmental cooperation and coordination with the private sector. Yet the aspects of such a program have not yet been stated.

How many aliens will actually come forward to claim legalization is anyone's guess. The creation of phony documents to prove residency prior to 1982 is likely to be immense.[10] Likewise, the new law virtually ignores the entire area of naturalization law, the "stepchild of immigration policy" that as always still needs attention (Cornelius and Montoya: 37–82; Bennett, D., 1985).

Another potential problem area involves the asylum issue and illustrates the elaboration of detailed procedures without stating a corresponding policy goal. What is the purpose of the new asylum procedures? Under what circumstances does the U.S. view itself as the country of first asylum? Having specifically trained people and elaborately detailed procedures to process asylum applicants does not constitute a policy response to challenges to the notion of asylum and refuge, nor do they imply policy to guide the nation on how to deal with instances of mass forced-migration. Such movements constitute an assault on current international law and on international response to refugee emergencies. The elaboration of detailed procedures at least implies that the intention of the drafters of the new law is that the new asylum offers and procedures are really put forth in order to discourage applications for asylum.

The new law does involve increases in spending to improve the enforcement capability of the border patrol and the INS, and additional allocations to carry out the added duties for the INS imposed by the law. It does not, however, contain the degree of improvement warranted by the current status of the INS and the border patrol. Both need vastly improved levels of performance just to be brought into the 20th century. The lack of adequate computerization of record-keeping, analysis of immigration data, and the correlation of such information is monumental (see Milton Morris or John Crewdson).

While the 1986 law entails some effort at upgrading the services, such improvements that are included remain far less than what seems so apparently necessary. Milton Morris, the Brookings Institution scholar who is a major but thoughtful critic of the INS, suggests the following reforms of the INS and the Bureau of Consular Affairs:

1. Drastically increase the INS budget to secure the people and equipment necessary to more effectively control illegal entries and to apprehend and expel illegal immigrants.

2. Speed up the planning and installation of automated data processing and storage systems to facilitate internal management, provide prompt and reliable service, and make reliable data available.

3. Create a strong planning and research unit within the INS.

4. Greatly increase the border patrol, both fixed and mobile stations, to reduce illegal entries.

5. Establish an outreach program of public education about the mission of the INS.

6. Develop computer-assisted screening of visa applications and machine-readable visas.

7. Establish a high-level task force to recommend improvements in the structure of the immigration bureaucracy to improve overall performance (Morris: 144–145).

It would seem more productive to impact upon the immigration problems discussed in this chapter by upgrading fair labor standards. Such an approach would tend to make many jobs now held by illegal aliens more competitive, and would thereby deter illegal immigrants from entering the U.S. labor market by reducing the economic incentive to hire them. This would be especially the case in urban commerce, where the FLSA and comparable state laws apply more rigorously nationwide. The natural deterrence through the competitive forces of the free labor market seems to be at least as promising as attempting to militarize our borders or making the INS a "hit squad" against U.S. businessmen (Cornelius and Montoya: 97).

In the final analysis, then, this historical review of immigration policy leads one to conclude that the new law is simply unlikely to work. The compromises, ambiguities and vague language necessary to get the bill passed into law contain the very seeds of the law's own problems that will ultimately result, a decade or two hence, in the need for a new broad-scale revision in U.S. immigration policy that will once again set off a "new phase" to replace what one might now call "the revolving-door era" of U.S. immigration policy.

NOTES

1. For a detailed discussion of the economic impact issue, see Kritz (ed.): 191–285, Chiswick (ed.): 251–358; Cornelius and Montoya, 1983; and North, 1978 and 1980. Additional viewpoints and elaborations on how to measure the labor impact are provided by seeing: Bonacich, 1976: 34–41; Piore, 1979; and Geschwender, 1978.

2. See: H.R. 1510 and S. 2222; Peters and Vega, 1986: 10.

3. See: *Congressional Quarterly Weekly Report,* October 18, 1986: 2595; Hart: 8; Villarreal, 1985; *Time,* July 8, 1985.

4. See: "Trying to Stem the Illegal Tide," *Time,* July 8, 1985, Special Edition Section; "Immigration Legislation Voted Down," *The Cumberland News,* September 14, 1985: Al; "Immigration Issue Heats Up Again," *The Washington Post,* Sunday, July 28, 1985: 8; Jeffrey Hart, "Illegal Immigration," *The Cumberland Evening Times,* Monday, July 22, 1985: 8; "Simpson Tackles Immigration Reform Again," *Minneapolis Star and Tribune,* Monday, June 24, 1985: 10A; and "Immigration Reform Elusive Goal," *Minneapolis Star and Tribune,* Monday, June 24, 1985, 10A.

5. See "Immigration Bill: How a 'Corpse' Came Back to Life," *The New York Times,* Monday, October 13, 1986: A-16; *Congressional Quarterly Weekly Report, October 18, 1986: 2595–2596;* "Conferees Agree on Vast Revisions in Laws on Aliens," *The New York Times,* Wednesday, October 15, 1986: A-1, B-11; and "House Passes Compromise Immigration Bill," *The Washington Post,* Thursday, October 16, 1986: A-5; "Hill Revises Immigration Law," *The Washington Post,* Saturday, October 18, 1986: A-1, 7–8.

6. For a thorough critique of the problems and prospects of the Simpson-Mazzoli approach, see: U.S. Commission on Civil Rights, *The Tarnished Door* (Washington, D.C.: U.S. Government Printing Office, September, 1980); Cornelius and Montoya (1983); Chiswick (1982); Kritz (1984); Morris (1985); Papademetriou and Miller (1984); and Glazer (1984).

7. See, for example: "Amnesty Program Means Phony Document Business Will Flourish," *The Cumberland Sunday Times,* Sunday, November 2, 1986: A-16; "Reaction to Immigration Bill Is Sharply Split," *The New York Times,* Thursday, October 16, 1986: B-15; "Surge in Bogus Papers Predicted in Wake of Change in Alien Law," *The New York Times,* Monday, October 20, 1986: A-1, 24.

8. See Carl Shwarz's analysis in Cornelius and Montoya: 83–97.

9. "U.S. Immigration Bill Assailed," *The New York Times,* Sunday, October 19, 1986: A-12.

10. "Trying to Reform the Border," *Newsweek,* October 27, 1986: 32, 35.

Appendix

MAJOR PROVISIONS OF THE IMMIGRATION BILL

The immigration bill (S 1200—H Rept 99-1000) contains sweeping changes in the way the United States treats aliens. Among its key features are a new system of penalties against employers who knowingly hire illegal aliens, amnesty for illegals who came to the United States before 1982, and $4 billion in appropriations to help states pay the costs of legalizing foreigners. It also creates a special program to ensure that growers have enough workers to harvest their crops.

As agreed to by conferees, S 1200:

Employer Sanctions

• Made it unlawful for any person knowingly to hire, recruit or refer for a fee any alien not authorized to work in the United States.

• Required employers to verify all newly hired people by examining either a U.S. passport, a certificate of U.S. citizenship, a certificate of naturalization or a resident alien card. If these documents are not available, verification could be established by a combination of papers showing authority to work and identity. For example, a person could show a driver's license in addition to either a U.S. birth certificate or a Social Security card.

• Required each employer to attest in writing under penalty of perjury that he saw such documentation before any hiring.

• Required the employee to attest in writing before being hired that he is authorized to work in the United States.

• Permitted the president to implement a more secure verification system upon notice and approval of Congress. The appropriate agencies were directed to study the feasibility of a system, like the one currently used to check credit cards, where employers could telephone a central number to get documents verified.

This information is taken from the *Congressional Quarterly Weekly Report,* October 18, 1986: 2597–2598.

- Established civil and criminal penalties for hiring illegal aliens but provided a six-month education period during which employers would not be subject to penalties. During the subsequent 12-month period, a violator would be given a warning citation for the first offense.
- Established the following fines for violations after the citation period:
  First offense—a civil fine of not less than $250 nor more than $2,000 per each illegal alien found to be hired.
  Second offense—a civil fine of not less than $2,000 nor more than $5,000 per illegal alien.
  Third offense—a civil fine of not less than $3,000 nor more than $10,000 per illegal alien.
- Authorized criminal penalties of up to six months' imprisonment and/or a $3,000 fine for a "pattern or practice" of knowingly hiring an illegal alien.
- Required employers, recruiters, and those who refer for employment to keep records. The bill established a civil fine of not less than $100 nor more than $1,000 for failure to keep records.
- Allowed employers charged with violating the law to defend themselves by showing that they had complied in good faith with the verification procedure.
- Required the attorney general to notify alleged violators of the infractions and, upon request, grant a hearing within 30 days before imposing any penalty.
- Required administrative law judges to conduct the hearings "at the nearest practicable place" to where alleged violators live and the infractions occurred.
- Required the judge to use a "preponderance of the evidence" as the standard for finding that a violation had occurred.
- Made the decision of the judge final unless the attorney general modifies or vacates the order within 30 days.
  Gave a violator 45 days from the time the order became final to challenge his penalty in a federal appeals court.
- Relieved employers from verifying a worker's credentials when a state employment agency had done so and the worker retained a certification of such verification.
- Terminated sanctions after three years if the comptroller general determined that sanctions resulted in discrimination in employment or had unduly burdened employers, and Congress enacts a joint resolution adopting that determination.
- Provided expedited procedures for Congress to consider a joint resolution terminating sanctions.

Anti-Discrimination Measures

- Created an Office of Special Counsel in the Justice Department to investigate and prosecute any charges of discrimination stemming from unlawful immigration-related employment practices.
- Barred employers from discriminating against legal residents simply because they were not full-fledged citizens. However, this provision would cover only those permanent or temporary residents who had shown an intention to become citizens.
- Made clear than an employer could not be sued if, between two equally qualified people, he chose the U.S. citizen over the legal resident who was not yet a citizen.

- Exempted employers of three or fewer workers from coverage.
- Authorized an administrative law judge, after a hearing, to order a violator to hire the aggrieved person, to award limited back pay if appropriate and to pay a penalty of $1,000 for each individual discriminated against.
- Terminated the anti-discrimination provisions if the employer sanctions are lifted. The anti-bias mechanism also could be ended if Congress, by joint resolution, determined that sanctions had not resulted in discrimination or that the process had "created an unreasonable burden on employers."

Increased Enforcement and Service

- Provided a two-year authorization for the Immigration and Naturalization Service (INS) providing an additional $422 million in fiscal 1987 and $419 million in fiscal 1988. The bill also authorized $12 million in fiscal 1987 and $15 million in fiscal 1988 for the Executive Office of Immigration Review to carry out added duties for the INS imposed by the bill.
- Beefed up criminal penalties for smuggling aliens into the United States. A violator could be imprisoned for up to five years per smuggled alien and could be fined in accordance with fines specified in the federal criminal code.
- Authorized a contingency fund of $35 million for use in immigration emergencies, such as the 1980 boat-lift from Cuba.
- Required states to verify the status of non-citizens applying for public aid, such as food stamps, welfare programs, public housing and unemployment compensation. Under the bill, states would be reimbursed 100 percent for the implementation costs of this provision. However, the secretaries of the appropriate departments, such as Agriculture, Health and Human Services, and Labor, could waive this verification rule.
- Required a search warrant for INS officers to enter outdoor agricultural operations to enforce the immigration laws.

Legalization

- Provided temporary resident status for aliens who have resided continuously in the United States since before Jan. 1, 1982, and who cannot be excluded for reasons specified in the immigration law.
- Allowed these temporary residents to become permanent residents after 18 months if they can show a minimal understanding of English and knowledge of history and government of the United States or are pursuing a course of instruction to gain such knowledge.
- Barred newly legalized aliens from most forms of public assistance for five years. Exceptions would be made for emergency medical care, aid to the aged, blind or disabled, for serious injury, or assistance that would be in the interest of public health.
- Provided permanent resident status for specified Cubans and Haitians who entered the United States prior to Jan. 1, 1982.
- Provided for administrative and judicial review of a denial of an application for legalization.

• Ensured the confidentiality of records by barring use of information in an application for any purpose other than determining the merits of the application or to determine whether fraud was involved.

• Allowed the attorney general to grant legal status to aliens who could show they had been in the United States prior to January 1972 and had lived in the country continuously since then. Under current law, the attorney general could grant legal status to those who could show they had been in the country since June 30, 1948.

• Appropriated $1 billion in each of the four fiscal years after enactment to reimburse states for the public assistance, health and education costs resulting from legalizing aliens. Unspent money from one year could be carried over to the next year. In addition, any of the unspent $4 billion at the end of fiscal 1991 could be carried over an additional three fiscal years. States would have to apply for the aid and the money would be allotted according to a detailed formula specified in the bill. The money paid to the states would be reduced by the Social Security and Medicaid that goes to newly legalized aliens.

• Reimbursed states for the costs of incarcerating certain aliens.

H-2 Workers

• Revised and expanded an existing temporary foreign worker program known as H-2. This program predominantly applies to farm workers.

• Required an employer to apply to the secretary of labor no more than 60 days in advance of needing foreign workers, and then required the employer to try to recruit domestic workers for the jobs that need to be filled. Current law requires an 80-day advance request.

• Required the labor secretary to decide on the request for labor no later than 20 days in advance of an employer's need.

• Provided an expedited procedure for getting workers if the labor secretary had determined that U.S. workers would be available at the time needed but the employer subsequently found that the workers were not qualified and available.

• Guaranteed agricultural H-2 workers certain benefits such as housing and worker compensation (if not available under a state program), travel and subsistence costs.

• Allowed H-2 workers to get help from the federally funded Legal Services Corporation in disputes over wages, hours and working conditions.

Special Seasonal Agricultural Workers

• Provided temporary resident status for up to 350,000 aliens who could prove they had lived in the United States for at least three years and who could prove they had worked at least 90 days in American agriculture in each of those years. They could adjust to permanent resident status after an additional year or within three years of enactment, whichever is later.

• Provided temporary status for aliens who have worked 90 days in agriculture between May 1985 and May 1986. They could become permanent residents two years after they received their temporary status or three years after enactment, whichever is later. Workers in both of these groups would not have to remain in agricultural jobs once they received their temporary status.

- Disqualified these workers from receiving welfare benefits.
- Provided for "replenishment" farm labor to replace those who left agriculture and allowed these new workers to enter the United States as temporary residents. They would have to work at least 90 days in agriculture for three years; after three years, they would apply to become permanent residents. They would be barred from receiving most public aid.
- Terminated the replenishment worker program seven years after enactment.
- Established a commission to study the availability of domestic farm labor and that industry's need for foreign workers.

Miscellaneous

- Increased the legal immigration ceilings for colonies from 600 to 5,000. This provision is designed to help immigrants from Hong Kong, which will become part of China in 1990.
- Provided special immigrant status to certain officers and employees of international organizations such as the United Nations and the World Bank and their immediate family members. This designation allows these people to remain if they are the surviving spouse or dependent of a covered employee and have been in the United States for a specified period.
- Authorized the attorney general and secretary of state to establish a three-year pilot program for up to eight countries allowing tourists from these countries to enter the United States without first obtaining a visa.
- Allowed a father to petition the government to bring his illegitimate child into the United States as an immediate relative.
- Made clear that an alien's "brief, casual and innocent" trips outside of the United States would not constitute a failure to maintain a continuous physical presence in the United States, thereby subjecting him to deportation.
- Adopted a sense of Congress that political prisoners from Cuba should be admitted to the United States.
- Required the expeditious deportation of convicted illegal aliens and required the government to list facilities available to incarcerate those aliens who are going to be deported.

Reports

- Required the president to submit several reports to Congress, including three studies on legal immigration, the program for granting visas. Among the other reports: one on the factors that cause illegal immigration, two on the legalization program established in the bill, and two on employer sanctions.
- Required the administration to submit reports on the H-2 program every two years.

- Required a report on the three-year visa waiver program.
- Required the attorney general to tell Congress the resources required to improve the INS.
- Stated a sense of Congress that Mexico should be consulted on the implementation of the immigration legislation.

Bibliography

Abbey, Sue Wilson. "The Ku Klux Klan in Arizona, 1921-25," *Journal of Arizona History*, 1973, 14 (1):10-30.

Abrams, Elliott and Abrams, Franklin S. "Immigration Policy—Who Gets In and Why?" *Public Interest*, 1975, (38):3-29.

Adamic, Louis, *Nation of Nations*. (New York: Harper Bros., 1945).

Allen, Leslie. *Liberty: The Statue and the American Dream*. (N.Y.: Statue of Liberty-Ellis Island Foundation, National Geographic Society, 1985).

"Aliens Become More Diverse Over Decades," *The Washington Post,* Sunday, June 10, 1984: A1, 16.

Amnesty Program Means Phony Document Business Will Flourish," *The Cumberland Sunday Times*, Sunday, November 2, 1986: A-16.

Anderson, James. *Public Policy-Making*. 2nd ed. (New York: Holt, Rinehart, and Winston, 1979).

Annals of the American Academy of Political and Social Science, 1979, 441: 55-81.

Archdeacon, Thomas J. *Becoming American: An Ethnic History*. (New York: Free Press, 1983).

"A Refugee's Despair," *Newsweek*, November 17, 1986: 12.

"Asian Indians Operating Many U.S. Hotels, Motels," *The Cumberland Times/News,* Thursday, September 12, 1985: 36.

Auerbach, Carl A., "Freedom of Movement in International Law and United States Policy," in McNeill and Adams (eds.), *Human Migration*. (Bloomington, Ind.: Indiana University Press, 1978):317-35.

Babcock, Kendrick C. *The Scandinavian Element in the United States*. (Urbana: University of Illinois Press, 1914).

Bach, Robert L. "Mexican Immigration and the American State," *International Migration Review*, 12 (Winter, 1978): 536-58.

Bailey, Thomas H. *Voices of America*. (New York: Free Press, 1976).

Baum, Dale. "Know-Nothingism and the Republican Majority in Massachusetts: The Political Realignment of the 1850s," *Journal of American History,* 1978, 64 (4):959-86.

Beals, Carleton. *Brass Knuckle Crusade*. (New York: Hasting House, 1960).

Bennett, Douglas C. "The Enforcement of Immigration Policy and the Meaning of Citizenship," paper delivered at the 1985 Annual Meeting of the APSA, New Orleans, August 29, 1985.

Bennett, Marion T. *American Immigration Policies: A History*. (Washington, D.C.: Public Affairs Press, 1963).

Bernard, William S. (ed.), *Immigration Policy: A Reappraisal.* (New York: Harper and Bros., 1950).

Betten, Neil. "Nativism and the Klan in Town and City: Valparaiso and Gary, Indiana," *Studies in History and Sociology,* 1973, 4 (2):3–16.

"Bilingual Education's Dilemmas Persist," *The Washington Post,* Sunday, July 7, 1985: A1, 12–13.

Billington, Ray A. *The Origins of Nativism in the United States, 1800—1844.* (New York: Arno Press, 1974).

Bleda, Sharon E. "Intergenerational Differences in Patterns and Bases of Ethnic Residential Dissimilarity," *Ethnicity,* 1978, 5 (2): 91–107.

Bodnar, John E. "The Procurement of Immigrant Labor: Selected Documents," *Pennsylvania History,* 1974, 41 (2):189–206.

Bogue, Alan G., "United States, the 'New' Political History," *Journal of Contemporary History* 11 (Jan., 1968): 5–27.

Bonacich, Edna, "Advanced Capitalism and Black/White Relations, A Split-Labor Market Interpretation," *American Sociological Review,* 41 (February, 1976): 34–41.

Bouvier, L. F. *The Impact of Immigration on U.S. Population Size.* (Washington, D.C.: Population Reference Bureau, 1981).

Bryce-LaPorte, R. S. (ed.), *A Scrapbook on the New Immigration.* (New Brunswick, N.J.: Transaction Books, 1981).

Brye, David L. (ed.), *European Immigration and Ethnicity in the United States and Canada: A Historical Bibliography.* (Santa Barbara, Ca.: Clio Press, Inc., 1983).

Burgess, Thomas. *Greeks in America.* (Boston: Sherman, French and Co., 1913).

Butz, William, *et al.,* "Demographic Challenges in America's Future," R-2911-RC. (Santa Monica, Calif.: The Rand Corporation, May, 1982), 40pp.

Candeloro, Dominic. "Louis F. Post and the Red Scare of 1920," *Prologue,* 1979, 11 (1):41–55.

Cherry, Robert. "Racial Thought and the Early Economic Profession in the U.S.A.," *Review of Social Economics,* 1976, 34 (2): 147–62.

Chiswick, Barry R. (ed.), *The Gateway: U.S. Immigration Issues and Policies.* (Washington, D.C.: American Enterprise Institute, 1982).

Claghorn, Kate H. *The Immigrants Day in Court.* (New York: Arno Press, 1969).

Clark, Malcolm, Jr. "The Bigot Disclosed: 90 Years of Nativism," *Oregon Historical Quarterly,* 1974, 75 (2):108–190.

Commission on the Wartime Internment and Relocation of Civilians, *Personal Justice Denied.* (Washington, D.C.: U.S. Government Printing Office, 1982).

"Conferees Agree on Vast Revisions in Laws on Aliens," *The New York Times,* Wednesday, October 15, 1986: A-1, B-11.

Congressional Quarterly Weekly Report, October 18, 1986: 2595–2598, 2612–2613.

Congressional Research Service, The Library of Congress, "Alien Eligibility Requirements for Major Federal Assistance Programs." (Washington, D.C.: The Library of Congress, January 9, 1981).

_____ , "Illegal/Undocumented Aliens," Issue Brief No. IB74137. (Washington, D.C.: The Library of Congress, September 14, 1981).

———, "Immigration and Refugee Policy," IP0164. (Washington, D.C.: The Library of Congress, October, 1981).

———, "Immigration and Refugee Policy," MB81244. (Washington, D.C.: The Library of Congress, September 16, 1981).

———, "The Immigration and Nationality Act—Questions and Answers," Report No. 81-65 EPW. (Washington, D.C.: The Library of Congress, March 10, 1981).

———, "Refugees in the United States: The Cuban Emigration Crisis," Issue Brief No. IB80063. (Washington, D.C.: The Library of Congress, August 6, 1981).

———, "U.S. Immigration and Refugee Policy: A Guide to Sources of Information," Research Guide JV6201. (Washington, D.C.: The Library of Congress, February 26, 1982).

Cornelius, Wayne and Ricardo A. Montoya. *America's New Immigration Law: Origins, Rationales and Potential Consequences.* (San Diego, Calif.: Center for U.S.-Mexican Studies, UC-SD, 1983).

———, "Illegal Mexican Migration to the United States: Recent Research Findings and Policy Implications," *Congressional Record* (July 13, 1977): H7061–7068.

Couch, Leslie F., "The Extent of Constitutional Protection Afforded Resident Aliens," *Albany Law Journal,* 19 (January, 1955): 62–73.

Craig, Richard B. *The Bracero Program: Interest Groups and Foreign Policy.* (Austin: University of Texas Press, 1971).

Crewdson, John. *The Tarnished Door.* (New York: Times Books, 1983).

Cross, Harry E. and James Sandos. *Across the Border.* (Berkeley, Institute of Government Studies, 1981).

"Closing the Golden Door," *Time*, May 18, 1981, p. 24.

Cuddy, Edward. "Are Bolsheviks Any Worse Than the Irish?" Ethno-Religious Conflict in America During the 1920s," *Eire-Ireland,* 1976, 11 (3): 13–32.

Daniels, Roger, "American Historians and East Asian Immigrants," *Pacific Historical Review* (November, 1974): 449–72.

———, and Harry Kitano. *American Racism.* (Englewood Cliffs, N.J.: Prentice-Hall, 1970).

———. *The Asian-American.* (Santa Barbara, Calif.: Clio Books, 1976).

Davis, Jerome. *The Russian Immigrant* (New York: Arno Press, 1969).

"Developments in the Law—Immigration Policy and the Rights of Aliens," *Harvard Law Review,* 96 (1983): 1268–1465.

Dimmitt, Marius, "The Enactment of the McCarran-Walter Act of 1952," (Ph.D. Dissertation, University of Kansas, 1970).

Dinnerstein, Leonard and Frederick C. Jaher. *Uncertain Americans: Readings in Ethnic History.* (New York: Oxford University Press, 1977).

Dinnerstein, Leonard and David Reimers. *Ethnic Americans.* (New York: Harper and Row, 1975).

DiNunzio, Mario and Galkowski, Jan T. "Political Loyalty in Rhode Island, a Computer Study of the 1850s," *Rhode Island History,* 1977, 36 (3):93–95.

Divine, Robert A. *American Immigration Policy, 1924—1952,* (New Haven: Yale University Press, 1957).

Dunlevy, James A., and Gemery, Henry A. "Economic Opportunity and the Response of 'Old' and 'New' Migrants to the United States," *Journal of Economic History,* 1978, 38 (4):901–917.

Dye, Thomas. *Understanding Public Policy,* 5th ed. (Englewood Cliffs, N.J.: Prentice-Hall, 1984).

Eisinger, Peter K. "Ethnic Political Transition in Boston, 1884-1933: Some Lessons for Contemporary Cities," *Political Science Quarterly,* 1978, 93 (2): 217-39.

Elles, Diana. *International Provisions Protecting the Human Rights of Non-Citizens.* (New York: The United Nations, 1980).

Fairchild, Henry. *Greek Immigration* (New Haven: Yale University Press, 1911).

Federal Writers Project. *The Italians of New York.* (New York: Arno Press: 1969).

Feingold, Henry L. *The Politics of Rescue: The Roosevelt Administration and the Holocaust, 1938-1945* (New Brunswick, N.J.: Rutgers University Press, 1970).

Feldstein, Stanley and Lawrence Costello (eds.), *The Ordeal of Assimilation: A Documentary History of the White Working Class, 1830s to 1970s* (Garden City, N.J.: Doubleday, 1974).

Fermi, Laura. *Illustrious Immigrants: The Intellectual Migration from Europe, 1930-1941.* (Chicago: University of Chicago Press, 1968).

Fine, Sidney, "Mr. Justice Murphy and the Hirabayashi Case," *Pacific Historical Review* (May, 1964): 195-209.

Fragomen, Austin T., Jr. "Alien Employment," *International Migration Review,* 1979, 13 (3): 527-31.

———, "Permanent Resident Status Redefined," *International Migration Review,* 1975, 9 (1): 63-68.

Franklin, Frank G. *The Legislative History of Naturalization in the United States* (New York: Arno Press, 1969).

Freedman, Morris and Carolyn Banks. *American Mix: The Minority Experience in America* (New York: J.B. Lippincott, 1972).

Fried, Charles (ed.), *Minorities: Community and Identity.* (New York: Springer-Verlag New York, Inc., 1983).

Friis, Erick J. (ed.), *The Scandinavian Presence in North America.* (New York: Harper and Row, 1976).

Fuchs, Lawrence. *American Ethnic Politics.* (New York: Harper, 1968).

Gallaway, Lowell E., *et al.* "The Distribution of the Immigrant Population in the United States: An Economic Analysis," *Explorations in Economic History,* 1974, 11 (3): 213-26.

Garza, E. (Kika) De La, *et al.* "Should People Stay Home? Regulation and Free Movement and Rights of Establishment Between the U.S., Canada, and Mexico," *American Society of International Law,* 1974, 68: 38-58.

General Accounting Office, "Information on the Enforcement of Laws Regarding Employment of Aliens in Selected Countries." (Washington, D.C.: U.S. Government Printing, August 31, 1982).

Geschwender, James A. *Racial Stratification in America.* (Debuque, Iowa: William C. Brown, 1978).

Gibson, William. *Aliens and the Law.* (Chapel Hill, N.C.: University of North Carolina Press, 1940).

Glazer, Nathan (ed.), *Clamor at the Gates: The New American Immigration.* (San Francisco: ICS Press, 1985).

——— and D.P. Moynihan. *Beyond the Melting Pot.* (Cambridge, Mass: Harvard University Press, 1973).

Goldstein, Robert J. "The Anarchist Scare of 1908: A Sign of Tensions in the Progressive Era," *American Studies,* (Lawrence, Kansas), 1974, 15 (2): 55–78.

Goodenow, Ronald K. "The Progressive Educator, Race and Ethnicity in the Depression Years: An Overview," *History of Education Quarterly, 1975,* 15 (4): 365–94.

Gordon, Charles, "The Alien and the Constitution," *California Western Law Review,* 9 (Fall, 1971).

Gordon, Charles, "The Need to Modernize Our Immigration Laws," *San Diego Law Review,* 13 (1975): 1–33.

Gordon, Charles E. and Harry N. Rosenfield. *Immigration Law and Procedure.* Rev. ed. (New York: Matthew Bender, 1980).

Gordon, Michael A., "The Labor Boycott in New York City, 1880–1886," *Labor History,* 16 (2): 184–229.

Grant, Madison. *The Passing of the Great Race.* (New York: Arno, 1916).

Green, Stephen, "Immigration, Politics," *The Cumberland Times News,* November 1, 1984: 13.

Gutman, Herbert. *Work, Culture and Society in Industrializing America.* (New York: 1977).

Halich, Vasyl. *Ukranians in the United States* (Chicago: University of Chicago Press, 1933).

Handlin, Oscar. *Boston's Immigrants.* (Cambridge: Harvard University Press, 1979).

———. *The Americans.* (Boston: Little, Brown, 1963).

———. (ed.), *Immigration as a Factor in American History.* (Englewood Cliffs, N.J.: Prentice-Hall, 1959).

———. *The Uprooted.* 2nd ed. (Boston: Little, Brown, 1973).

Hansen, Marcus Lee. *Atlantic Migration, 1601–1860.* (New York: Harper Torch-books, 1961).

———. *The Problem of the Third Generation Immigrant.* (Rock Island, Ill.: Augustana Historical Society, 1938).

Harney, Robert F. "The Padrone and the Immigrant," *Canadian Review of American Studies,* 1974, 5 (2): 101–118.

Harper, Elizabeth J. *Immigration Laws of the United States.* 3rd ed. (Indianapolis: Bobbs-Merrill, 1975).

Hart, Jeffrey, "Illegal Immigration," *The Cumberland Evening Times,* Monday, July 22, 1985: 8.

Harwood, Edwin, "Can Immigration Laws Be Enforced?" *The Public Interest,* 17 (Summer, 1983): 105–123.

Helbush, Terry J., "Aliens, Deportation and the Equal Protection Clause," *Golden State University Law Review,* 6 (Fall, 1975): 23–77.

Herberg, William. *Protestant, Catholic, Jew.* (Garden City, N.J.: Doubleday, 1955).

Hewlitt, S. "Coping With Illegal Aliens," *Foreign Affairs,* 60 (1981): 358–78.

Higham, John (ed.), *Ethnic Leadership in America.* (Baltimore: Johns Hopkins University Press, 1978).

———. *Send These To Me.* (New York: Atheneum, 1975).

Higham, John. *Strangers in the Land: Patterns of American Nativism, 1860–1925.* (New Brunswick: Rutgers University Press, 1955).

"Hill Revises Immigration Law," *The Washington Post*, Saturday, October 18, 1986: A-1, 7–8.

"Hispanic Americans Haven't Found Their Pot of Gold," *The Washington Post National Weekly Edition*, May 28, 1984: 9–10.

Hoerder, Dirk (ed.), *American Labor and Immigration History, 1877–1920*. (Urbana, Ill.: University of Illinois Press, 1982).

Hofstadter, Richard and Michael Wallace. *American Violence*. (New York: Knopf, 1971).

Holt, Michael F. "The Politics of Impatience: The Origins of Know-Nothingism," *Journal of American History*, 1973, 60 (2): 309–331.

Hosokowa, William. *Nisei: The Quiet Americans*. (New York: William and Morrow, 1969).

"House Approves Compromise Bill on Illegal Aliens," *The New York Times*, Thursday, October 16, 1986: B-15.

"House Passes Compromise Immigration Bill," *The Washington Post*, Thursday, October 16, 1986: A-5.

Howe, Irving. *World of Our Fathers*. (New York: Simon and Schuster, 1976).

Hutchinson, Edward P. *Legislative History of American Immigration Policy, 1798–1965* (New Brunswick, N.J.: Rutgers University Press, 1970).

———. *Immigrants and Their Children*. (New York: Wiley, 1956).

"Illegal Aliens: Invasion Out of Control," *U.S. News and World Report*, January 29, 1979: 38–43.

Illich, Richard. *The Human Rights of Aliens in Contemporary International Law*. (Manchester: Manchester University Press, 1984).

"Immigrants in Washington," *The Washington Post Magazine*, April 10, 1983.

"Immigrants: The Changing Face of America," *Time* (Special Edition, July 8, 1985).

"Immigration Bill Approved; Bars Hiring Illegal Aliens, But Gives Millions Amnesty," *The New York Times*, Saturday, October 18, 1986: A-1, 8.

"Immigration Bill: How 'Corpse' Back to Life," *The New York Times*, Monday, October 13, 1986: A-16.

"Immigration Bill Mixed Blessing for Aliens," *The Washington Post*, Sunday, June 24, 1984: Cl, 7.

"Immigration Issues Heats Up Again," *The Washington Post*, Sunday, July 28, 1985: A 15.

"Immigration," *Law and Contemporary Problems*, Duke University School of Law, 21, Spring, 1956: 211–426.

"Immigration Legislation Voted Down," *The Cumberland Times/News*, Saturday, September 14, 1985: A 1.

"Immigration Measure Produces Sharp Division in House Hispanic Caucus," *The Washington Post*, Sunday, March 18, 1984, A 2.

"Immigration Reform and Control Act," HR 1510, 98th Congress, First Session (The Simpson-Mazzoli Bill). (Washington, D.C.: U.S. Government Printing Office).

Iorizzo, Luciano and Salvatore Mondello. *The Italian-Americans*. (New York: Twayne Publishing, 1971).

"Is Hatred of Japanese Making A Comeback?," *The Washington Post*, Sunday, July 7, 1985: B1, 4.

Janis, Ralph. "Flirtation and Flight: Alternatives to Ethnic Confrontation in White Anglo-American Protestant Detroit, 1880-1940," *Journal of Ethnic Studies,* 1978, 6 (2): 1-17.

Jones, Charles O. *An Introduction to the Study of Public Policy,* 3rd ed. (Monterey, Calif.: Brooks, Cole, 1984).

Jones, Maldwyn Allen. *American Immigration.* (Chicago: University of Chicago Press, 1960).

Jordan, Philip D. "Immigrants, Methodists and a 'Conservative' Social Gospel, 1865-1908," *Methodist History,* 1978, 17 (1): 16-43.

Kamin, Leon J. "The Science and the Politics of I.Q.," *Social Research,* 1974, 41 (3): 387-425.

Keefe, Thomas M. "The Catholic Issue in the Chicago Tribune Before the Civil War," *Mid-America,* 1975, 57 (4): 227-45.

Keely, Charles. *U.S. Immigration: A Policy Analysis.* (New York: Population Council, 1979).

Keely, Charles, "Illegal Migration," *Scientific American,* 246 (March, 1982): 31-37.

Keller, Morton. *Affairs of State.* (Cambridge, Mass.: Harvard University Press, 1977).

Kettner, James H. *The Development of American Citizenship, 1608-1870.* (Chapel Hill, N.C.: University of N.C. Press, 1978).

Kilpatrick, James J., "Looking At 'Immigrant'," United Press Syndication, Tuesday, February 21, 1984: A2.

Kitano, Harry. *Japanese Americans: The Evolution of a Subculture* (Englewood Cliffs, N.J.: Prentice-Hall, 1969).

_____ . *Race Relations.* (Englewood Cliffs, N.J.: Prentice-Hall, 1984).

Knickrehm, Kay M. "Congress, The Executive, and Immigration Policy," Paper Delivered at the Annual APSA Meeting, New Orleans, August 29, 1985.

_____ and G. Hastedt, "State Terrorism, Development and Refugee Flows," in G. Lopez and M. Stohl (eds.), *Development, Dependence, and State Repression.* (Westport, Conn.: Greenwood Press, 1985).

Konvitz, Milton R. *The Alien and the Asiatic in American Law.* (Ithaca, N.Y.: Cornell University Press, 1946).

_____ , *Civil Rights in Immigration.* (Ithaca, N.Y.: Cornell University Press, 1953).

_____ , *First Amendment Freedoms, Select Cases on Freedom of Religion, Speech, Press, Assembly.* (Ithaca, N.Y.: Cornell University Press, 1963).

Kramer, Jane M. "Due Process Rights for Excludable Aliens Under U.S. Immigration Law and the United Nations Protocol Related to the Status of Refugees: Haitian Aliens, A Case in Point: The *Pierre* and *Sannon* Decisions," *New York Journal of International Law and Policy,* 10 (1): 203-240.

Kritz, Mary M. *U.S. Immigration and Refugee Policy: Global and Domestic Issues,* Lexington: Lexington Books, 1983.

Lane, A. TR. "American Labor and European Immigrants in the Late Nineteenth Century," *Journal of American Studies,* 1977, 11 (2): 241-60.

Latham, Earl. *The Group Basis of Politics.* (New York: Octagon Books, 1965).

Leibowitz, A. "The Refugee Act of 1980: Problems and Congressional Concerns," *Annals of the American Academy of Political and Social Science* (1983): 163-171.

LeMay, Michael. *The Struggle for Influence.* (Lanham, Md.: University Press of America, 1985).

Leventman, Seymour. *The Ghetto and Beyond.* (New York: Random House, 1969).

Levy, Mark and Michael Kramer. *The Ethnic Factor.* (New York: Simon and Schuster, 1972).

Lieberson, Stanley. *A Piece of the Pie.* (Berkeley, Calif.: University of California Press, 1980).

Lineberry, Robert L. *American Public Policy.* (New York: Harper and Row, 1977).

Linkh, Richard M. *American Catholicism and European Immigration.* (New York: Center for Migration Studies, 1975).

Litt, Edgar. *Ethnic Politics in America.* (Glenview, Ill.: Scott, Foresman, 1970).

Lopata, Helena Znaniecki. *Polish Americans.* (Englewood Cliffs, N.J.: Prentice-Hall, 1976).

Lungren, Daniel, "Immigration Reform: If Not Now, When?," *The Washington Post National Weekly Edition,* September 24, 1984: 28.

Mamot, Patricia R. *Foreign Medical Graduates in America.* (Springfield, Ill.: Charles Thomas, 1974).

Mann, Arthur. *The One and the Many.* (Chicago: University of Chicago Press, 1979).

Manning, B., "The Congress, the Executive and Intermestic Affairs: Three Proposals," *Foreign Affairs,* 55 (1977): 306-324.

"Marcos' Filipinos Flock to America," *The Cumberland Times/News,* Wednesday, July 17, 1985: 7.

"Marriages of Convenience," *The Washington Post,* Sunday, October 21, 1984: A1, 18-19.

McBride, Paul. "Peter Roberts and the YMCA Americanization Program, 1907-World War I," *Pennsylvania History,* 1977, 44 (2): 145-62.

McCarthy, Kevin, "Immigration and California: Issues for the 1980s," P-6846. (Santa Monica, Calif.: The Rand Corporation, January, 1983), 11pp.

———— , and R. Burciaga Valdez, *Current and Future Effects of Mexican Immigration in California,* R-3365-CR, Santa Monica, Cal.: The Rand Corporation, May 1986, 104pp.

McClemore, Dales S. *Racial and Ethnic Relations in America.* (Boston: Allyn and Bacon, 1980).

McClellan, Grant S. (ed.), *Immigrants, Refugees, and U.S. Policy.* (New York: H. W. Wilson, 1981).

McClymer, John F. "The Federal Government and the Americanization Movement, 1915-1924," *Prologue,* 1978, 10 (1): 23-41.

McGouldrick, Paul F. and Tannen, Michael B. "Did American Manufacturers Discriminate Against Immigrants Before 1914?," *Journal of Economic History,* 1977, 37 (3): 723-46.

McKenna, George. *A Guide to the Constitution That Delicate Balance.* (New York: Random House, 1984).

McSeveny, Samuel T., "Ethnic Groups, Ethnic Conflicts, and Recent Quantitative Research in American Political History," *The International Migration Review,* VII (Spring, 1973): 14-33.

Meister, Richard J. *Race and Ethnicity in Modern America.* (Lexington, Mass.: D. C. Heath, 1974).

"Melting Pot Boiling From Racial Tension," *The Cumberland Evening Times,* Tuesday, January 10, 1984: 5.

"Mexico's People Boom," *The Cumberland Evening Times,* Friday, October 4, 1984: A10.

Miller, R. M. and T. D. Marzik (eds.) *Immigrants and Religion in Urban America.* (Philadelphia, Pa.: Temple Univ. Press, 1977).

Mohl, Raymond A. "The Saturday Evening Post and the 'Mexican Invasion'," *Journal of Mexican-American History,* 1973, 3 (1): 131–38.

Montero, Darrel. *Vietnamese Americans.* (Boulder, Colorado: Westview Press, 1979).

Morris, M. *Immigration—The Beleagured Bureaucracy.* (Washington, D.C.: The Brookings Institution, 1985).

Moskos, Charles C. *Greek Americans.* (Englewood Cliffs, N.J.: Prentice-Hall, 1980).

Murphy, Caryle. "Sanctuary: How Churches Defy Immigration Law," *The Washington Post National Weekly Edition,* September 17, 1984: 8–9.

National Geographic Society. *We Americans.* (Washington, D.C.: National Geographic Society, 1975).

Nelli, Humbert. *Italians in Chicago, 1830-1930* (New York: Oxford University Press, 1970).

Neely, Mark E. "Richard W. Thompson: The Persistent Know Nothing," *Indiana Magazine of History,* 1976, 72 (2): 95–122.

Nevins, Allan. *Ordeal in the Union: A House Dividing.* (New York: Charles Scribners Sons, 1947).

Nord, Douglas C. "The 'Problem' of Immigration: The Continuing Presence of the Stranger Within Our Gates," *American Review of Canadian Studies,* 1978, 8 (2): 116–33.

North, David S. "The Growing Importance of Immigration to Population Policy," *Policy Studies Journal,* 1977, 6 (2): 200–207.

_____ and Allen LeBel. *Manpower and Immigration Policies in the United States.* (Washington, D.C.: U.S. National Commission for Manpower Policy, Special Report 20, The Commission, 1978).

_____ . *Immigration and Income Transfer Policies in the United States: An Analysis of a Nonrelationship* (Washington, D.C.: New Trans Century Foundation, 1980).

North, David S. *Seven Years Later: The Experiences of the 1970 Cohort of Immigrants in the U.S. Labor Market.* (Washington, D.C.: New Trans Century Foundation, 1978).

Novak, Michael. *The Rise of the Unmeltable Ethnics.* (New York: Macmillan, 1972).

O'Brien, Kenneth B., Jr. "Education, Americanization and the Supreme Court: the 1920s," *American Quarterly,* XIII (Summer, 1961): 161–71.

O'Connor, Thomas. *The German Americans.* (Boston: Little, Brown, 1968).

O'Grady, Joseph D. *How the Irish Became Americans.* (New York: Twayne, 1973).

"One-Time Internee Returns to Camp," *Cumberland Evening Times,* Thursday, August 15, 1985: 38.

Orback, William. *The American Movement to Aid Soviet Jews* (Amherst, Mass.: University of Massachusetts Press, 1979).

Orth, Ralph and Alfred Ferguson (eds.), *The Journals and Miscellaneous Papers of Ralph Waldo Emerson*. (Cambridge: Harvard University Press, 1971).

Papademetriou, Demetrious G. and Mark J. Miller (eds.), *The Unavoidable Issue* (Philadelphia: Institute for the Study of Human Issues, 1984).

"Paper Provides Homeland News to Indian Immigrants," *The Cumberland Times/News*, Wednesday, July 17, 1985: 7.

Parlin, Bradley W. "Immigrants, Employers, and Exclusion," *Society*, 1977, 14 (6): 23–26.

Parrillo, Vincent. *Strangers to These Shores*. (Boston: Houghton Mifflin Co., 1980).

Perlmutter, Philip. "The American Struggle With Ethnic Superiority," *Journal of Intergroup Relations*, 1977, 6 (2): 31–56.

Peters, Ronald M., Jr. and Arturo Vega, "The Role of House Democratic Party Leaders on Non-Party Position Legislation with Partisan Consequences: The Immigration Bill," Paper Presented at the 1986 Meetings of the American Political Science Association, August 28–31. 1986, Washington, D.C.

Piore, Michael. *Birds of Passage: Migrant Labor and Industrial Societies*. (New York: Cambridge University Press, 1979).

Piott, Steven L. "The Lesson of the Immigrant: Views of Immigrants in Muckraking Magazines, 1900-1909," *American Studies*, 1978, 19 (1): 21–33.

Pitkin, Thomas M. *Keepers of the Gate*. (New York: New York University Press, 1975).

Poulson, Barry W. and James Holyfield, Jr. "A Note on European Migration to the United States: A Cross-Spectral Analysis," *Explorations in Economic History,* 1974, 11 (3): 289–310.

"President Endorses Immigration Proposal," *The Washington Post,* Friday, October 17, 1986: A-4.

Preston, William Jr. *Aliens and Dissenters, Federal Suppression of Radicals, 1903-1933*. (Cambridge, Mass.: Harvard University Press, 1963).

Prpic, George. *South Slavic Immigration in America*. (Boston: Twayne, 1978).

"Quiz Traps Fraudulent Immigrants," *The Cumberland Sunday Times,* November 3, 1985: A 3.

"Raids Nab High-Pay Aliens, Make Jobs, Outrage Clergy," *The Washington Post,* May 2, 1982, p. A 10.

"Reaction to Immigration Bill Is Sharply Split," *The New York Times*, Thursday, October 16, 1986: B-15.

"Reagan Said to Favor Signing New Aliens Bill," *The New York Times*, Friday, October 17, 1986: A-2.

Renner, Richard W. "In a Perfect Ferment: Chicago, The Know-Nothings, and the Riot for Lager Beer," *Chicago History*, 1976, 5 (3): 161–69.

Research Institute on Immigration and Ethnic Studies, "Caribbean Immigration to the United States," RIIES Occasional Papers No. 1. (Washington, D.C.: Smithsonian Institution Press, 1983).

———, "Female Immigrants to the U.S.," RIIES Occasional Papers No. 2 (Washington, D.C.: Smithsonian Institute Press, 1981).

———, "Pacific Migration to the U.S.," RIIES Bibliographic Studies, No. 2. (Washington, D.C.: The Smithsonian Institution Press, 1977).

———, "Quantitative Data and Immigration Research," RIIES Research Notes, No. 2. (Washington, D.C.: Smithsonian Institution Press, 1979).

———— , "Recent Immigration to the United States: The Literature of the Social Sciences," RIIES Bibliographic Studies No. 1. (Washington, D.C.: The Smithsonian Institution Press, 1976).

———— , "Return Migration and Remittances: Developing a Caribbean Perspective," RIIES Occasional Papers, No. 3. (Washington, D.C.: The Smithsonian Institution Press, 1982).

"Right Versus Right: Immigration and Refugee Policy in the United States," *Foreign Affairs,* (Fall, 1980).

Ringle, Ken, "What Did You Do Before the War, Dad? *The Washington Post Magazine,* (December 6, 1981): 54–62.

Ringer, Benjamin B. *"We the People" and Others.* (New York: Tavistock Publications, 1983).

Rippley, LeVern T. *The German Americans.* (Chicago: Claretian Press, 1973).

Rischin, Moses (ed.), *Immigration and the American Tradition.* (Indianapolis: Bobbs-Merrill, 1976).

Rivera, Jose A. "Aliens Under the Law: A Legal Perspective," *Employer Relations Law Journal,* 3 (Summer, 1977): 12–37.

Roberts, Peter. *Immigrant Races in North America.* (New York: Association Press, 1912).

Rosenblum, Gerald. *Immigrant Workers: Their Impact on American Labor Radicalism.* (New York: Basic Books, 1973).

Rostow, Eugene V. "The Japanese American Cases—A Disaster," *Yale Law Journal* (June, 1945): 489–533.

Rostow, Eugene, "Our Worst Wartime Mistake," *Harper's Magazine* (September, 1945): 193–201.

Roucek, Joseph S. and Bernard Eisenber (eds.), *America's Ethnic Politics.* (Westport, Conn.: Greenwood Press, 1982).

Rubin, Jay. "Black Nativism: The European Immigrant in Negro Thought, 1830–1860," *Phylon,* 1978, 39 (3): 193–202.

Samuel, Joseph. *Jewish Immigration to the U.S.: 1881–1910.* (New York: Arno Press, 1969).

Satariano, William A. "Immigration and the Popularization of Social Science, 1920–1930," *Journal of History of the Behavioral Sciences,* 1979, 15 (4): 310–20.

Saveth, Edward N. *American Historians and European Immigrants, 1875–1925.* (New York: Free Press, 1938).

Scanlon, Joseph and G. Loescher, "Mass Asylum and Human Rights in American Foreign Policy," *Political Science Quarterly,* 97 (1982): 39–56.

Schander, Edwin R. "Immigration Law and Practice in the U.S.: A Selective Bibliography," *International Migration Review,* 1978, 12 (1): 117–27.

Schuck, Peter H. "The Transformation of Immigration Law," *Columbia Law Review,* 84, 1 (January, 1984): 39–56.

Schwartz, Abba P. *The Open Society.* (New York: William Morrow, 1968).

Scott, Franklin D. *The Peopling of America: Perspectives on Immigration.* (Washington, D.C.: American Historical Association, Pamphlet #241, 1972).

Select Commission on Immigration and Refugee Policy, *Final Report.* (Washington, D. C.: U.S. Government Printing Office, 1981).

Shaw, Albert (ed.), *Messages and Papers of Woodrow Wilson*. (New York: 1924).

Sibley, Mulford Q. *The Transformation of American Politics, 1840-1860*. (Englewood Cliffs, N.J.: Prentice-Hall, 1967).

Siegel, Mark, "Ethnics: A Democratic Stronghold?," *Public Opinion* (September/October, 1978).

Sieghart, Mary Ann, "Border Patrol: A Revolving-Door Policy," *The Washington Post National Weekly Edition,* September 17, 1984: 7.

"Simpson Tackles Immigration Reform Again," *Minneapolis Star and Tribune,* Monday, June 24, 1985: A10.

Simpson: the 'Anglo' Behind the Immigration Bill," *The Washington Post,* Sunday, October 19, 1986: A-8-9.

Smith, James M. *Freedom's Fetters: Alien and Sedition Laws* (Ithaca: Cornell University Press, 1956).

Smith, Theodore C. *Politics and Slavery* (New York: Negro University Press, 1969).

Smith, T. and Lynn and Vernon J. Parenton, "Acculturation Among the Louisiana French," *American Journal of Sociology,* 44 (November, 1938): 130pp.

Soloutos, Theodore. *The Greeks in the United States* (Cambridge: Harvard University Press, 1964).

Sowell, Thomas (ed.), *Essays and Data on American Ethnic Groups.* (Washington, D.C.: Urban Institute Press, 1978).

––––––. *Ethnic America: A History.* (New York: Basic Books, 1981).

Staley, Joseph, "Law Enforcement and the Border," in Erb, Richard D. and Stanley R. Ross, *United States Relations With Mexico.* (Washington, D.C.: American Enterprise Institute, 1981): 106-120.

Steinberg, Peter L. *The Great "Red Menace," United States Prosecution of American Communists, 1947-1952.* (Westport, Ct.: Greenwood Press, 1984).

Stephenson, George M. *The Religious Aspect of Swedish Immigration* (New York: Arno Press, 1969).

Stevens, Rosemary. *The Alien Doctors* (New York: Wiley and Sons, 1978).

Stipanovich, Joseph. "Immigration and American Social History," *Journal of Urban History,* 1978, 5 (1): 133-42.

Stolzenberg, Ross M., "Occupational Differences Between Hispanics and Non-Hispanics," N-1889-NCEP. (Santa Monica, Calif.: The Rand Corporation, July, 1982), 107pp.

Stout, Harry H. "Ethnicity: The Vital Center of Religion in America," *Ethnicity,* 2(June, 1975): 204-224.

Strange, Steven L. "Private Consensual Sexual Conduct and the 'Good Moral Character' Requirement of the Immigration and Nationality Act, *Columbia Journal of Transnational Law,* 1975, 14 (2): 357-81.

"Study Shows Indochina Refugees Doing Well," *The Cumberland Times/News,* Wednesday, July 24, 1985: 5.

"Surge in Bogus Papers Predicted in Wake of Change in Alien Law," *The New York Times,* Monday, October 20, 1986: A-1, 24.

Tanton, John. *Rethinking Immigration Policy.* (FAIR Immigration Paper I. (Washington, D.C.: Federation for American Immigration Reform, 1980).

Taylor, Philip. *The Distant Magnet: European Emigration to the U.S.A.* (New York: Harper and Row, 1971).

Teitelbaum, M. "Rights Versus Rights: Immigration and Refugee Policy in the United States," *Foreign Affairs,* 59 (1980): 21-59.

"The Gatekeepers," *The Wall Street Journal,* Thursday, May 9, 1985: 1-2, 7.

"The New Immigrants," *Newsweek,* July 7, 1980: 26-31.

Thernstrom, Stephen. *Harvard Encyclopedia of American Ethnic Groups.* (Cambridge, Mass.: Harvard University Press, 1980).

Thompson, James J. Jr. "Southern Baptists and Anti-Catholicism in the 1920s," *Mississippi Quarterly,* 1979, 32 (4): 611-25.

"Thousands Eligible for Alien Amnesty Across Maryland," *The Cumberland Times/News,* Tuesday, November 11, 1986: A-10.

Tomasi, S. M. (ed.), *Perspectives in Italian Immigration and Ethnicity.* (New York: Center for Migration Studies, 1977).

"Tortilla Curtain Fails to Stem Tide of Illegal Aliens," *The Washington Times,* Monday, May 13, 1985: 8a.

"U.S. Border Patrol Going 'High Tech'," *The Cumberland Times/News,* Thursday, October 17, 1985: 23.

U.S. Congress. Senate. Committee on the Judiciary. *The Immigration and Naturalization Systems of the United States.* (Washington, D.C.: U.S. Government Printing Office, 1950).

United States Commission on Civil Rights, *The Tarnished Door: Civil Rights Issues in Immigration.* (Washington, D.C.: U.S. Government Printing Office, 1980).

United States Congress, House of Representatives, "Immigration Reform and Control Act of 1983," [The Mazzoli Bill], HR 1510, 98th Congress, 1st Session, February 17, 1983: 1-63.

U.S. Department of Justice, Immigration and Naturalization Service, "1979 Statistical Yearbook of the INS." (Washington, D.C.: U.S. Government Printing Office, 1980).

"U.S. Hispanics 'Melting' But Not Prospering," *The Washington Post,* Sunday, May 13, 1984: A 1, 8.

U.S. Immigration Commission. "Brief Statement of the Investigations of the Immigration Commission, With Conclusions and Recommendations and Views of the Minority," U.S. Senate Doc. 747, 61st Congress, 3rd Session. (Washington, D.C.: U.S. Gov't Printing Office, 1910-911).

U.S. Interagency Task Force on Immigration Policy. *Staff Report.* (Washington, D.C.: Departments of Labor, Justice, and State, March, 1979).

U.S. President's Commission on Immigration and Naturalization. *Whom Shall We Welcome: Report.* (Washington, D.C.: U.S. Government Printing Office, 1953).

U.S. President's Select Commission on Immigration and Refugee Policy. *U.S. Immigration Policy and the National Interest: Final Report.* (Washington, D.C.: U.S. Gov't Printing, March 1, 1981).

_____ . *U.S. Immigration Policy and the National Interest: Staff Report.* (Washington, D.C.: U.S. Government Printing Office, April 30, 1981).

Vecoli, Rudolph and Joy K. Lintelman, *A Century of American Immigration, 1884-1984.* (Minneapolis: University of Minnesota Continuing Education and Extension, 1984).

_____ , "Prelates and Peasants: Italian Immigrants and the Catholic Church," *Journal of Social History,* 2 (Spring, 1969): 217–68.

Vialet, Joyce. "A Brief History of U.S. Immigration Policy," *Report 80-223 EPW.* (Education and Public Welfare Division, INS, Washington, D.C.: December, 1980).

Vittoz, Stan. "World War I and the Political Accommodation of Transitional Market Forces: The Case of Immigration Restriction," *Politics and Society,* 1978, 8 (1): 49–78.

Walters, Robert, "Immigrants and Jobs," *The Cumberland Times/News,* Friday, October 25, 1985: 8.

Walton, Gary M. and Ross M. Robertson, *History of the American Economy.* 5th ed. (New York: Harcourt, Brace, Jovanovich, Inc., 1983).

Wang, Peter H. "Farmers and the Immigration Act of 1924," *Agricultural History,* 1975, 49 (4): 647–52.

_____ , "The Immigration Act of 1924 and the Problem of Assimilation," *Journal of Ethnic Studies,* 2 (3), 1974: 72–75.

Wareing, J. "The Changing Pattern of Immigration Into the United States, 1956–1975," *Geography,* 1978, 63 (3): 220–24.

Weinberg, Daniel E., "Ethnic Identity in Industrial Cleveland: 1900–1920," *Ohio History,* 86, 13 (Summer, 1971).

_____ . "Greek Americans Score Big in Carter/Mondale Campaign, *Greek World,* (Nov./Dec., 1976).

_____ . "The Ethnic Technician and the Foreign Born: Another Look at Americanization Ideology and Goals," *Societas,* 1977, 7 (3): 209–227.

Weiser, Marjorie P. *Ethnic America.* (1978).

Weiss, Richard. "Ethnicity and Reform: Minorities and the Ambience of the Depression Years," *Journal of American History,* 1979, 66 (3): 566–85.

Weissbrodt, David. *Immigration Law and Procedure.* (St. Paul, Minn.: West Publishing Co., 1984).

"Where the Family Comes First," *Parade Magazine,* June 2, 1985: 4–6.

White, Jerry C. *A Statistical History of Immigration.* (Immigration and Naturalization Reporter, V. 25, Summer, 1976).

Williamson, Jeffrey G. "Migration to the New World: Long-Term Influences and Impact," *Exploration in Economic History,* 1974, 11 (4): 357–89.

Wittke, Carl. *We Who Built America.* (Akron, Ohio: Case Western Reserve University Press, 1967).

Woll, Peter. *Public Policy.* (Cambridge, Mass.: Winthrop, 1974).

Wyman, David S. *Paper Walls: America and the Refugee Crisis.* (Amherst, Mass.: University of Massachusetts Press, 1968).

Yzaquirre, Raul, "What's Wrong With the Immigration Bill," *The Washington Post National Weekly Edition,* December 12, 1983:29.

Ziegler, Benjamin M. *Immigration: An American Dilemma.* (Lexington, Mass.: D.C. Heath, 1953).

Index

acculturation, 46–48, 51, 116

Adamic, Louis, 69, 150

Africa, 33, 80, 82

Alabama, 31, 89, 92

Alaska, 47, 50

alien, 10, 20–21, 57, 63–64, 67, 69, 74, 77–78, 79–80, 84–85, 86–87, 97, 100–101, 106, 107, 109, 111–12, 116, 128–29, 130, 131–32, 133–35 136–37

Alien Acts, 9, 21, 29

America, 1–4, 5–6, 10, 21, 23, 25–26, 28, 39, 42–43, 44–45, 48, 52, 56, 58, 78, 79–80, 83–85, 90, 97, 111–14

American Coalition, 88, 94, 95, 110, 119

American Communist Party, 51, 94

American Federation of Labor, 13, 26, 67, 68, 70–71, 74, 81, 82, 83, 88, 93, 95

"Americani", 42

American Jewish Committee, 13, 52, 95

American Legion, 13, 70–71, 77–78, 81, 82, 94, 95, 110, 120

American Miners Association, 26, 81

American party, 31, 33, 56

American Protective League of True Americans, 55, 58, 71, 119

"Americanization Movement", 12, 74, 78, 80

amnesty, 15–16, 137, 140–42, 143, 147

Anderson, James, 150

anti-Bolshevik, 50–51

anti-Catholicism, 4, 10, 31–32, 36, 55, 71

anti-Chinese, 53–54, 67

anti-foreign reaction, 9–10, 71

anti-Greek, 46

anti-immigrant, 9, 31–32, 36, 55–56, 68, 131, 146

anti-Japanese, 63, 67, 71, 85

anti-Jewish, 43, 51–52, 71, 74

Anti-National Origins Clause League, 81, 89, 119

anti-slavery movement, 24, 32

Arizona, 91, 97, 125, 131

Asia(ns), 1, 3, 5, 12, 14, 67–68, 71, 80, 82, 84, 104, 106, 108, 114–15, 115–16, 118, 119, 120–21, 123–24

Asian Exclusion League, 67, 119

Asian-Pacific Triangle, 104–07, 112

assimilation, 6, 10, 23, 28–29, 38, 44, 46, 52–53, 55–56, 104, 119–20, 123, 125

asylum, 6–7, 15–16, 28, 121, 123, 132, 138–39, 147–48

Atlantic Ocean, 41, 47

Austria, 99, 114

Bailey, Thomas, 32

Baltimore, 10, 32, 47, 50, 51, 58

Beals, Carleton, 10, 32

Bennett, Douglas, 131, 150

Bennett, Marion, 53, 54, 66, 67, 81, 84, 99–100

Bernard, William, 58, 59, 68, 69, 72, 79

Billington, Ray, 10

Blacks, 25, 92, 123, 125, 133, 141

B'nai B'rith, 52, 66

Board of Special Inquiry, 64

Bolshevism, 12, 70, 73

Border Patrol, 13, 16, 100, 127, 128–29, 130, 131, 137, 148–49, 151

Boston, 10, 39, 43, 47, 50, 58, 82, 87

Box, Representative John (R.-Tex), 88, 90

Bracero Program, 13, 14–15, 107, 134–35, 139–40, 147

British, 21–23, 24–25, 28

British Isles (U.K.), 1, 4, 7, 21, 41, 114, 121

Buffalo, 39, 47, 49

Bulgarians, 46, 84

Bureau of the Census, 76

Bureau of Immigration, 58, 65, 70

Burgess, Thomas, 46

California, 10, 29–30, 35, 41, 42–43, 50, 53–54, 56, 63, 67, 68, 70–71, 74, 84, 93–94, 121, 124–25, 128, 133–35, 145

California Alien Land Act, 70–71

Calvinists, 23, 29

Canada, 34, 47, 67, 81, 92, 100, 106, 137

Carolinas, 29, 41

Castle Garden, 54, 56, 58

Catholics, 4, 9–10, 11, 24–25, 32, 36, 38, 49, 74, 95, 100, 119

Celler, Representative Emmanuel, 104, 111

Chicago, 24, 39, 41, 43–45, 47, 49, 50, 56, 69, 88, 127, 134

China, 56, 99, 104, 115, 123, 127

Chinese, 10, 13, 25, 27, 29, 30, 35, 42, 45, 53–54, 56–58, 62, 63, 65, 66–67, 68, 109, 123

Chinese Exclusion Act of 1882, 11, 54–55, 56–57, 58, 71, 99

Chiswick, Barry, 13, 107, 108–09, 110, 114, 151

Civil Rights, 14, 109–10, 130–31, 135–36, 142

Civil War, 10, 23, 24, 26, 33–34, 41, 44, 47, 118

Cleveland, 39, 43, 47

Cold-War Era, 6, 14, 101–03, 106, 118

Commissioner General of Immigration, 58, 65, 66, 70

Congress, 9, 11–15, 20–21, 34, 35–37, 53, 54–55, 56–58, 59, 63–64, 65, 68, 69, 70–71, 73, 77, 78, 80, 81–82, 83, 84, 92–94, 95, 98, 99–103, 106, 107–11, 115, 118–19, 122–23, 126, 135, 136–37, 138, 139, 140, 142

Connecticut, 31, 90

Constitution, 7–9, 20–21, 31, 63–64, 99

Cornelius, Wayne, 135, 138, 139–40, 144, 146, 148–49

Crewdson, John, 127, 128–29, 130, 132, 134, 139

Cuban, 15, 104, 109, 114–15, 119, 123, 125, 129

Cuban boatlift, 15, 114–15, 128, 129, 137

Cuban Refugee Program, 109

Czar Alexander II, 39, 50

Czechs, 46, 84, 123

Daughters of the American Revolution, 81, 88, 110

Davis, Jerome, 50

Delaware, 26, 31, 145

Democrats, 9, 21, 23, 32, 33, 36, 44–45, 48, 53, 74, 108, 111, 140–41

Denmark, 26

Department of Labor, 70, 135, 139

Detroit, 24, 39, 43, 47, 49, 50

DeWitt, Lt. General John L., 97–98

Dickstein, Senator Samuel, N. Y., 94

Dillingham Commission, 11–12, 69, 77, 104, 116

Dinnerstein, Leonard, 30, 42–43, 48, 51, 52

Displaced Persons Act, 13, 38–39, 100, 103, 109

Divine, Robert, 55, 59, 65, 69, 78, 81, 85, 88–90, 92–95

"Door-Ajar Era", 6, 10–11, 36, 38, 39, 41

Dutch, 7, 9, 27–28

"Dutch-Door Era", 6–7, 14–16, 102–04

Eastern European, 46, 51, 52, 59

Eastern Hemisphere, 14–15

Economic depression, 10, 36, 44, 55, 58, 67, 72, 77–78, 82–83, 92, 118
Economic recession, 10, 36, 55, 92, 109–110, 116, 118, 143
"economic refugees", 115–16
Ellis Island, 58, 60, 65, 67, 70, 82, 113
El Salvador, 16, 145
emigration, 3, 25, 38–39, 50, 62, 67–68, 73–74, 84
employer sanctions, 16, 118–19, 137, 139, 140–47
England, 1, 23, 28, 79–80
English, 28, 31, 42, 62, 84, 85, 120, 132–33, 136
English language proficiency, 11, 136
Ervin, Senator Sameul, 111, 112
"ethnic association", 33–34, 81, 83, 89, 104, 120, 145–46
"ethnic theory", 78, 79
eugenics, 71, 88–89, 90
Europe, 1–4, 9, 12, 20, 21–23, 27, 33–34, 35, 77–78, 79–82, 83, 94–95, 96, 100, 114, 118–19
European, 7, 10, 13, 26, 27–28, 31, 33, 62, 81, 86–87, 89, 92, 104, 115, 120, 123, 147
excluded categories, 82, 85, 86–87, 106, 107, 119
Executive Order 9066, 98–99

Fairchild, Henry, 46, 79
Federalist Party, 9, 21, 29
Federal Writers Project, 41–42
Federation for American Immigration Reform [FAIR], 16, 119
feudal system, 3, 39
Florida, 41, 45, 121, 123, 125, 129, 135, 145
Ford, Henry, 12, 74
Fourteenth Amendment, 80
France, 27–28, 79–80
French, 7, 21, 27, 28
French Canadians, 27–29
French Revolution, 21, 28–29
Fuchs, Lawrence, 6, 24

"gatekeeping function", 6
Gentlemen's Agreement, 67, 84
Georgia, 31, 41, 48, 84, 89–90
German(s), 4, 21–24, 32, 35, 41, 47–48, 52, 68, 95, 97, 99, 108
Grant, Madison, 69, 79, 82, 88
Great Depression, 13, 74, 92, 118
Greece, 45, 84
Greeks, 45–48, 55, 108, 114
Greek Orthodox, 11, 38
green card, 127, 128–29, 130, 137
Green, Stephen, 16
Guest Worker Program [H-2], 16, 137, 138–40, 142

Haiti, 114–15, 119, 123, 128, 129, 132
Hall, Prescott, 64, 82
Handlin, Oscar, 36, 58, 68
Harper, Elizabeth, 111, 112
Hawaii, 62, 67–68
Hebrew Sheltering and Immigration Aid Society, 66, 94–95, 119
Henderson v. *New York* (1876), 34, 36, 54
Higham, John, 31, 34, 35, 71, 74, 77–78, 80, 81, 83
Hispanic Americans, 115, 120–21, 123, 124–25, 132, 134, 139, 140–41
Hofstadter, Richard, 32
Holland, 27–28
Homestead Act of 1862, 24, 35
Hong Kong, 29–30, 109, 138
Hosokowa, William, 98
House of Representatives, 16, 45, 58, 63, 77, 79, 80, 81, 84, 85–86, 88, 89–90, 94, 95, 104, 106, 107–08, 111 112, 114, 135, 137, 138–40, 142
Howe, Irving, 52
Hungarians, 36, 47–48, 108, 116, 123

"illegal aliens", 13, 16, 128–29, 133–35, 136–137, 138–39, 140, 141–42, 145–46
illegal immigration, 15, 16, 100, 103–04, 107, 115–16, 121, 123,

125-26, 128-29, 131, 132-33,
135-37, 140-41, 144, 145-46, 148-49
Illinois, 27, 29, 42, 47, 121
immigration, 1, 3-7, 10, 11-15, 16-22,
24-25, 28, 29, 32-33, 37, 41, 46-47,
48, 50, 51, 52-56, 57-59, 62, 63,
65-68, 70-77, 80-84, 85-86, 89-94,
95, 96-97, 103-04, 106, 107,
109-10, 111-12, 113-16, 118,
119-20, 121, 124, 126-27, 129,
132-34, 135-36, 136-37, 142-44,
148-50
Immigration Act of 1882, 11, 55
Immigration Act of 1906, 11
Immigration Act of 1907, 67, 69
Immigration Act of 1917, 12, 73, 82,
86, 100, 106
Immigration Act of 1921, 47, 74, 82,
83, 91-92
Immigration Act of 1924, 13, 62, 74,
82, 84, 86-87, 88, 89, 91-92
Immigration and Nationality Act of
1952, 14-102, 104, 107, 118
Immigration and Nationality Act of
1965, 14, 106, 109-10, 111-12,
113-15, 118, 120-21
Immigration Act of 1976, 114-15
Immigration and Naturalization Service [INS], 15, 16, 123, 125-32,
133-34, 136-37, 138-39, 140, 142,
144, 145-46, 148, 149
Immigration Control and Reform Act
of 1982, 135, 137, 139-40
immigration law, 4, 11, 14, 57, 71,
74, 107, 108-09, 112-15, 118-19,
129, 130-31, 135-36, 142, 143-44
immigration policy, 9-10, 11-20,
33-34, 59, 69, 73, 84-85, 86, 88, 99,
102-04, 106, 108, 116, 118-19, 120,
121-22, 126-27, 135, 142, 143, 144,
149
immigration process, 1, 16, 116, 120,
129
Immigration Restriction League, 59,
65, 69, 81, 82, 119
Immigration Service, 60, 67-68, 70,
86, 100-02

immigrants, 9-11, 13, 20, 24-28, 29, 31,
32, 33-34, 35-36, 38-42, 43-44, 45,
46-48, 49, 50-52, 53-54, 55-56,
57-59, 62-63, 64-65, 66-67, 68-70,
71-72, 74, 78-79, 82, 83-84, 86-87,
89, 91-92, 94, 99-102, 108-09,
112-14, 119-20, 121-23, 124, 129-30,
133-34, 136-39, 140-41, 146-47
Indians, 8, 90, 114
Indochinese Refuge Resettlement Program, 115, 122
interest groups, 119-20, 142-43
Internal Security Act [1950], 101-02,
107
Iorizzo, Luciano, 41-42, 43-44
Iowa, 27
Iranian Hostage Crisis, 127-28
Irish, 4, 9-10, 21, 24-26, 32-33, 35,
44, 47, 49, 62, 68, 114
Italian(s), 36, 41-42, 43-44, 45-47, 51,
59, 64, 80, 81, 84, 97, 99-100, 108
Intalian-Americans, 41, 43-45, 49, 62
Italy, 36, 41, 42

Japanese, 13, 59-62, 65, 66, 67-68, 70,
71, 80, 84-85, 87, 97-98, 99, 106,
118
Japanese-Americans, 97-99, 106, 124
Japanese and Korean Exclusion League,
67, 71
Jewish, 11, 51-52, 86
Jews, 23, 38-39, 50, 51-52, 95, 100,
115, 116, 119, 121
Johnson, Representative Albert, 77,
81-83, 88
Johnson, Senator Hiram, 10, 77, 89, 94
Johnson-Reed Act, 12, 81-82, 86-87,
88, 91
Jones, Charles, 10
Jones, Maldwyn, 54-55, 58-59, 65-67,
70-71, 95, 99-100, 108-109
Junior Order of United American
Mechanics, 81, 89

Kansas, 35, 145
Kennedy, Senator Edward, 110-11,
135, 139

Kitano, Harry, 70
Knickrehm, Kay, 121, 122
Knights of Labor, 26, 29, 55, 59
Know-Nothing party, 10, 24, 31-33, 53, 119
Korea, 104, 114-15, 121, 127
Korean War, 118
Korematsu v. *United States*, 99
Kritz, Mary, 6, 14, 16, 121
Ku Klux Klan, 44, 46, 52, 71, 74, 77, 81, 83, 86, 119

LaGuardia, Governor, 44, 94
Latin America, 14-15, 81, 88, 89-90, 104, 106, 114-15, 120, 123
Laughlin, Dr. Harry, 79, 82, 90
League of Nations, 77, 95
Leibowitz, A., 121, 139
LeMay, Michael, 36, 51-52, 53-54, 55, 59, 102, 125
Leventman, Seymour, 51-52
Lieberson, Stanley, 38
literacy bill, 11-12, 65-66, 68, 70-71, 73
literacy test, 11-12, 58-59, 65, 68-69, 70-71, 74, 119
Lodge, Senator Henry Cabot, 58-59, 64-65, 77, 85
Lopata, Helena, 48
Los Angeles, 47, 53, 121, 125, 129, 133-34, 135
Louisiana, 29, 31, 42-43
Louisville, 10, 32

Maine, 84, 145
"Marriages of Convenience", 130
Maryland, 24, 31, 32
Massachusetts, 25, 31, 34, 51, 145
Mazzoli, Representative, 140-41, 143-44
McCarran-Walter Bill, 14, 103-04, 106
McClemore, Dale, 68, 97, 98, 102
McClellan, Grant, 109, 121
"melting pot", 28, 76, 80, 126
Mennonites, 23, 50
Mexican American Legal Defense Education Fund [MALDEF], 139, 142-43

Mexico, 13, 67, 88, 89-90, 92, 100, 104, 115, 121-22, 125, 127, 128, 131, 133-34, 137
Michigan, 27-29, 34, 56, 111
Middle East, 14, 115
Migration and Refugee Assistance Act, 14, 110
Milwaukee, 24, 47, 49, 128
Mississippi, 30, 31, 95
Mississippi River, 24, 47
Mongolian, 85
Montana, 35, 145
Montero, Darrel, 115
Morris, Milton, 126
"mortgaging" [quotas], 13, 100, 109
Moskos, Charles, 45, 45-46
Murphy, Caryle, 16

National Academy of Science Report, 123
National Association of Manufacturers, 12, 65, 81, 82-83
National Grange, 70-71, 81, 94
National Industrial Conference Board, U.S. Chamber of Commerce, 81, 82-83
national origins quota system, 7, 12-15, 73-74, 80-81, 86-89, 90-91, 102-06, 107, 108-09, 110-13, 118-19
National Origins Act, 13, 59, 81, 86, 88, 90-91, 93, 96
nativist sentiment, 10, 29, 31-33, 36, 56, 65-66, 80-81, 87, 107, 147-48
Nazi Germany, 59, 104
Nelli, Humbert, 44
Netherlands, 27
Nevada, 35, 145
Nevins, Allan, 31
Newark, 32, 39
New England, 29, 34, 45, 47
New Hampshire, 31, 52
"new" immigrants, 4, 10-11, 36, 39-41, 58-59, 84
New Jersey, 25, 27, 47, 50, 58, 121
New Orleans, 43, 58

New York, 10, 24, 25–26, 27, 29, 32–33, 39–41, 42–48, 50, 52, 56, 65, 83, 94, 95, 121, 125, 134
New York City, 26, 39, 43–45, 47, 50, 51, 52, 82, 87, 94, 121, 124, 126, 134
New York Times, 79, 86
nonquota immigrants, 86–87, 92, 95, 99–100, 103, 104, 108, 111
North, David, 10, 12, 30, 36, 38, 41, 74, 82, 89, 96, 104, 119
Norway, 26

Oceania, 82
O'Connor, Thomas, 31
O'Grady, Joseph, 25–26
Ohio, 24, 47, 95
"old" immigrants, 3, 11, 21, 27, 29, 31, 58
Omaha, 35, 46
"One Hundred Percenters", 12, 71, 78
"Open-Door Era", 6, 13, 14–15, 20, 27, 32, 71–72, 73, 78
Orth, Ralph, 33
Ozawa Case, 71, 80
padrone system, 44–46, 48
Palmer Raids, 51, 77
Panic of 1873, 43, 53
"parole" program, 15, 109, 115
Parrillo, Vincent, 28–29, 45, 48, 68
"patriotic" associations, 81, 88, 119–20
Patriotic Order of the Sons of America, 81, 88
Pennsylvania, 24–25, 29, 31, 34, 36, 42, 47, 48, 50, 56
"Pet-Door Era", 7, 12, 73
phases of immigration, 6–7, 16, 19, 36, 73, 74, 102–04, 118, 120
Philadelphia, 10, 39, 47–50, 51, 58, 126
Philippine Islands, 89, 92–94, 100, 104, 114–15, 121, 124
Pitkin, Thomas, 56, 58, 64–65
Pittsburgh, 39, 47, 49
pograms, 39, 50, 52
Poland, 49, 99–100, 123, 127
Poles, 33, 46, 49–50, 79, 82, 108

Polonia (Polish-America), 49
potato famine, 4, 23, 25, 32
post-Civil War period, 10, 23, 33–34, 36
Powderly, Thomas, 26, 65
"preference system", 14, 100, 110, 111–13, 114–15, 119–20, 136, 147–48
President John Quincy Adams, 21
President Arthur, 54
President Carter, 135
President Cleveland, 11, 58, 65
President Coolidge, 83, 86
President Eisenhower, 103, 108–110
President Millard Fillmore, 31–32
President Harding, 12–13, 71, 81
President Harrison, 58
President Hayes, 54
President Hoover, 91
President Lyndon Johnson, 111–13
President Kennedy, 26, 109–10
President Lincoln, 24, 35
President McKinley, 66
President Reagan, 5, 116, 136, 138–39, 144
President Franklin D. Roosevelt, 95, 98
President Theodore Roosevelt, 65, 67, 69, 94
President Taft, 12, 68, 70
President Truman, 13–14, 99–100, 106, 107–08
President Washington, 5, 8, 31
President Wilson, 12, 45, 63, 71, 73, 77, 81
"procedural justice", 16
Progressive party, 44, 47
"Project Jobs", 133–35
Protestants, 4, 10–11, 28, 29, 31–32, 95, 119
Providence, 10, 47
pseudo-scientific, 11–12, 71
pull factors, 2, 29, 39, 42, 45, 56
push factors, 2, 29, 39, 42, 45, 56, 122

Quota Act of 1921, 12–13
quota system, 13, 48, 69, 71–72, 74, 78–79, 80–84, 85–89, 91–96, 100–02, 103–06, 108–11, 119–20, 121

racist theories, 10–11, 12, 59, 70, 71–72, 88–89, 92–94, 97
Red Scare, 12, 71, 73, 77, 118
Reed, Senator, 77, 83, 85–87, 88, 89, 94
Refugee Act of 1980, 15, 114–15, 121, 123
refugees, 14, 15–16, 19, 95–96, 99–100, 103, 108–09, 111–12, 114–16, 118–19, 121–23, 131–32, 137–38, 147–48
refugee-escapees, 14, 108, 109
Refugee Relief Act of 1953, 108–09
Reimers, David, 30, 38–39, 48, 51, 53, 116
relocation camps, 96–99
Republican party, 24, 32, 33, 35, 41, 44–45, 66, 71, 74, 83, 86, 107, 116
restrictions, 10, 11, 34, 36–37, 38, 48, 53, 55–56, 58–59, 65–66, 69–70, 71–72, 73–78, 82, 85, 86–89, 89–90 91–95, 103–106, 109, 119
restrictive policy, 5–7, 12–13, 20, 29, 53, 66, 67, 71–72, 77, 85, 89–90, 109, 118–19, 130
Revolutionary War, 4, 23, 28, 41, 47
"Revolving-Door Era", 16
Ringer, Benjamin, 54, 56–57, 58, 62, 67–68, 71, 78, 80, 85, 98
Roberts, Kenneth, 78, 82, 88
Rodino, Representative Peter, 135, 142
Rodino-Mazzoli Bill, 142, 143–44
Roucek, Joseph, 9
Russia(ns) 2, 39, 46, 49–52, 62, 67, 70–71, 77, 84, 115, 116, 123
Russian Orthodox Church, 38, 50
Russian Revolution, 50–51, 70–71, 72

Salvadorians, 16, 121
San Francisco, 10, 25, 34, 43, 45, 47, 53, 58, 67
Saturday Evening Post, 16, 78, 88–89
Scandinavians, 21, 26–27, 35
Schurz, Carl, 24, 69
Scots, 9, 27, 29, 84
Scotch-Irish, 27, 29, 36
Scott Act, 57
"Screen-Door Era", 16

Select Commission on Immigration and Refugee Policy, 9, 10, 115–16, 135–36, 138–39, 148
Senate, 12, 16, 54, 63, 77, 81–83, 85–86, 88, 89, 92, 94, 104, 107–08, 110–11, 112, 114, 135, 137, 139–40, 142
Shaler, Nathaniel, 55, 59
Shortridge, Senator, 77, 85
Simpson, Senator Alan, 135, 138, 141–42
Simpson-Mazzoli Bill, 16, 135, 138, 139–41, 142, 143–44, 147, 149–50
SIN, 139 142–43
Slavic peoples, 46–49, 50, 51
Smith, James, 31
sojourner, 42, 45, 47, 48–49
Sons of the American Revolution, 81, 88
South America, 41, 127
Southeastern Europe [S/C/E Europe], 4, 10, 12–13, 36, 38, 45, 51, 68, 74, 83–86, 96, 104, 107, 108–09
Soviet Union, 6, 15, 72
Sowell, Thomas, 63
Spanish, 8, 66, 90, 121, 132–33
Statue of Liberty, 1, 11, 55–56, 78, 112
St. Louis, 10, 24, 47
Stoddard, Lothrop, 82, 88
"strangers", 6, 11
Superintendent of Immigration, 58–59
Supreme Court, 9, 20, 34, 36, 54, 56–57, 59, 63, 64, 70, 71, 80, 99
Sweden, 26, 33

Task Force on Immigration and Refugee Policy, 136–37, 138–39
Taylor, Philip, 77
Texas, 24, 31, 49, 121, 125, 127, 134
The Passing of the Great Race in America, 69, 79
Thernstrom, Stephen, 45
Time, 57, 123, 124, 126, 130, 131–32, 133
Treasury Department, 58, 65, 66
Trevor, John D., 82–83, 88
Turkey, 45, 84

undocumented aliens, 15–16, 45, 116, 122–23, 125–26, 127, 128, 130–31, 135–36, 139–40, 141, 145–46

United States, 1–6, 11, 13, 15, 19–24, 25, 28, 29, 30, 38–42, 45–46, 50, 51, 56, 57, 62, 63–64, 65, 67, 70, 73–77, 78, 80–81, 82, 83, 86, 87, 89, 92–94, 95–97, 98–100, 103–06, 108–09, 111–13, 114, 115, 118, 120–21, 122–23, 124, 126, 126–27, 128, 129–30, 131, 132–33, 135–37, 138–39, 140, 141, 142, 144–45, 147–49

United States Chamber of Commerce, 83

Union Pacific, 29, 30, 35

urban political machine, 11, 32, 43–44

Utah, 46

Vecoli, Rudolph, 36, 44, 56, 62, 71

Vialet, Joyce, 4

Vietnamese, 15, 114–16, 121, 123, 124

Vietnam War, 118

Virginia, 31, 41, 145

War-Brides Act of 1946, 13, 99

"waves" of immigration, 2–5, 21, 52–53, 119, 123, 125–26

Webb-Henry Bill, 70

Weinberg, Daniel, 45–46

Welsh, 27, 29, 84

West Coast, 10, 53, 67, 84, 99

Western Hemisphere, 4–5, 14–15, 89, 104, 107, 112, 114, 115

Wisconsin, 27, 29

"worker-identification card", 137, 140, 141, 144

Workingmen's Party, 53

World Refugee Survey, 121–22

World War I, 12, 39, 44, 45, 47, 48, 49, 59, 63, 65–66, 69, 70–71, 74, 78, 118

World War II, 13–14, 45, 51, 96–97, 109, 116, 118, 140

Wright, Representative James, 140–41

Wyoming, 29, 35

xenophobia, 4, 10, 11–12, 21, 56, 66, 73

"Yellow Peril" (Menace), 29, 53, 57, 67, 68, 84

Yugoslavia, 84, 123

Zero Population Growth, 16, 119, 143

About the Author

Michael C. LeMay is Professor and Head of the Department of Political Science at Frostburg State College. Dr. LeMay has served in that capacity since 1974. He has previously published several articles in journals, and a chapter on Allegany County politics in a book entitled, *Western Maryland: A Profile.* His other book, published in 1985, is entitled *The Struggle for Influence: The Impact of Minorities on Politics and Policies in the United States.* In addition to his teaching at Frostburg State College, Professor LeMay has taught at the University of Wisconsin-Milwaukee, and at the Seido Juku Language Institute in Japan. He is a 1966 graduate of the University of Wisconsin-Milwaukee and earned a master's degree there in 1967. He was awarded a doctorate in Political Science by the University of Minnesota in 1971.